An Introduction to Syntax

Also available from Continuum:

An Introduction to Syntactic Theory, Edith Moravcsik

An Introduction to Syntax

Fundamentals of Syntactic Analysis

Edith Moravcsik
University of Wisconsin-Milwaukee

continuum
LONDON • NEW YORK

To the memory of my parents
Gyula Moravcsik and Edith Fleissig Moravcsik

Continuum

The Tower Building
11 York Road
London SE1 7NX

80 Maiden Lane
Suite 704
New York
NY 10038

British Library Cataloguing-in-Publication Data
A catalogue record for this book is available from the British Library.

ISBN: 0–8264–8945–1 (hardback)
       0–8264–8946–X (paperback)

Library of Congress Cataloging-in-Publication Data
A catalog record for this book is available from the Library of Congress.

Typeset by Servis Filmsetting Ltd, Manchester
Printed and bound in Great Britain by MPG Books Ltd, Bodmin, Cornwall

Contents

Preface

1 Goals

What kind of syntax should be taught in an introductory syntax course? Different textbooks offer different alternatives. Most authors select a single approach; others feel that students should be exposed to a variety of points of view and present more than one framework; and there are a few books that search for a shared middle ground among the various syntactic theories.

This book takes this third tack by offering a theory-neutral framework designed as a simple tool for a convenient abbreviatory record of syntactic facts. The approach is theory-neutral in that it is founded only on two assumptions about language, both shared by all syntactic theories. One assumption is that sentences are **semiotic objects** – that is, they have form and meaning; the other is that syntactic forms are **complex objects** – that is, they consist of parts that fall into categories.

The book is intended as a textbook for undergraduate and graduate courses. A first course in linguistics is presupposed. Gramatically English example sentences mostly reflect American usage. Some of the relevant terminology is introduced in the text and defined in the glossary, other terms are assumed. For basic terms of syntactic analysis, the following works are particularly useful references:

James R. Hurford. 1994. *Grammar. A Student's Guide.* Cambridge: Cambridge University Press.

Robert Lawrence Trask. 1993. *A Dictionary of Grammatical Terms in Linguistics.* London: Routledge.

2 Focal points

Here are five points that the approach is based on, described for prospective instructors (for student readers, this section may not be fully understandable because of unfamiliar terminology). The idea behind the first four points is that, in order to explore a relationship between two things, each must be described independently of the other.

(a) The syntactic form of sentences can be and must be described **apart from their meanings.**

It is both possible and necessary to describe syntax independently of meaning. That this is possible is shown by many analogous examples: one can describe the syntax of manual gestures of sign languages independently of what they express, or the formal composition of a rosary without specifying what prayers the beads stand for. The necessity of describing form independently of meaning is in turn dictated by the further goal of accounting for the relationship between form and meaning and exploring the ways in which meaning shapes form. This is because, as noted above, one cannot study the relationship between two entities unless each is first characterized independently of the other.

(b) Sentences can be and must be described **apart from their functions**.

The possibility of describing sentences regardless of the various uses they are put to is again suggested by analogous instances of other symbol systems. For example, one can describe the forms and meanings of traffic signs without considering how they function in actual use. The necessity of describing objects apart from their functions in turn follows from the further goal of wanting to account for the relationship between structure and function and to explore the extent to which function explains structure.

(c) Sentences can be and must be described **apart from the psychological and physical mechanisms** underlying their structure and use.

From the perspective taken here, sentences are objects: more like artifacts – tools – than like activities. Describing language in this way is seen as a necessary prerequisite for the further step of studying the ways in which the structure and use of language are anchored in human cognition and physiology.

(d) Sentences can be and must be described **apart from how they change**.

Just as any object can be described without regard to how it arises and how it evolves, sentences, too, can be analysed in purely synchronic terms. Traffic signs may serve as an example once again: one can describe both the form and the meaning of traffic signs without considering how they were first created, how they subsequently evolved in history, and how their form, meaning and use are acquired by children. The purely synchronic description of objects is necessitated by the further goal of describing change.

If describing change means specifying the directed relationships between synchronic states, then each synchronic state needs to be first described independently of the others.

(e) Syntax can be described in a relatively **theory-neutral** way and such descriptions have some utility.
Any account of any set of facts must, by definition, be based on some assumptions; no account can be entirely theory-neutral. Nonetheless, as noted above, the approach taken in this book is neutral to theories of syntax in that it does not make any assumptions about language other than two uncontroversial ones: that sentences have form and meaning, and that syntactic form is complex (i.e., analysable into parts which in turn fall into categories).

Accordingly, syntactic accounts as viewed in this book consist of four kinds of information: the **inventory** of syntactic categories, **selectional dependencies** among categories in sentences, their **linear order**, and the **symbolic correspondence** relations between syntactic form and meaning, and syntactic form and sound form.

The usefulness of theory-neutral descriptions is seen in the relatively objective record of the facts that they provide, on which theories may be built; and in serving as a common denominator for the comparison of different theories. Also, since the framework is applicable not only to describing syntax but also to describing other complex objects and other semiotic objects, it highlights a basic similarity between language and many other things in the world.

3 Overview

Chapter 1 illustrates what syntax is about and situates syntactic analysis within the context of linguistic research and human inquiry in general.

The topic of Chapters 2–5 is synchronic syntactic description. Proceeding from the more obvious to the more abstract, Chapter 2 discusses linear order, Chapter 3 takes up selection, and Chapter 4 motivates syntactic categories. Chapter 5 is about the relationship of syntactic form to meaning, on one hand, and to sound form, on the other.

Chapter 6 takes up syntactic variation and change, both historical and developmental. Chapter 7 proceeds from description to explanation: it discusses and illustrates three ways of explaining syntactic patterns.

Following each chapter, there is a set of exercises for students to work on.

4 Acknowledgements

Many people have provided indispensable help for this project. First and foremost, it is with very special gratitude that I think of Joseph H. Greenberg and Gerald A. Sanders, whose views on language and linguistics will be apparent throughout the book.

Joseph Greenberg's pioneering oeuvre encompassing many fields of linguistics and anthropology is well known. In this book, I have mostly relied on his work in language typology, major highlights of which are the recognition and fruitful use of implicational statements as the principal means of capturing constraints on language variation, and the elaboration of the claims of markedness theory.

Gerald Sanders' 1972 book *Equational Grammar* presents a comprehensive theory of grammar. In it, several ideas that have since been independently proposed and now prominently figure in several current syntactic approaches were first put forth and synthesized within a coherent and principled framework. These include the insights that syntactic and phonological rules, just as lexical entries, express symbolic equivalence relations between meaning and form; that rules of syntactic selection and linear order must be separately formulated; that linear order be recognized as a feature of phonetic form; that order statements be surface-true and thus invariant in the course of grammatical derivations; that the application of rules should be motivated by the requirement of full phonetic and semantic interpretability; and that the discourse, rather than the sentence, is the proper domain of linguistics.

I also want to thank my other professors and mentors in linguistics as well as my teachers of Hungarian grammar in elementary and high school in Budapest for all that I have learnt from them. From among my colleagues and friends, I am particularly grateful to my present and past colleagues at the University of Wisconsin-Milwaukee – especially Pamela Downing, Fred Eckman, Michael Hammond, Gregory Iverson, Patricia Mayes, Michael Noonan and Bert Vaux – for their support; and foremost of all, to Jessica R. Wirth for many stimulating discussions, for her sense of orderly argumentation, and for her keen insights. For interesting discussions over many years, I am grateful to the members of the Cognitive Science Reading Group at UWM. My heartfelt thanks go to friends and colleagues at the Linguistic Research Institute of the Hungarian Academy of Sciences, the Department of Linguistics at the Eötvös Lóránd University in Budapest, the Max Planck Institute for Evolutionary Anthropology in Leipzig, the EUROTYP programme, and the World Atlas of Language Structures (WALS) project. I am much indebted to Konrad Koerner, who steadfastly encouraged me to complete my syntax book projects over several years, and to my relatives and friends for their unflagging support.

Suggestions on previous versions of some of the chapters by Jean Acevedo, Kimberly Barskaitiki, Dina Crockett, Kasumi Kato, Min Sook Kim, and Katalin É. Kiss have been very valuable. Eun Hee Lee provided a thorough and insightful commentary on several of the chapters, for which I am particularly grateful. Many thanks to András Kertész for his thoroughgoing and insightful commentary on parts of the book. I am indebted to Claudia Barreto, Peter Dunn and Xinping Qiu for their generous help with the zoological examples; and to Gusztav Bayerle, Shigekazu Hasegawa, Motomi Kajitani and Catherine Rethi for help with the Turkish, Persian, Japanese and French examples.

Finally, I am profoundly grateful to all my students in Stanford, Los Angeles, Vienna, Salzburg, Honolulu, Giessen, Budapest and Milwaukee for providing the basic motivation for writing this book and for their ideas. My sincere thanks also to Jenny Lovel and her colleagues at Continuum for their help and encouragement.

Edith A. Moravcsik
July 2005

Department of Foreign Languages and Linguistics
University of Wisconsin-Milwaukee, USA
Milwaukee, WI 53201-0413
(edith@uwm.edu)

Symbols and Abbreviations

Symbols

In interlinear glosses:

- indicates morpheme boundaries
: indicates morpheme boundaries in the English gloss that are not shown in the object-language words
. indicates two words in English for one word in the object language
& indicates temporal precedence: 'A & B' means 'A directly precedes B'
, indicates co-occurrence in some unspecified linear order: 'A, B' means 'A and B co-occur'
* precedes an ungrammatical construction
? indicates constructions of questionable grammaticality

Abbreviations:

These abbreviations mostly follow those given in the Leipzig Glossing Rules (www.eva.mpg.de/lingua/files/morpheme/html).

ABL	ablative case
ABS	absolutive case
ACC	accusative case
ADJ	adjective
ADP	adposition
ART	article
AUX	auxiliary
CL1	noun class 1
CL2	noun class 2
CM	case marker
DAT	dative case
DEF	definite
DEM	demonstrative
DET	determiner
DO	direct object or direct object case marker

ERG	ergative case
FEM	feminine gender
GEN	genitive case
INDEF	indefinite
INF	infinitive
IO	indirect object or indirect object case marker
M	modality
MSC	masculine gender
NEG	negative
NEU	neuter gender
NOM	nominative case
NP	noun phrase
OBJ	object or object marker
P_1	first person plural
P_2	second person plural
P_3	third person plural
PASS	passive
PERF	perfective
PL	plural
PP	prepositional phrase
PREP	preposition
PST	past tense
Q	question particle
REFL	reflexive
REL	relative clause marker
S_1	first person singular
S_2	second person singular
S_3	third person singular
SBJ	subject case marker
SG	singular
you(r)_P	plural 'you(r)'
you(r)_S	singular 'you(r)'

Chapter One

What is Syntax?

There are three men on a train. One of them is an economist and one of them is a logician and one of them is a mathematician . . . (T)hey have just crossed the border into Scotland . . . and they see a brown cow standing in the field . . . And the economist says, 'Look, the cows in Scotland are brown.' And the logician says, 'No. There are cows in Scotland of which one at least is brown.' And the mathematician says, 'No. There is at least one cow in Scotland, of which one side appears to be brown.'

(Haddon 2003: 142)

1 Preliminaries

You have just arrived at the airport in Ankara, Turkey, and are standing at the baggage carousel waiting to be re-united with your possessions. Since the belt fails to disgorge your luggage, you go to the service counter to inquire about it. How do you say 'Where are my two suitcases?' in Turkish? Well, this should be easy: first, you look up each word in your English–Turkish pocket dictionary. This is what you find:

(1) 'where'   *nerede*
    'are'   *var*
    'my'   *benim*
    'two'   *iki*
    'suitcase-s' *bavul-lar*

You then put the words together in some reasonable order, such as what English has, and come up with the following:

(2) *Nerede var benim iki bavullar?*
    where are my   two suitcases

The chances are good that the clerk at the service counter will understand what you are trying to say; however, from the point of view of grammaticality, the sentence is a disaster. The correct version is this:

(3) *Iki bavul-ım   nerede?*
    two suitcase-my where

In other words, for the meaning of 'Where are my two suitcases?', Turks say the equivalent of 'Two suitcase-my where?'

What this example shows is what all travellers know: if you want to speak a language, a dictionary is not enough because the meaning you are trying to express does not fully determine word choice and word order. Here is the additional information not generally included in dictionaries that you need to formulate (3):

(4) (a) The word *var* 'are' must not occur after *nerede* 'where?'.
    (b) The word form *bavullar* 'suitcases' must not occur after *iki* 'two'.
    (c) The word *benim* 'my' may or may not occur before the word for 'suitcase' but either way, the form of the word for suitcase must be *bavul-ım*.
    (d) The word *nerede* 'where?' must come after *bavulım* 'my suitcase'.

Instructions of this kind, which specify the choice and ordering of words and word forms, make up the **syntax** of a language.

This much characterizes the (minimal) content of syntax. However, actual syntactic rules as formulated by linguists radically differ from those in (4) in the manner in which they are stated. The problem with the rules in (4) is that they are too specific. This is for two reasons. First, the rules in (4) mention individual words. But syntactic rules are better formulated in reference to **classes** (also known as categories, or types) **of words**. Here is the categorial re-statement of (4):

(5) (a) Forms of the verb for 'be' must not follow question words that ask about location. (These verb forms are used only to say 'there exist(s)'.)

(b) Nouns following numerals (e.g. 'two') must occur in singular form. (Plural forms are used only for un-numbered quantities.)

(c) Possessed nouns (e.g. 'my suitcase') must occur with a suffix showing the person and number of the possessor. (Possessive pronouns occur before nouns only if the pronouns are emphasized, such as in 'my suitcase, not yours'.)

(d) Question words must occur at the end of the sentence.

The rules of (5) differ from those in (4): where (4) says *bavullar* 'suitcases', (5) says 'nouns'; where (4) says *iki* 'two', (5) says 'numerals'; where (4) says *nerede* 'where', (5) says 'question words'; and so forth. Thus, (5) is a more useful description than (4) because the rules in (4) describe only the Turkish sentences that include the particular words mentioned in the rules, but (5) helps us formulate many other Turkish sentences as well, such as 'Where are your three houses?' *Üç kitab-ı nız nerede?* or 'Where are his five friends?' *Beş arkadas-ı nerede?* These sentences employ different words but follow the same general mould. Rules stated on classes of words highlight the shared template beneath the sentences which, on the face of it, would seem different just because the words are different.

The same point can be made if we take the English sentences in (6):

(6) (a) *Jack should buy a hat.*
(b) *Catherine must wash the dress.*

A word-token-based description as (4) above would fail to capture the similarity between (6a) and (6b). These two sentences differ in word tokens but consist of the same word categories: *Jack* and *Catherine* are both nouns, *should* and *must* are both auxiliaries, *buy* and *wash* are both verbs, and *a* and *the* are both articles.

Descriptions that mention classes of words rather than individual word tokens are useful not only for stating regularities that hold within a language but also for formulating generalizations across languages. Consider the following sentences of French:

(7) FRENCH
(a) *Jacques faudrait acheter un chapeau.*
Jack   should to:buy a   hat
'Jack should buy a hat.'

(b) *Catherine doit   laver   la   robe.*
Catherine must to:wash the dress
'Catherine must wash the dress.'

The English and French sentences in (6) and (7) contain different words but follow the same pattern in terms of word categories. Word–token-based rules would need to be formulated separately for the two languages – for example, that in English, *must* has to come before *wash* and in French, *doit* 'must' has to come before *laver* 'wash' – but a single category-based rule saying that the auxiliary has to come before the verb defines a uniform blueprint for the two languages. Similarly, the fact that English *a* and *the* and French *un* and *la* come before the noun can be taken care of by a single categorial rule according to which the article comes before the noun in both languages.

However, even categorial rules may miss some similarities among sentences; and this is the second reason why rules like those in (4) are not optimal. Consider translations of the English and French sentences in (6) and (7) into German and Hungarian:

> (8) GERMAN
> > (a) *Johannes* **soll** *einen Hut* **kaufen.**
> > Jack **should** a hat **to:buy**
> > 'Jack should buy a hat.'
>
> > (b) *Katherine* **muss** *das Kleid* **auswaschen.**
> > Catherine **must** the dress **to:wash**
> > 'Catherine must wash the dress.'

> (9) HUNGARIAN
> > (a) *Jánosnak* **vennie kellene** *egy kalapot.*
> > Jack **to:buy should** a hat
> > 'Jack should buy a hat.'
>
> > (b) *Katinak* **mosnia kell** *a ruhát.*
> > Catherine **to:wash must** the dress
> > 'Catherine must wash the dress.'

Are these sentences cut by the same template as their equivalents in English and French in (6) and (7)? The answer is yes and no. On the one hand, all these sentences are very much alike in that they all include a verb and an auxiliary as well as two nouns and an article. But on the other hand, they are also different since, as the use of bold makes it clear, the order of the auxiliary and verb is not the same: in English and French, auxiliaries directly precede verbs, in German, they indirectly precede them, and in the Hungarian sentences, they directly follow them. Here are the three order patterns:

> (10) (a) ENGLISH and FRENCH:
> > Noun & **Auxiliary & Verb** & Article & Noun
> (b) GERMAN:
> > Noun & **Auxiliary** & Article & Noun & **Verb**
> (c) HUNGARIAN:
> > Noun & **Verb & Auxiliary** & Article & Noun

(The & sign stands for 'immediately precedes'. For example, (10a) reads: 'The noun must immediately precede the auxiliary, which must immediately precede the verb, which must immediately precede the article, which must immediately precede the noun.')

The problem with (10) is that it specifies three different sentence templates. But, as noted above, the three structures are not entirely different: while they differ in the order of some of the categories selected, they agree in the selection of the categories. This similarity among the four languages can be made explicit if we specify selection separately from order, as in (11). (In (11a), the comma is used to indicate co-occurrence between categories without specifying their linear order: (A, B) stands for 'A and B must co-occur in some yet unspecified order'.)

(11) (a) RULE OF SELECTION:
           – for ENGLISH, FRENCH, GERMAN, AND HUNGARIAN:
           (Noun, **Verb**, **Auxiliary**, Article, Noun)
      (b) RULES OF ORDER
           – for ENGLISH AND FRENCH:
           Noun & **Auxiliary** & **Verb** & Article & Noun
           – for GERMAN:
           Noun & **Auxiliary** & Article & Noun & **Verb**
           – for HUNGARIAN:
           Noun & **Verb** & **Auxiliary** & Article & Noun

Thus, (11) breaks down the notion 'combination of word categories' into two components: 'selection of word categories' and 'ordering of word categories'. The selection rule in (11a) abstracts away not only from the specific words but also from the specific order in which they appear. Thus, (11) succeeds in capturing both similarities and differences among sentences that differ in word order but contain the same categories. Their similarity is made explicit by the selection schema in (11a) while their difference is shown by the order schemata in (11b).

That the selection of words and their ordering are distinct components of grammaticality is evident also from the fact that there are ungrammatical sentences that violate constraints on order but not on selection. Suppose somebody wants to say in English 'Peter has found a lizard in the yard' and comes up with *Peter has found a lizard yard the in*. This sentence is selectionally sound – it has all the right kinds of words – but is ungrammatical because it does not observe the right order of the noun, article and adposition. Another ungrammatical alternative is **Peter has found a lizard in yard*. The sentence is flawed in a more basic way: it is ungrammatical by selection because the article *the* is not mis-ordered but simply left out.

In sum: syntactic rules specify the selection and order of words. For the rules to be general, they have to be stated on word classes rather than individual words and with selection information separated from ordering. Just as different words are concrete manifestations of word categories, different orderings of the same words are concrete manifestations of selection patterns: the ordered strings 'Auxiliary & Verb' and 'Verb & Auxiliary' are tokens of a single selectional structure 'Verb, Auxiliary', just as the individual words *boy* and *book* are tokens of the general category 'Noun'.

Before closing this brief introduction to the concept of syntax, it is worth noting the broad applicability of the term 'syntax': in the sense in which we defined the term, all complex objects have syntactic structure. Here are some syntactic rules for a meal at dinner:

(12) (a) RULE OF SELECTION:
Soup, salad, meat course and dessert may make up a dinner.
(b) RULE OF ORDER:
Soup must precede salad, which must precede the meat course, which must precede dessert.

Cooking recipes are also 'syntactic descriptions': American cookbooks even follow the two-part format by first listing the ingredients selected and then giving the order in which they need to be mixed. Just as sentences can be selectionally grammatical but ungrammatical in order or ungrammatical even by selection, a cake can also be ruined because the right ingredients have been mixed in the wrong order – such as adding flour to the egg whites before beating them – or because the very choice of the ingredients is incorrect – such as using salt instead of sugar. Images, too, have their own syntax. For example, the picture of a chicken may be ill-formed either by the choice or by the arrangement of the parts. The picture of a chicken fitted with human legs is ill-formed by selection; one with both eyes on one side of the head is selectionally correct but it suffers from an ill-formed arrangement of the parts.

As we are about to embark on a more detailed discussion of syntactic descriptions, an obvious question that arises is about the purpose of all this. What is the goal of the entire endeavour of describing the syntax of sentences? And why should descriptions be general as was suggested in the preceding discussion? In attempting to answer these questions, we will first look at the big picture: the goals of science in general (Section 2). Following that, we will explore how these goals apply to the science of linguistics (Section 3) and then to syntax in particular (Section 4).

2 Studying the world

2.1 EXPLANATION

2.1.1 Why-questions

On a Saturday morning, 1 February 2003, the space shuttle Columbia was on its way back to Earth when it exploded in mid-air killing all of its seven crew members. As the event was replayed on TV over and over again with the world watching in horror, there was one question on most people's mind: why did this happen?

The impact of the disaster was different for people depending on what their expectations had been. Those who did not know that a similar disaster destroyed the space shuttle Challenger 17 years earlier might have thought that the explosion of the Columbia was simply impossible. If in turn you had asked people old enough to remember the Challenger catastrophe, they probably would have said it was possible that the Columbia would explode but certainly not that it was necessary or even likely. And some of the engineers at the National Aeronautics and Space Administration who had raised doubts earlier about the space-worthiness of the Columbia might have considered the crash likely – but not that it would necessarily happen.

During the weeks and months following the Columbia disaster, reports about the subsequent investigation were splashed on front pages of newspapers everywhere. Just as the people around the globe, the investigative board also asked the question: why did it happen? Their task was to show that the crash was not only possible and not even just probable but that there were factors involved that rendered it necessary.

A host of different circumstances were considered and their status as the cause for the crash kept fluctuating between being impossible, possible and likely. As one newspaper article reported, 'The board has emphasized that everything is under consideration, no matter how seemingly irrelevant or obscure or unimaginable' (*The Milwaukee Journal Sentinel*, 20 February 2003: 12A). That the shuttle was hit by space debris, a meteorite, or lightning, that its old age was the problem, that there had been undue budget pressures on the project and that poor management decisions had been made were all considered unlikely but possible. Even sabotage, which was first ruled out as impossible by the investigative board, was later brought back into the realm of possibilities. The idea that a bit of foam insulation peeled off the fuel tank and struck the craft's left wing at take-off allowing hot gases to penetrate the wing upon return was first tentatively suggested; then ruled impossible; then revived as a possibility, until it eventually emerged as the most probable cause for the crash.

The impact of Columbia's crash on ordinary people and scientists alike and the thinking that underlay the subsequent investigation aiming to find the cause illustrate an important universal characteristic of the human mind. Throughout our lives, we notice things around us and wonder why they are the way they are. Although our desire to know may sometimes be fuelled by some further aspiration – wanting to improve things in the world, such as in the case of the Columbia investigation, or seeking money or prestige for ourselves – often there is no such ulterior motif. When people send inquiries to the science columns of newspapers about why leaves turn colour in autumn, this is out of sheer curiosity. Or, if you notice one October morning that the cup of water left on the backyard table froze overnight but the cup of wine standing next to it did not and you ask yourself about the reason for this difference, this may again be without any further goal: you simply want to understand.

The kind of curiosity that permeates our everyday life about why things are the way they are is the ultimate basis of scientific endeavour. The difference between what an everyday person does and what the scientist does is only that the latter takes a more persistent, more rigorous and more systematic approach to inquiry than the rest of us.

What exactly do we mean when we are asking for an explanation of something? The need for an explanation arises in a person's mind when there is a mismatch between the way he observes reality and the way he expects it to be. In other words, a why-question emerges from a gap between the actual world as we see it and the contents of our mind. The Columbia disaster is a case in point: as noted above, many people had believed it could not happen, some had imagined it was possible, a few may have thought it was likely to happen, but nobody had thought it necessary. Yet, it did happen, proving everybody wrong and giving rise to the question 'why?'.

An analysis of this example shows that the mismatch between what is experienced and what is expected may vary in depth. First, at times, the way things are seem likely but not necessary. Second, the gap is wider if the actual state of affairs seems possible but not necessary and not even likely. And, third, something may seem impossible – that is, totally beyond the realm of conceivable alternatives – even though it is real.

Let us further illustrate these three scenarios. In winter, retail prices of fruits and vegetables can be expected to go up. It is likely that this would happen but, given the complexity of the factors that influence pricing, it is not necessary.

For the second scenario, take the example of the water and the wine left outdoors overnight. That the water should have frozen is not miraculous provided you know that H_2O freezes at 32 degrees Fahrenheit and that overnight temperatures dipped below 32 degrees. But what about the wine? Why should water freeze sooner than wine? Wine is like water in many ways: it can be boiled, it seems to have similar viscosity, it quenches thirst as water does, and so forth. But wine is also different from water in some ways, such as in colour and taste. Therefore, when it comes to freezing, we have some reason to expect wine to behave like water but also to expect it to behave unlike water. Reality, however, comes down hard on one side: water will freeze before wine will. In this case, both the freezing and the non-freezing of the wine at 32 degrees F seem possible and the problem is why, of two equally likely alternatives, one is true and the other is not.

The example of leaves turning colour exemplifies the third type of gap between thought and reality: for the botanically uninitiated, the way things actually happen may seem not even possible. Since from March to September, oak trees show a bright green colour, one would expect them to remain verdant for the rest of the year just as evergreens do. The colour change of oak leaves thus might appear entirely beyond expectations: reasoning and reality go separate ways, this time even more radically than in the previous examples, and we ask 'why?'.

'Why X?' always means 'why X rather than Y?'. Asking a why-question requires detachment from the here and now and the ability to see alternatives to it, whether from past experience or from imagination. As long as we are prisoners of a particular view of the world, the possibility that things could be otherwise is dimly or not at all perceived: the very notion of an alternative is beyond our grasp. It is only when we are able to distance ourselves from a given situation and approach it from the angle of other conceivable alternatives that we come to realize that it is not necessary that it be the way it is. A person whose musical experience does not extend beyond bluegrass music is not likely to wonder why bluegrass is the way it is; in fact, he may not even be aware of the special conventions of this genre. But somebody coming to bluegrass from a different musical style will be struck by these constraints and is bound to ask why they are the way they are.

The fact that a why-question presupposes the inquirer's ability to see alternatives to the way things are throws light on why it is such an interesting experience to meet new people, to visit foreign countries and to learn new languages. In the course of these experiences, alternatives to known patterns come into vision and prompt us to take an outsider's look at our own ways and ask why they are the way they are. Science fiction offers a similar experience in that it takes us into a different world and thus inspires questions about our own. Reading about human-like creatures with two heads makes us realize that we, too, could have two heads and makes us wonder why we just have one.

By way of a summary, (1) provides a schematic representation of the mental scenarios that prompt why-questions. X stands for a state of affairs, such as leaves turning colour. In (a), (b) and (c) are shown the three kinds of gaps in order of increasing size that may separate reality and expectation: in (a), it is thought that something is probable but not necessary; in (b), it is believed that something is possible but not necessary and not even probable; and in (c), what is observed is thought to be entirely beyond the realm of possibilities.

(1) • OBSERVATION: 'X exists'
    • THREE ALTERNATIVE REACTIONS TO THE
      OBSERVATION:

	'X is possible'	'X is likely'	'X is necessary'
(a)	YES	YES	**NO**
(b)	YES	**NO**	**NO**
(c)	**NO**	**NO**	**NO**

    • THE RESULTING QUESTION: 'Why does X exist?'

2.1.2 *Answers to why-questions*

Since a why-question sprouts from a gap between what is observed and what is expected, what an explanation must do is close or at least narrow this gap.

Minimally, all that an explanatory attempt achieves is to bring the observed fact into the realm of possibilities, without showing that it is necessary or even likely. In other cases, the explanation goes one step further towards a tighter fit between fact and expectation: it renders the observed fact likely but not necessary. And optimally, an explanation renders the observed fact necessary so that all conceivable alternatives are ruled out.

Here are examples of the three degrees of explanation. Suppose that you have just moved from California to Chicago and on a May morning you wake up to snow covering the ground. Snow in May might seem impossible to you; but if the locals tell you that this has happened before, your expectations change: the statement 'Snow may fall in Chicago in May' renders the observed fact possible, although not likely and certainly not necessary. We will call this kind of explanation **permissive**: it permits something to happen but does not require or even probabilitize it.

To illustrate the second kind of explanation, let us assume that the day you see snow on the ground in Chicago is in January rather than May. In this part of the world, snowfalls are frequent in the winter months and this generalization renders the observation likely. We will call this a **probabilistic** explanation.

The third and most satisfying type of explanation renders an observation not only possible and not only probable but necessary. This is so if the scene is the Arctic region rather than Chicago. For that part of the world, there is an exceptionless generalization which says the ground is always packed with snow, and thus the observation about snow on one particular day is an inevitable consequence of this general truth. We will call this kind of explanation law-like, or **nomological** (from the Greek word *nomos* 'law').

Additional examples of nomological explanations come from two of our earlier scenarios: water freezing before wine and leaves turning colour. A nomological explanation for why water freezes before wine would appeal to the chemical composition of wine: while wine contains some water, it also contains alcohol, whose freezing-point is known to be lower than that of water. As a result of this recognition, the fact that appeared mysterious before – that wine does not freeze when its twin substance, water, does – now seems natural: things have 'fallen into place'. Before the explanation, the observation seemed possible but not necessary. After an explanation has been offered and accepted, the real state of affairs remains the only possible option and thus a necessary one, with all counterfactual alternatives ruled out.

Similarly, leaves of oak trees turning colour in autumn can be explained nomologically. The colour change comes about in response to the leaves gradually separating from the branch – a process triggered by the lessening of daylight hours and the coldness of nights. Once the leaves are cut off from the nourishment coming from the trunk, photosynthesis cannot take place any more to produce chlorophyll – the substance responsible for the green of the leaves. Other colours such as yellow and red thus far masked by the green then show up. Given that we understand that the conditions needed for the production of the chlorophyll gradually disappear, the colour change is inevitable: the leaves could not but lose their green. As Hercule Poirot, musing at his lifelong efforts to explain 'The Murder', remarks: 'when the right solution is reached, everything falls into place. You perceive that **in no other way** could things have happened' (Agatha Christie 1986; emphasis original).

In (2) there is a summary of the three types of answers to why-questions as they close the gap between fact and expectation to varying degrees, proceeding from minimal to maximal explanatory force: (a) schematizes permissive explanations, (b) schematizes probabilistic explanations and (c) represents nomological explanations.

(2) • WHY-QUESTION: 'Why does X exist?'
   • THREE ALTERNATIVE ANSWERS TO THE QUESTION:
    'X exists because it follows from Principle P that . . .

	. . . X is possible.'	. . . X is likely.'	. . . X is necessary.'
(a)	**YES**	NO	NO
(b)	**YES**	**YES**	NO
(c)	**YES**	**YES**	**YES**

Exactly how does an explanation effect this crucial transformation in the mind? The key notion is **generalization**. All explanations must include three crucial components: a fact to be explained – called an **explanandum**; at least one generalization to which appeal is made – called the **explanans**, or explanatory principle – and at least one additional statement called the **bridge statement** that shows how the explanans ties in with the explanandum. An explanation renders an observed fact possible, likely or necessary by revealing that the object under study belongs to a class some, most, or all members of which exhibit the observed characteristic(s).

Here is the explanatory schema for the water and wine example:

(3) EXPLANANDUM:
Wine freezes at a lower temperature than water.

EXPLANATORY PRINCIPLE:
Alcohol freezes at a lower temperature than water.

BRIDGE STATEMENT:
Wine is a kind of alcohol.

However, explaining things is a much more complex endeavour than it might seem. First, an explanation may appeal to more than one general principle. Thus, in the chlorophyll example, it is not enough to invoke the principle that photosynthesis requires water: other relevant principles having to do with how trees sense the shortening of days and so on are also at play. Second, things may have several competing explanations. Thus, an alternative attempt at explaining the colourful autumn foliage may be made by positing little fairies that paint the leaves yellow and brown in the depth of the night. Although in this particular instance it would not be difficult to show that the latter theory lacks independent support and thus is inferior to the former, the task of choosing between alternative explanations may in other cases be much more difficult.

Third, explanations are never ultimate: the explanans itself is also in need of an explanation. To say that wine does not freeze at 32 degrees Fahrenheit because it is a kind of alcohol is a low-level explanation in that it raises the question of why alcohol does not freeze at 32 degrees even though water does? A higher-level explanation would have to do with the molecular composition of alcohol and water and the behaviour of the ingredient atoms and their component particles under varying temperatures. But even these principles would call for further explanations. The existence of complex explanations and of alternative explanations, and the need to search for explanations of explanations render science a forever challenging and, in the final analysis, forever elusive pastime of human beings.

In sum: Section 2.1 discussed why-questions and what it takes to answer them. Explanations are called for when there are mismatches between observation and expectation. If an observed fact is deemed possible but not probable, or is seen as probable but not necessary, the explanation needs to narrow the range of expectations to the one state of affairs actually observed. If the observed fact is not even deemed possible, then the explanation first needs to broaden the spectrum of conceivable alternatives before narrowing it to the one that holds true. In either case, an explanation succeeds if it eliminates the conflict between perceived reality and the human mind: by changing the mind's content it re-aligns the two.

In order for something to be explained, it first has to be observed and described. The next two sections will take a look at the notions of observation and description.

2.2 OBSERVATION

A why-question asks about something that has been observed; that is, it presupposes that somebody has looked at the world and has singled out a certain portion of it for attention. Thus, for instance, asking a question about leaves turning colour in the autumn presupposes that we see leaves as separate from the trunk and from the insects that crawl on them, and their colours as separate from their shapes; or asking why Jim is absent in class implies that Jim has been perceived as an entity separate from his classmates and separate also from the chair that he usually sits on in class. Accordingly, the first step in scientific inquiry is observation: delimiting an object as a separate part of the world.

Facts and observations about facts are not the same thing: an observation reflects how facts are perceived. Observations are our images formed of reality rather than reality itself. No matter how much we try to make perceptions be true to reality, they always carry the stamp of the observer. As the Danish physicist Niels Bohr is reputed to have said: 'It is not enough for us to explain what things seem like; we need to explain what things really seem like.' Bohr did not contrast how things 'seem' with how things 'are' but with how things 'really seem'. The tongue-in-cheek expression 'really seem' is self-contradictory and it reflects Bohr's doubts as to whether the true nature of reality can ever be revealed to the observer.

The observer's effect on perception is shown by the fact that things are perceived differently depending on the observer and his goals and means. For example, newborn babies may not see their caretakers as separate from themselves and may not perceive their own hands and feet as parts of their own body. Dogs and bees are colour-blind and thus miss out on some properties of things that humans readily perceive – just as we miss out on nuances of smell that dogs are adept at picking up.

The human capacity to observe things is in fact greatly constrained by our limited abilities: we cannot observe things that are too big, or too small, or too distant, or that are inside objects too dense to be penetrated by our senses. These limits can be stretched somewhat by telescopes, microscopes, X-ray machines, radar, sonar, MRI and other instruments but the fact remains that it is only a part of reality that is open to human observation. Since scientific inquiry pertains only to things that can be observed, the entire endeavour of science is limited to the humanly observable portion of the world.

2.3 DESCRIPTION

Before an observation can become an explanandum, it must be put in verbal form. Verbal renderings of observations are called **descriptions**.

As shown by the three observers' different ways of recording their observation regarding the brown cow in the epigraph at the start of this chapter, descriptions may be couched at different levels of generality. The mathematician's statement – that there is at least one cow in Scotland, of which one side appears to be brown – is the most cautious and most factual one, the economist's – 'The cows in Scotland are brown' – is the most general, and the logician's take on the facts falls between the two.

In its simplest form, the description of a set of objects may be enumerative, simply presenting each object in its entirety. Good descriptions, however, are analytic rather than enumerative: they describe objects by dissecting them into component parts and properties. Analytic descriptions reduce an apparently unique object to a unique combination of non-unique components and thus relate it to various other things.

Suppose, for example, that I am asked to describe lemons. I may offer the following analytic description: 'Lemons are a tropical fruit of the size of a small apple, yellow by colour, their consistency similar to that of an orange and their flavour like grapefruit laced with vinegar.' This description characterizes lemons by six properties: general type, provenance, size, colour, consistency and flavour. By situating lemons along each of these descriptive parameters, I assign them to classes of things. When I say lemons are a fruit, I am relating them to pears, bananas and strawberries. By saying that they are tropical, I am relating them to crocodiles and rain forests. By saying that the size of lemons is that of a small apple, I am lumping them together with apples, potatoes, eggs and small balls of yarn. By describing them as yellow, I am linking them with bananas and sunflowers. By describing their consistency, I am relating lemons to oranges, grapefruits and limes; and by describing their flavour, I am assigning them to yet another class which consists of acidic substances. This characterization captures both the uniqueness of lemons and also their relatedness to other things in the world. On the one hand, there are many other things that have the same colour as lemons *or* the same size *or* the same flavour *or* the same consistency *or* the same provenance *or* the same fruitiness. But there is nothing else that has the same size *and* the same colour *and* the same flavour *and* the same consistency *and* the same provenance *and* the same fruitiness. Lemons, in other words, are non-unique in their individual properties but are unique in the combination of their properties.

That scientific descriptions are analytic is important since analysis is an indispensable tool of explanation. Here is an example of how the two are related. Consider the case of a patient who reports to his doctor that he has allergic reactions to the following kinds of food: chicken salad, potato salad, eggnog, Hollandaise sauce, custard pie, chicken soup and ham-and-noodles casserole. The doctor's job is to explain why the patient is allergic to just these foods but not, say, to beef bouillon or turnip salad. This requires working out what it is that the seemingly diverse foods have in common. Since they are all distinct as wholes, their similarity must reside in their parts. Analysis of the respective recipes will reveal that two of them – chicken salad and potato salad – contain mayonnaise. Two of the other foods also have an ingredient in common: both chicken soup and ham-and-noodles casserole contain noodles. But breaking down four of the seven kinds of food into their immediate ingredients does not yet solve the problem since mayonnaise is still distinct from noodles and both are distinct from eggnog, Hollandaise sauce and custard pie. Additional analysis reveals, however, that noodles, mayonnaise, eggnog, Hollandaise sauce and custard pie all share a single ingredient: eggs, which must therefore be the cause of the patient's allergy.

This example shows how analytic descriptions are instrumental in explaining things. In addition, note that the doctor's job is not only to explain why the patient gets sick from certain foods, but he also needs to be able to predict what other food items are likely to evoke the same reaction so that he can warn the patient against them. Prediction is a by-product of explanation and, as such, it becomes possible only by analysis. In this instance, the prediction is that any food that contains eggs will cause problems for the patient.

In addition to explanation and prediction, there is a third benefit to analytic descriptions: they are the only descriptive option if the set of things to be described is infinite in size. There are many such things: the infinite variety of human fingerprints, human faces, human diseases, snowflakes, birch trees, cloud configurations and hair patterns of giraffes. Members of such infinite sets could never be 'enumeratively described' – that is, presented in their entirety – but they can be described in terms of their finite number of properties.

Constructing useful descriptions is difficult. The example of the doctor's task to find the crucial food ingredient that causes the allergy illustrates this. In order for the description to become a tool of explanation and prediction, the analyst must hit upon the right kind of parts and properties of things and find the right level of analysis. First, note that foods could be described in many ways other than in terms of their ingredients – such as their colour, taste and consistency. But none of these analyses would be helpful in finding the common denominator of the offending food items in our example and thus explaining and predicting the patient's allergic reactions. Second, even if the analysis undertaken is on the right track by breaking the food items down into their ingredients, the crucial ingredient responsible for the allergy would be missed if the analysis did not go far enough but ended with identifying mayonnaise as being an ingredient in some of those foods. Thus, finding the right description that will make explanation and prediction possible is not a mechanical task: it takes insight to hit upon the right parts and properties and to zero in on the right level of analytic depth.

Hidden behind the idea of describing an object as the sum of its parts, properties and their relationships lies the assumption that a whole equals the sum of its parts and their relations. This assumption is known as the principle of **compositionality**. Although in many instances, compositionality turns out to be a fruitful assumption, it does not always hold. Is the full nature of a lemon really accounted for by the sum of its properties? Can the behaviour of a crowd of people be reduced to the behavioural features of the individuals that make it up? And does the sum of the characteristics of your best friend do full justice to what he or she is really like? Similarly, how could the idiomatic meanings of expressions like *kick the bucket* or *spill the beans* be accounted for in terms of the meanings of the words they are made up of? Compositionality is an empirical hypothesis about things in the world and it may or may not always work.

Let us summarize Section 2. Scientific inquiry is rooted in two realities. One is outside the human mind – the world; the other is inside it – the mind that perceives reality and wants to explain it. We make observations, describe them and then ask why they are the way they are. Observations are limited by the observer's goals and means. Descriptions must be analytic for three reasons. First, infinitely large sets of phenomena cannot be described individually but analytically. Second and third, descriptions are tools of explanations and predictions.

Asking a why-question is a creative activity in and of itself since it means that the person asking it is capable of visualizing alternatives. Since a why-question arises from a gap between what the observer perceives and what he expects, an explanation must close the gap by showing, minimally, that the observed fact is possible; or, better, that it is probable, and, optimally, that it is necessary.

3 Studying language

3.1 OVERVIEW

In Section 1, two basic points were made about syntax: syntactic statements specify the choice and ordering of words; and they have to be formulated in a maximally general way. Section 2 served to place the generality requirement in a broader context in that it showed how this requirement was dictated by the goals of scientific inquiry in general. Next, we will return to the first point: the content of syntax, and view it within a larger context of linguistics – the science of natural human languages.

As all other artifacts – objects constructed for a purpose, such as chairs, houses or computers – sentences, too, have three basic types of properties: structure, function and location. Structure refers to composition out of smaller parts; for sentences, these are sounds, morphemes, words and so on. An observation about language structure is that the verbal affix -*ing*, as in *singing*, must follow the verb stem that it goes with rather than precede it. Function means utility: what sentences are used for. An observation about sentence function is that certain sentences, such as *Can you tell me what time it is?*, may be used both as questions and as requests. The third concept, location, refers to the spatial and temporal context in which sentences occur. For example, you can note that double negatives, such as *I did not see nothing*, occur in twenty-first-century non-standard dialects of English as well as in standard versions of Russian and Serbo-Croatian.

The study of these three basic domains of linguistic observation is divided among the various subfields of linguistics. Structure is the concern of descriptive linguistics. Language function is studied in semantics, pragmatics, stylistics, psycholinguistics and sociolinguistics. The textual, spatial, temporal, natural, social and physiological context in which sentences occur is the subject of discourse analysis, dialectology, areal linguistics, historical linguistics, developmental linguistics, sociolinguistics, psycholinguistics and neurolinguistics.

In the next three sections, we will take up the three concepts of linguistic structure, function and location in more detail.

3.2 STRUCTURE

An object has structure if it can be analysed into component parts. As was noted in Section 1, any complex object has structure. By recognizing that sentences have structure – they consist of words – we recognize their fundamental similarity to all other complex phenomena in the world: minerals, galaxies, plants, human bodies, societies and religions.

Sentences are not the largest units of speech, they are themselves components of larger chunks called discourses. A discourse is a coherent sequence of sentences produced either by a single person, such as a diary, lecture, poem or novel, or by a set of interlocutors, such as a conversation or exchange of letters. Although descriptive linguistics may ultimately adopt the discourse as its most fruitful domain, in this book we will follow the dominant tradition and restrict our analysis to sentence-size chunks while delegating the study of discourse context to the study of the location of sentences (see Section 3.4 below).

The description of a language cannot simply be a dictionary-like listing of all the sentences that it consists of; instead, what is needed is an analytic description that describes parts and properties of sentences. This is not only because, as we saw in Section 2.3, analytic descriptions facilitate explanations and predictions but also because the number of sentences that any language consists of is infinite and, as also noted above, infinite sets cannot be enumerated.

There are several sources of infinity for the set of sentences making up a language, many of which have to do with the infinite set of ideas that can be expressed. First, note that it is possible to talk about an infinite number of things. Thus, one can say: *Sammy owns two houses, Sammy owns three houses, Sammy owns twenty million houses*, and so on. If we run out of numerals, we can always name the largest number available and add *plus one, plus two* and so on. Second, we can talk about an infinite number of events or states, as in *I know that Sammy is a jerk, I know that you know that Sammy is a jerk, I know that you know that I know that Sammy is a jerk*, and so on. Third, even a single event can have an infinite number of instances that differ in length: *The cougar ran, The cougar ran and ran, The cougar ran and ran and ran*, and so on. And, fourth, degrees of intensity are also infinite in number, as in *The hunter was tired, The hunter was very tired, The hunter was very, very tired*, and so on. It is the unlimited repeatability of certain meaningful elements in a sentence that enables language to express an infinite number of thoughts by using a finite stock of items.

How exactly do analytic descriptions of linguistic structure work? Consider first an enumerative description – one where sentences are not analysed into parts. In such an account, each statement pertains to one sentence only, as is the case in (1).

(1)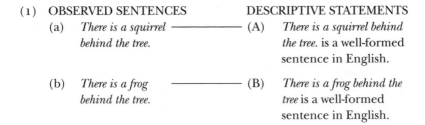

	OBSERVED SENTENCES		DESCRIPTIVE STATEMENTS
(a)	*There is a squirrel behind the tree.*	—— (A)	*There is a squirrel behind the tree.* is a well-formed sentence in English.
(b)	*There is a frog behind the tree.*	—— (B)	*There is a frog behind the tree* is a well-formed sentence in English.

(c)   *Is there a squirrel* —————— (C)   *Is there a squirrel behind*
      behind the tree?   *the tree?* is a well-formed
                                           sentence in English.

(d)   *Is there a frog* —————— (D)   *Is there a frog behind*
      behind the tree?   *the tree?* is a well-formed
                                           sentence in English.

As the lines indicate, there is one 'rule' for every sentence in this account and each rule applies to one sentence only. In an analytic account, on the other hand, there is a many-to-many relationship between descriptive statements and objects to be described: each descriptive statement pertains to only one portion of a sentence, but each applies across sentences.

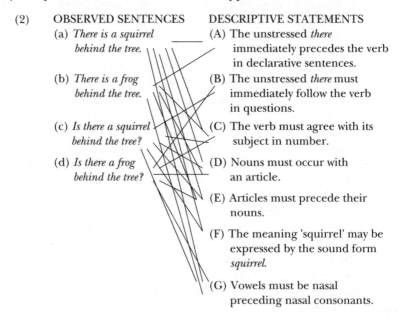

(2)   OBSERVED SENTENCES   DESCRIPTIVE STATEMENTS
         (a) *There is a squirrel*   (A) The unstressed *there*
             behind the tree.   immediately precedes the verb
                                               in declarative sentences.

         (b) *There is a frog*   (B) The unstressed *there* must
             behind the tree.   immediately follow the verb
                                               in questions.

         (c) *Is there a squirrel*   (C) The verb must agree with its
             behind the tree?   subject in number.

         (d) *Is there a frog*   (D) Nouns must occur with
             behind the tree?   an article.

                                         (E) Articles must precede their
                                               nouns.

                                         (F) The meaning 'squirrel' may be
                                               expressed by the sound form
                                               squirrel.

                                         (G) Vowels must be nasal
                                               preceding nasal consonants.

Additional rules stating that certain words or phrases are repeatable any number of times will allow for an infinite number of sentences.

The rules in (2) make reference to various kinds of structural characteristics: the presence of certain words (as in (D)), the presence of an ending in a word (as in (C)), the sound form that goes with a meaning (as in (F)), and details of pronunciation (as in (G)). The branches of descriptive linguistics analysing sound form are called **phonetics** and **phonology**. (While phonetics and phonology have distinct domains – phonetics analyses individual speech sounds and phonology analyses their sequences – the term phonology may be used broadly so as to include both.) The analysis of meanings is called **semantics**. Meaning-form linkages are formulated as rules of the **lexicon**, **morphology** and **syntax**. How these components fit together will be discussed in Section 4.

3.3 FUNCTION

All complex objects have structure but not all of them have function. Artifacts, such as spoons, books and trains, are functional; natural objects, such as rocks, mountains or thunderstorms, are not – unless somebody presses them into service, such as using a rock to crack open a nut.

Language is a human artifact and it does have functions. The most obvious purpose that language serves is communication – that is, for rendering thoughts public and addressing them to somebody.

Communication includes three components: an idea that the speaker has, a form in which he expresses the idea and an addressee that the idea is communicated to. While all three of these factors may be prominent in an act of communication, there are uses of language where only one or two of them stand out, with the others receding or not present at all. Thus, in puns and in poetry, form may acquire supreme significance that may outweigh content. In small talk, both literal content and form are underplayed – the very fact of exchanging a few words with somebody on an inconsequential topic such as the weather can communicate goodwill and camaraderie. Also, simply expressing thoughts may be de-coupled from wanting to convey them to somebody else, such as when writing a diary. And in thinking, neither addressing another person nor even trying to express one's thoughts is present.

While communication is the most obvious function of language, human language is neither necessary nor sufficient for human communication. Postures, gestures, facial expressions and various kinds of bodily contact may not only complement – or cancel – a verbal message but may also entirely replace it. Besides, language may not even be the best means for communicating some messages. The process of fitting ideas into linguistic form is often frustrating: a stream of thoughts is somewhat like a waterfall which, when reaching the foot of the mountain, loses its power by being forced to split into rivulets that follow already existing ruts in the ground. Linguistic expression forces the speaker to utilize publicly agreed-upon means for bringing forth what is on his mind and thus possibly to compromise some of the intended content.

Identifying the functions of artifacts is important if we want to explain structure: the structural characteristics of artifacts must support or at least be compatible with their function. For example, it would be hard to understand why bicycles were built the way they are if we did not know what they were used for. Does language function similarly leave its marks on language structure? This question will be taken up in Section 4 of Chapter 7.

3.4 LOCATION

Everything – both simple and complex objects and objects with or without function – occurs somewhere. In other words, everything has a location. The location of an object can be specified in terms of space, time, and natural and social context. For example, boats are normally found in water; and two legs as a means of locomotion are located in humans and birds. The location of a set of objects relative to their surrounding conditions is called their **distribution**. For example, one can describe the distribution of oak trees in Wisconsin by referring to the areas where they grow and the distribution of different hair colours among people by specifying the body type and age factors that condition them.

The location, or distribution, of sentences is definable in reference to linguistic and extralinguistic context. What is the **linguistic context** in which sentences are located? First, sentences are generally not used in isolation: they occur as parts of sentence sequences forming coherent discourses, such as conversations, lectures, poems or novels. Second, sentences are part of a language that includes many other sentences that are all similar: they share grammatical characteristics with each other. We will call the first type of context **syntagmatic** and the second, **paradigmatic**. Here are non-linguistic examples for the clarification of these terms. Paprika and whipped cream share the paradigmatic context of Western cuisine since they are both available in that style of cooking even though they may never be used together in any one dish; while whipped cream and powdered sugar share not only paradigmatic but also syntagmatic context since whipped cream is generally sweetened with powdered sugar.

Apart from the linguistic context, the other factor defining the location of sentences is the **extralinguistic context**: the particular speech situation in which a particular sentence is uttered and, more generally, the natural and social environment in which the language is used.

Just like function, the location of an object or phenomenon can also serve to explain aspects of structure: the structure of an object or phenomenon may in part be determined by the context in which it occurs. For example, the kinds of trees that grow in some areas are limited and thus predictable by the climatic and soil conditions available. Similarly, languages reflect the general natural and social conditions under which they are used; and the structure of sentences is influenced by the particular speech situation where they are spoken.

Within a given speech situation, the identity of the speaker – whether male or female, whether a child, a young adult or an old person, whether college-educated or not, what region of a given country a person is from, and their current physical and psychological state – will influence how a person speaks. In addition, an individual's particular style of speech will also depend on the identity of the addressee and other attendant conditions.

The aspect of language structure that most clearly reflects surrounding natural and social conditions is vocabulary. For example, it is well known that Eskimo languages have an extensive set of terms for various kinds of snow. Another example: the Shona people of Zimbabwe and Mozambique, forming an agricultural society, have at least 20 different words for walking, such as for 'walk with a squelching noise through a muddy place', 'walk while making a noise of breaking sticks', 'walk naked or almost naked' and so on.

4 Why do languages have syntax?

Let us now return to the first-mentioned property of sentences: structure. In Section 3.2, five types of rules were mentioned as instrumental in describing sentence structure: phonetic-phonological, semantic, lexical, morphological and syntactic. What exactly is the contribution of each of these rule types? Are all of them necessary?

The description of any symbolic object – such as body gestures, traffic signs or religious rituals – must, by definition, include information about meaning, form and the correspondence between the two. Sentences are symbolic objects: every sentence has a form and a meaning. It thus follows that any description of sentence structure must include three kinds of information: about meanings, about sound forms and about what meanings go with what sound forms. As noted above, these components of grammar are called phonology, semantics and the lexicon, respectively. These three components are therefore indispensable, logically necessary parts of grammar. Let us consider each in turn.

Both phonological and semantic descriptions include in some form an inventory of basic components, rules of selection and rules of arrangement. For example, the **phonology** of English will say that English has both /s/ and /p/, that they can be selected to introduce a syllable, and if they are so selected, the /s/ must precede the /p/ (cf. words like /spɪl/ (spelled *spill*) but none like */psɪl/). Similarly, the **semantic** description of English will characterize meanings in terms of the selection and arrangement of components. The principal components include 'predicate', 'argument' and 'tense'. What is meant by 'predicate' is the action, event or state that the sentence is about; 'arguments' are the participants in the action, event or state; 'tense' refers to time. For example in *Joe wrote a letter*, 'wrote' is the predicate, 'Joe' and 'a letter' are the arguments, and the tense is past. Relying on these concepts, semantic descriptions will say that 'predicate', 'argument' and 'tense' may be selected together to form a sentence meaning, and that tense must go with predicates and not with arguments.

The third logically necessary component of grammar is the **lexicon**. Lexical rules show symbolic correspondence relations between small units of meanings and sounds: they assign the right sound forms to the right meanings.

How small should the chunks of form and chunks of meaning be that lexical rules relate to each other? It is easy to imagine symbolic systems where lexical rules apply to the entire meanings and entire forms of symbols. For example, in the system of traffic lights, the colours – red, green and amber – cannot be broken down into components that would separately symbolize parts of the meanings 'wait', 'go' and 'prepare to stop'. In other symbol systems, however, bits of form are separately associated with bits of meaning. A ritual meal is an example: while the whole meal has a meaning, each food item has its own symbolic significance.

Sentences are like ritual meals in that they consist of recurrent parts each of which carries meaning by itself. Thus, lexical rules are best stated not on entire sentences but on the smallest recurrent meaningful parts of sentences called morphemes. For example, the meaning-form relation underlying the sentence *The squirrels nibbled at the acorns* does not have to be stated by a single rule for the entire sentence: a separate rule can be formulated for each morpheme, such as DEFINITE = *the,* SQUIRREL = *squirrel,* PLURAL = *s,* and so on (all capitals stand for meaning representations, orthography stands for sound form). The lexicon is thus a set of symbolic correspondence rules stating the meanings and forms of morphemes.

At this point in our argument, we have three components of grammar: **phonology** describing the sound forms of sentences, **semantics** describing the meanings of sentences, and the **lexicon** relating sound form and meaning for the smallest bits of form that are meaningful – morphemes. Do these three types of rules suffice to describe what well-formed sentences are like?

The answer is 'no' for two reasons. First, well-formed sentences must include well-formed words; but simply having a list of morphemes for a language does not tell us how to put words together out of them. Whether a word is grammatical or not depends on whether the morphemes that make it up have been properly selected and properly ordered. Thus – unless in a language every word consists of a single morpheme only (such as English *pumpkin* or *turn*), or unless both the selection and the order of words are completely free – an additional rule type is needed. The rule type that specifies the selection and order of morphemes in words is called **morphology**.

Morphology tells us how words are formed out of morphemes. If we now consider how sentences in turn are formed out of words, we find a similar picture. First, just as many words consist of more than one morpheme, most sentences consist of more than one word. There are, to be sure, one-word sentences – such as English *Sit!* – but they are not typical of English or any other language. Second, as we already saw in Section 1, the selection and ordering of words is not free: *Johnny fast* is not well-formed because of the wrong selection of words and *Johnny fast runs* is not well-formed because of the wrong ordering of words. These facts point at the second reason why phonology, semantics and the lexicon are not enough to account for the well-formedness of sentences. This is where **syntax** comes in: as morphology does for morphemes, syntax specifies the proper selection and order of words.

The five components of grammar thus stack up as follows:

- logically necessary for all languages: semantics
  phonology
  lexicon
- not logically necessary for all languages: morphology
  syntax
  - morphology:
    - impossible in languages that have only monomorphemic words

- possible in languages with at least some polymorphemic words
- necessary if the selection and order of morphemes in words is not free
- syntax:
  - impossible in languages that have only one-word sentences
  - possible in languages with multi-word sentences
  - necessary if the selection and order of words in sentences is not free

In addition to describing well-formed sentences, syntax also needs to account for what the sentences mean. The lexicon does provide the meanings of the morphemes contained in sentences; but, as we saw in connection with the Turkish sentence in Section 1, the meaning of the entire sentence is not always the simple sum of the meanings of the words. Similarly, the sum of the phonological forms of words does not always equal the phonological forms of the entire sentence: that the word *cafeteria* may have rising intonation in the sentence *Where is the cafeteria?* cannot be part of the lexical entry of that word since it does not always carry this intonation pattern. Thus, in addition to rules of syntactic structure that describe the selection and order of words, we also need syntactic correspondence rules that relate syntactic structures to meanings, on the one hand, and to phonological form, on the other.

Syntax, therefore, complements the other components of grammar – semantics, phonology, the lexicon and morphology – in two ways. On the one hand, it describes the selection and order of words for producing well-formed sentences; on the other hand, it describes the correspondence between sentence structure and sentence meaning, and sentence structure and sentential sound form.

Here are some examples of syntactic rules for English:

(1) (a) syntactic structure rules:
- word selection: Every concrete common noun in the singular must occur with an article.
- word order: The article must precede the noun.

(b) syntactic correspondence rules:
(i) between syntactic structure and meaning:
- In sentences where the predicate has a negative meaning, if they contain no auxiliary, a form of the verb *do* has to be included.
- In sentences whose meaning is a basic weather statement, there must be an *it*-subject.

(ii) between syntactic structure and sound form:
- Yes-no questions carry rising intonation.
- The two syntactic constituents *is* and *not* can make a single phonological word *isn't*.

The two tasks of syntax are presented in diagram (2):

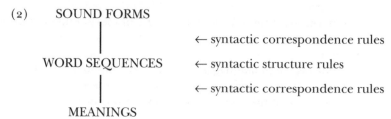

(2)   SOUND FORMS

← syntactic correspondence rules

WORD SEQUENCES   ← syntactic structure rules

← syntactic correspondence rules

MEANINGS

In sum, why do languages have syntactic rules? Because

- most sentences consist of more than one word
- the selection and order of the words in sentences are not free
- the sum of the word meanings does not always equal the meaning of the entire sentence and the sum of the word forms does not always equal the phonological form of the entire sentence

5 Conclusions

This chapter discussed syntax in the context of linguistics and of science in general. Here are the major points that have emerged.

On science

'Only when we are able to find life-as-we-know-it in the larger context of life-as-it-could-be will we be able to understand the nature of the beast' (Langton 1995: 2). The basic message of this statement applies to any branch of science including linguistics: what we want to know is how things are as opposed to how they could be. There are thus two cardinal factors that define the space within which any inquiry – whether in science or in everyday life – takes place: one is external reality and the other is the human mind that observes things, describes the observations, compares what it sees with other logical possibilities and, puzzled when there is no match, asks 'why?'. What an explanation does is to bring about a change in our expectations so that what seems impossible is rendered possible, what seems possible but unlikely is rendered likely and, optimally, what seems possible and perhaps likely but not necessary is revealed as the only option and thus a necessary one. Asking a why-question is asking for a reconciliation between reality and the mind. A true explanation succeeds by resolving the conflict through altering the content of the mind so that harmony between the two is restored.

On descriptive linguistics

Linguistics is a science dedicated to the study of the structure, function and location of sentences. Descriptive linguists focus on language structure and aim at providing maximally general analytic descriptions called grammars. A grammar has five basic components, three of which are logically necessary in descriptions of a language just as they are in the descriptions of any other symbols systems. These three are phonology (or, for symbolic systems that are not sound-based, such as sign language, the description of the particular medium they utilize), semantics and the lexicon. Phonetics and phonology describe the proper selection and order of phonetic form elements. Semantics sets limits to the proper selection and arrangement of meaning elements. The lexicon spells out the minimal pairings of meanings and forms. If words include more than one morpheme and the selection and order of morphemes is not free, rules of morphology are needed to specify how morphemes can be selected to make a word, how they should be ordered, and what the exact meanings and pronunciations of the resulting words are. And given that sentences include more than one word with selection and order constrained, an additional rule component, called syntax, is called for.

ON SYNTAX

Minimally, syntax describes the selection and order of words that make well-formed sentences and it does so in as general a manner as possible so as to bring out similarities among different sentences of the same language and of different languages and render them explainable. Since sentences are not just complex objects but symbolic objects that convey meanings, syntactic rules also need to account for the relationship between strings of word meanings and the entire sentence meaning, on the one hand, and the relationship between strings of word forms and the entire sentential phonetic form, on the other.

Structural syntax – describing word selection and ordering – will be detailed in Chapters 2–4; correspondence syntax – describing the relationship between syntax, meaning and phonetic form – will be taken up in Chapter 5.

Notes

Section 1   Preliminaries
The term 'syntax' is used in two ways in the literature: in reference to a particular aspect of grammatical structure and in reference to the subfield of descriptive linguistics that describes this aspect of grammar.

Section 2.1   Explanation
The concept of explanation known as the deductive-nomological, or covering-law, model associated primarily with Carl Hempel's name (see Hempel and Oppenheim 1948) has been adopted in this book because of its intuitive appeal and for lack of a clear alternative. Nonetheless, it should be noted that this is only one of the several concepts of explanation that have been

entertained by philosophers of science and it has been shown to be unsatis-factory in some ways. A brief and clear summary of the issues surrounding the goals and means of scientific explanations is Newton-Smith (2000). More will be said about linguistic explanations in Chapter 7.

Section 2.3   Description
On the infinite number of hair patterns of giraffes, see *National Geographic Magazine*, September 1977: 403–4.

Section 3.1   Overview
For concise summaries of the various branches of linguistics, consult the web site of the Linguistic Society of America (www.lsadc.org).

Section 3.2   Structure
For arguments for discourse, rather than sentence, being the natural domain of linguistics, see Sanders 1970a. On discourse analysis, see for example Beaugrande and Dressler 1981 and Givón 1997.

Section 3.4   Location
For the Shona walking verbs, see Comrie *et al.* 1996: 89.

Section 4   Why do languages have syntax?
The definition of the concept 'word' is actually more complex than given in this chapter; see Dixon and Aikhenvald 2002.

Exercises

1. Choose a foreign language unfamiliar to you. Translate a couple of English sentences into the language by looking up the words in a bilingual dictionary. Show your sentences to somebody who knows the language and ask for the actual translation. Do your translations and the real ones differ? If so, do they differ in the selection of words or in their ordering or both?

2. Consider the following ungrammatical sentences and determine whether they are ungrammatical because of word order, because of word selection, or both.

   (a) *The rabbits have ran back to the hole.*
   (b) *The rabbits run have back to the hole.*
   (c) *They not have enough to eat.*
   (d) *Squirrels hide nuts and underground.*
   (e) *Nuts and acorns are hide underground.*
   (f) *Are the nuts where?*
   (g) *Acorns grow on.*
   (h) *Who do you think who ate the nuts?*
   (i) *What you think squirrels eat nuts and?*

3. Consider the following common reactions of people to an event:

(a) 'If you had told me before it would happen, I would not have believed it!'
(b) 'Well, it has happened before!'
(c) 'I could not believe my eyes!'
(d) 'Don't tell me this!'
(d) 'No-o-o-o-o!!!'
(e) 'I just KNEW this would happen.'
(f) 'Didn't I tell you???'

What are the initial expectations that can be reconstructed from these reactions? Did the person think that it was impossible for the event to happen, or possible, or probable or necessary?

4. Find an explanation in everyday life or in a science book and spell out its structure by identifying the explanandum, the explanatory principle(s) and the bridge statement(s).

5. Under certain conditions, drivers honk their horn. Describe the distribution of horn-honking in your town. Factors that may determine the distribution may be specific parts of the town, certain stretches of streets, the kind of vehicle, the place where the driver is heading and the driver's state of mind.

6. At the world-famous Niagara Falls, a small sightseeing boat takes visitors deep inside the enormous horseshoe-shaped waterfall. In the midst of the boiling waters, with the towering backside of the falls already in sight through the mist and with people on board scrambling to put on their rain gear to protect themselves against the deluge of water droplets blown at them by the winds, the boat comes to a precarious bobbing halt and the captain's solemn voice is heard announcing: 'Ladies and gentlemen, this is Niagara Falls.' Needless to say, the announcement has no information value – yet, it has an emotional impact on people. What do you think is the function of this announcement and why does it have the effect that it has?

Chapter Two

Linear Order

Our task is not to penetrate in the essence of things, the meaning of which we don't know anyway, but rather to develop concepts which allow us to talk in a productive way about phenomena in nature.

(Niels Bohr in a letter of 20 July 1955, cited in Pais 1994: 45)

1 Preliminaries

Words of a sentence are pronounced one after the other. We will call the temporal sequencing of words their **linear order**.

Linear order relations in language boil down to the temporal order of the articulatory events that produce speech. For example, as you say the word *sleep*, the alveolar constriction which produces the /s/ precedes the partial alveolar closure of the /l/. Although the way articulatory events are produced in time involves complex overlaps, for simplicity's sake we will assume that individual articulatory gestures cluster into simultaneous bundles – that is, phonetic segments – and that phonetic segments are ordered one after the other like beads on a string.

As we say a sentence, how do we know in what order to pronounce the phonetic segments that make it up? There are four types of constraint that determine phonetic segment order: phonological, lexical, morphological and syntactic. First, for an example of a phonological order constraint, let us take a closer look at the word *sleep*. Why does the /s/ precede the /l/ rather than in reverse? This is not an isolated fact in English: the word-initial /sl/ cluster also shows up in many other words such as *slender* or *slogan*. On the other hand, there are no English words starting with /ls/: if a word is to start with a sequence of /s/ and /l/, their order must be /sl/. The word-initial /s/-before-/l/ order is thus a **phonological** constraint.

Second, consider now the word *cat*. Why should /k/ precede /æ/ rather than the other way around? There is no phonological reason for this: words like *act* show that word-initial /æk/ is as easily pronounceable in English as word-initial /kæ/. All that can be said about the sequence /kæ/ in *cat* is that it is required by the meaning of this particular word: if you want to refer to a *cat*, /k/ must come before /æ/ and not in reverse. In this case, we are dealing with a **lexical** restriction on the order of phonetic segments.

Third, not all segment sequences are the result of phonological or lexical constraints. Take the word *cats*. Why does /t/ precede /s/? It is not for reasons of pronunciation: *cast* is as pronounceable as *cats*. Nor is it a lexical constraint since *cats* is not a single lexical item. The reason is that in *cats*, the /s/ is the plural marker, which is an inflectional morpheme and all inflectional morphemes in English follow the stem. In this case, it is a **morphological** rule that effects the order of /t/ before /s/.

Fourth, consider the sequence /ik/ in the middle of the phrase *furry cat*. There is no phonetic constraint against the opposite order in English: /ki/ occurs, for example, in the middle of *black eagle*. Nor can this order be a lexical stipulation since the two phonetic segments belong to different words; and, for the same reason, no morphological rule is involved here, either. There is nonetheless a generalization that dictates the /ik/ sequence. The relevant rule is that in English, adjectives precede their nouns. Since the /i/ happens to be the final segment of the adjective *furry* and the /k/ happens to be the first segment of the noun *cat*, /i/ will end up immediately preceding /k/ in *furry cat*. The same rule that puts /i/ before /k/ in *furry cats* will place /i/ before /d/ in *furry dogs*, /d/ before /k/ in *old computers*, and so on. Here, phonetic segment order is the result of a **syntactic** ordering rule.

The four types of rules determining the order of phonetic segments in language have parallels in other areas. Take music. First, just as two phonetic segments may be ordered in a particular way because of the pronunciation conventions of a language, two notes may be sequenced so as to conform to the permitted successions of notes in a given musical style.

Second, if two notes are part of a musical motif – for example, the 'signature' of a character in a Wagner opera – the order is irreversible because the meaning assigned to the motif would not come through otherwise. This is the equivalent of lexical ordering. And, for an analogy of morphological and syntactic ordering, picture a singer's performance. The last note of the first song will precede the first note of the next song simply because the entire unit that one note is part of precedes the entire unit that contains the other note.

In sum, syntactic word order rules have the same function as phonological, lexical and morphological linearization constraints: they determine the order in which certain phonetic segments are to be pronounced in a sentence. Phonetic and lexical specifications directly order phonetic segments; morphological and syntactic order rules refer to larger units – morphemes and words – that consist of sequences of segments so that the phonetic segments, being parts of words, get a 'free ride'.

Since this book is about syntax, we will discuss only syntactic order rules: the ordering of words. As we saw in Chapter 1, the ultimate goal of any scientific study is to explain the facts observed; and a fact calls for an explanation if it is counter to expectation. Accordingly, our discussion in this chapter falls into three parts. In Section 2, we will explore the range of logically possible patterns of word order. Section 3 will look at some actual patterns of syntactic order. In the concluding section, we will summarize the generalizations that emerge about how actual facts and logical possibilities differ and attempt an explanation for one syntactic order pattern.

2 Temporal relations: some possibilities

2.1 The general schema

All temporal relation statements – whether in or outside language – are instances of the following schema:

> (1) **(M) If (A, B), then A t B /W**
> In prose: in context W, given A and B, they must (or may, or must not) be in temporal relation t.

The formula involves four components. A and B refer to the events to be arranged in some temporal relation: they are the **terms** of the relation. t is the **temporal relation** that is to hold between A and B. W, which may be null, specifies the **context** within which the relation is to hold. M is the **modality** of the statement: whether the given temporal relation must or may hold or must not hold. In (2) there are two examples from the ordering of food courses in a meal.

> (2) (a) MUST: (Entrée, Dessert) → Entrée & Dessert
> (b) MAY: (Entrée, Salad) → Entrée ~ Salad /Lunch

In (2a), the entrée must precede the dessert. The terms are entrée and dessert; the relation is immediate precedence (symbolized by the ampersand &); there is no context specified; and the modality is 'must'. In (2b), the terms are entrée and salad; the relation is simultaneity (symbolized by ~); the context is lunch; modality is 'may'. It says that entrée and salad may be served simultaneously for lunch.

We will now consider the various logically possible realizations of the general schema in (1) by looking at what temporal relations and their terms, contexts and modalities may be.

2.2 RELATIONS

Let us take a closer look at temporal relations. Simultaneity and immediate precedence, illustrated in (2), are only two of the ways in which events can be linked to each other in time. To explore the entire range of options, let us take the two events of driving a car and of listening to the car radio. What are possible temporal relations that may hold between the two?

First, there is the familiar option of immediate precedence (see (2a) above): you first drive somewhere and when you get there, you turn on the radio; or you first listen to the radio and then you begin to drive. Another possibility, exemplified in (2b), is that the two events are simultaneous: you turn on the radio as soon as you turn on the engine and you turn the radio off at the end of the trip.

There are three additional possibilities. One event may include the other, such as if the radio is switched on after the engine was turned on and is switched off before the end of the trip. Or the two events may overlap: the music is turned on after starting the trip and is left on after the engine is turned off. Finally, if you drive for a while, then stop the car and listen to the radio, then turn off the radio and resume driving, the two events are interlocked.

In (3) are diagrams showing all five relations. D stands for 'driving', L stands for 'listening to music'. The three dots in (e) show the possible additional portions of driving and listening to music resulting in a multiple interlocking pattern.

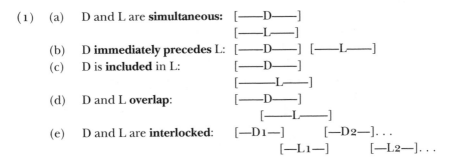

(1) (a) D and L are **simultaneous:**   [——D——]
                                        [——L——]
     (b) D **immediately precedes** L: [——D——] [——L——]
     (c) D is **included** in L: [——D——]
                                         [———L———]
     (d) D and L **overlap:**   [——D——]
                                           [——L——]
     (e) D and L are **interlocked:**   [—D1—]   [—D2—]...
                                              [—L1—]   [—L2—]...

These five relations are not equally basic. Inclusion, overlap and interlocking are complex relations composed out of simultaneity and immediate precedence that hold between subparts of the two events. Interlocking involves the immediate precedence of parts; inclusion and overlap involve both simultaneity and immediate precedence.

This leaves us with two basic relations that make up the others: simultaneity and immediate precedence. While neither can be reduced to the other, immediate precedence, as its name suggests, is further analysable as the combination of adjacency and precedence. Adjacency (the 'next-to' relation) and precedence (the 'before' relation) are two distinct notions that may vary independently: one event may precede another regardless of whether they are adjacent or not and, conversely, two events may be adjacent regardless of whether one precedes the other or the other way around. Neither adjacency nor precedence by itself defines a unique position for an event in relation to the other, but the two together do, yielding immediate precedence.

Let us now relate these general considerations to the order of words. The five relations – simultaneity, immediate precedence, inclusion, overlap and interlocking – are logically possible temporal arrangements for events in general: but can all of them apply to words? It is clear that a word can follow another in immediate sequence; but can, say, an adjective and a noun be simultaneous, or one include the other, or one overlap the other, or can the two be interlocked?

These in-principle possibilities are shown in (2). A stands for Adjective, such as *black*, N stands for Noun, such as *dog*, A_1 and A_2 are parts of Adjective; N_1 and N_2 are parts of Noun.

(2)   (a)   A and N are simultaneous: [——A——]
                                        [——N——]
      (b)   A immediately precedes N: [——A——] [——N——]
      (c)   A is included in N: [——A——]
                                       [———N———]
      (d)   A and N overlap: [——A——]
                                          [——N——]
      (e)   A and N are interlocked: [—A_1—]   [—A_2—]. . .
                                          [—N_1—]   [—N_2—]. . .

It is easy to see that three of these options are excluded for words. By definition, a word is an independently pronounceable unit of speech. Just as it is not possible for most people to sing two different notes at the same time, the articulatory organs cannot be set in two conflicting configurations simultaneously as would be required if words or their parts were to be pronounced simultaneously. Thus, words can occur only in immediate precedence and interlocking since these are the two that do not involve simultaneity.

In sum, there are five logically possible temporal relations for events in general and of those five, two are available to words: immediate precedence and interlocking.

Having surveyed the possible temporal relations among words, we will turn to the possibilities regarding the second component of the general temporal relations schema given in (1) above: the terms that are in a temporal relation.

2.3 TERMS

The most straightforward way of defining the temporal relationship between two items is by direct reference to the items themselves. For an example, take the waiting room of a walk-in clinic. Ann and Sue arrive at the same time; who will be admitted first? The doctor may decide to take Ann before Sue because of his personal preference for Ann. If so, he goes by the simple 'rule': Ann before Sue. In this case, the two people are ordered as individuals: **tokens are ordered as tokens** (where 'token' refers to a specific member of a class).

Individuals may also be referred to indirectly, in terms of some of their characteristics. This can happen in several ways. First, we can refer to an item by the type that it belongs to. The scene is once again the doctor's office with Ann and Sue waiting to be called. Suppose the office has a policy that patients over 60 are admitted before patients under 60. This general rule, which makes no reference to Ann and Sue in particular, will nonetheless define their order if Ann happens to be 62 and Sue is 58. Here Ann and Sue are **tokens ordered by reference to their types**.

Another way of referring to individuals indirectly is in terms of the part–whole relations they participate in: either by the wholes that they belong to or by the parts that they contain. Suppose the order in which members of couples are admitted to the doctor's office is based on their combined age. Thus, either member of a couple whose combined age exceeds 90 years is admitted before either member of another couple whose combined age falls below 90. In this manner, Ann may be younger than Sue but she will still precede Sue if she has an old enough husband. (In actual practice, doctor's offices do not of course adopt such weird policies; but we are considering logical possibilities here.) This example illustrates that two terms may be ordered by characteristics that do not hold for them as individuals but only for the larger unit that they belong to: **parts are ordered by reference to their wholes**.

Then there is the reverse possibility. Suppose the scene is the office of a family counsellor who sees couples together. He has adopted the rule that a couple is admitted first if at least one of its members is over 60. By this rule, a larger unit – a couple – is given priority over another because of a characteristic of a part of that unit: **wholes are ordered by reference to one of their parts**.

In all these instances, each individual in the ordering relation was identified in some way. Consider now a case where the doctor decides to see one particular patient before all others regardless of who the others are. In such cases, one individual's position is defined numerically as 'first' relative to the other individuals who are not specified at all. This order pattern may be called **numerical ordering**. In addition to first position, there are many other possibilities: second, third, fourth, last, one-before-last and so on.

In numerical ordering, one specific individual is ordered relative to one or more unspecified ones. Is it possible for both terms of an ordering rule to be unspecified? What such a rule would say is that any individual may precede any other individual. This is the case if a dinner host announces that there is no set seating arrangement around the table: 'just sit wherever you would like'. This is an instance of **free ordering**.

In sum, we have found six ways in which temporal relation rules may refer to their terms:

(a) terms are ordered as individuals
(b) terms are ordered by virtue of the types they belong to
(c) terms are ordered by virtue of the wholes they belong to
(d) terms are ordered by virtue of a part that belongs to them
(e) a specified term is ordered in relation to unspecified terms (numerical order)
(f) unspecified terms are ordered relative to each other (free order)

All these ways of identifying terms are logically possible in syntax as well: words might be ordered as individual lexical items, or by reference to their taxonomic (i.e., type-token) and partonomic (i.e., whole–part) properties. Similarly, there is no reason why words could not be ordered numerically or allowed to occur in free order.

Having considered temporal relations and their terms, we will now turn to the a third component of temporal relation statements: possible contexts in which a temporal relation is said to hold.

2.4 CONTEXT

How two events are ordered may depend on the situation. In some cultures, husbands are expected to go before their wives when entering a restaurant but they will yield to their wives when entering their home. Thus, neither of the two orders 'husband entering before wife' and 'wife entering before husband' holds in all situations but each holds under certain conditions.

The order of words can be similarly context-dependent. Conceivable contexts may be a particular sentence type or a particular style in a language or a particular language. For example, the auxiliary in English follows the subject in declarative sentences but precedes it in yes–no questions; and adjectives precede nouns in English but generally follow them in French.

2.5 MODALITIES

In Section 2.1, we saw that the general schema for temporal relation statements contains four components: relation, terms, context and modality. In the preceding three sections, we discussed the first three; what remains is modality.

Modality (just as context) is not specific to temporal relation rules: it is a factor in all rules regardless of what they say. There are three modality options:

- two terms **must** occur in a particular relation
- two terms **may** occur in a particular relation
- two terms **must not** occur in a particular relation

For example, when designing a seating arrangement for a formal dinner party, you may decide on any of the following guidelines:

- husbands and wives **must** sit next to each other
- husbands and wives **may** sit next to each other
- husbands and wives **must not** sit next to each other

We will call the three types of modalities **requirement, permission** and **prohibition**. The fourth logical possibility – **may not** – means the same as 'must not'.

When it comes to ordering words, there is again no reason for any one of these logical possibilities to be barred.

2.6 Summary

In sum, here are the logical possibilities of relations, terms, contexts and modalities for word order:

(1) (a) RELATIONS:
  - immediate precedence
  - interlocking

(b) TERMS:
  - referred to as tokens
  - referred to by virtue of the types tokens belong to
  - referred to by virtue of the wholes tokens belong to
  - referred to by virtue of a part that belongs to tokens
  - one term specified, the other term unspecified
  - both terms unspecified

(c) CONTEXTS:
  - sentence type
  - style
  - language, and so on

(d) MODALITIES:
  - must
  - may
  - must (or may) not

In (2) are shown (partly hypothetical) examples of some of these logical options for ordering the two words *new* and *puppy*. The rules in (2) fall short of illustrating all logical possibilities surveyed above in that, of the two relations that can hold in syntax – immediate precedence and interlocking – they illustrate immediate precedence only and, of the available modalities, they employ MUST as an example. Context is omitted. Furthermore, they do not exemplify the various combinations of the basic options, such as one of the terms referred to one way and the other in another way (e.g. one term is a token, another is a type). Each rule is first stated as a formula and then in prose.

(2) (a) TOKENS ORDERED AS TOKENS
  - MUST: (*new, puppy*) → *new* & *puppy*
  - Given the words *new* and *puppy*, *new* must immediately precede *puppy*.

  (b) TOKENS ORDERED BY THEIR TYPES
  - MUST: (Adjective, Noun) → Adjective & Noun
  - Given an adjective and a noun, the adjective must immediately precede the noun.

  (c) PARTS ORDERED BY THEIR WHOLES
  - MUST: (Adjective Phrase, Noun) → Adjective Phrase & Noun
  - Given an adjective phrase and a noun, the adjective phrase must immediately precede the noun.

  (d) WHOLES ORDERED BY THEIR PARTS
  - MUST: ([n . . .], [p . . .]) → [n . . .] & [p . . .]
  - Given two words one starting with /n/ and another starting with /p/, the /n/-initial word must immediately precede the /p/-initial word.

  (e) NUMERICAL ORDER
  - MUST: (new, X) → new & X
  - The word *new* must be first – that is, must precede everything else.

  (f) FREE ORDER
  - MUST: (X, Y) → X & Y
  - Given the two words *new* and *puppy*, either must precede the other.

The question that now arises is which of these possibilities actually occur in the word order patterns of human languages? It is logically possible to order words individually as tokens; but are there languages that actually do this? Are words ever ordered by reference to their parts? Or by reference to the wholes they belong to? We will now embark on an investigation of some of these questions.

3 Temporal relations in syntax: some facts

3.1 RELATIONS

3.1.1 Immediate precedence

As seen in Section 2.2, the two temporal relations that are available for words are immediate precedence and interlocking. One might expect both to be equally common in word order patterns. In fact, however, immediate precedence is far more common. Rules of immediate precedence are exemplified from English in (1).

(1) (a) MUST: (Adjective, Noun) → Adjective & Noun /English
In prose: The adjective must immediately precede the noun in English.
Examples: *pretty penny*
inexhaustible resources

(b) MUST: (Adverb, Adjective) → Adverb & Adjective /English
In prose: The adverb must immediately precede the adjective in English.
Examples: *very big (storm)*
hardly surprising (event)

(c) MUST: (Verb, Object) → Verb & Object /English
In prose: The verb must immediately precede the object in English.
Examples: *(The mechanic) fixed the landing gear.*
(The boys) were picking apples.

As was noted in Section 2.1, the immediate precedence relation may be analysed into two distinct components: adjacency and precedence. The question is whether, for purposes of formulating rules of word order, it is better to view them as a single basic relation or to separate the two components. For example, should the Adjective & Noun order in English be stated in terms of a monolithic rule as in (1a) above, or in terms of two rules as in (2)?

(2) (a)   ADJACENCY RULE:
            The noun and the adjective must be adjacent in English.
     (b)   PRECEDENCE RULE:
            The adjective must precede the noun in English.

How can we decide which description is better, (1a) or (2)? Here is the answer. If the two relations – adjacency and precedence – consistently co-vary, there is no reason to posit two separate relations; but if they vary independently from each other, they need to be recognized as separate relations. In other words, if it turns out that, given two syntactic units A and B, if A precedes B, A is always immediately next to B, there is no reason to talk about adjacency and precedence as separate relations. But if, when A precedes B, the two may or may not be adjacent, or when A and B are adjacent, they can occur in either order, this would show that adjacency and precedence are independent of each other and we need to be able to talk about them as such.

What are the facts to decide this issue? There are cases where adjacency and precedence are jointly constrained. For example, the English demonstratives *this, that, these* and *those* both precede and adjoin the rest of the noun phrase; for example, *these red tulips* and not *red tulips these* or *red these tulips*. If all instances of syntactic ordering were like this, it would be pointless to split the concept of immediate precedence into adjacency and precedence since there would never be a need for a rule to refer to one without the other.

However, there are many instances where adjacency and precedence part ways: either of the two relations may be restricted while the other can go either way. An example of adjacency being invariant but precedence going either way is the order of sentence adverbs and clauses in English: the sentence adverb may precede or follow the clause but, either way, it has to be adjacent to it.

(3) (a)   ADVERB & CLAUSE:
            (i)   *I told Jack that **tomorrow, there is a holiday**.*
            (ii)   *I told Jack that **mornings, it is difficult to park**.*
     (b)   CLAUSE & ADVERB:
            (i)   *I told Jack that **there is a holiday tomorrow**.*
            (ii)   *I told Jack that **it is difficult to park mornings**.*

If immediate precedence were to be construed as an atomic, unanalysable concept, we could not talk about adjacency and precedence separately and, therefore, the ordering of sentence adverbs and clauses could only be described as two distinct relation patterns: Adverb & Clause and Clause & Adverb, with the two having nothing in common. But if adjacency and precedence are identified as two distinct relations, we gain a generalization: the precedence relation between adverb and sentence differs but their adjacency is the same.

The independence of adjacency and precedence is also shown by cases of the opposite kind, where precedence is invariant but proximity varies. For example, the relative clause in English always follows the head noun but it may or may not be adjacent to it.`

(4) (a) NOUN & RELATIVE CLAUSE:
   (i) ***The software that you lent to me*** *is indispensable.*
   (ii) ***A man who was in a bad mood*** *visited me.*

(b) NOUN . . . & . . . RELATIVE CLAUSE:
   (i) ***The software*** *is indispensable* ***that you lent to me.***
   (ii) ***A man*** *visited me* ***who was in a bad mood.***

Precedence and adjacency can independently vary not only within languages, as seen in (3) and (4), but even more across languages. Here are three examples. First, while in English most adjectives precede their nouns, in Spanish, French and Italian most adjectives follow the noun. Nonetheless, in all four of these languages, adjectives remain adjacent to their nouns. If we separate adjacency and precedence, we can reduce differences between the patterns Adjective & Noun and Noun & Adjective to a difference in precedence while highlighting their shared relation: adjacency.

Second, the precedence relation of nouns and relative clauses also varies across languages: in English and French the relative clause follows but in Turkish and Japanese it precedes the head noun. Nonetheless, the adjacency relation between noun and relative clause is normally adhered to in all these languages.

For a third example showing the utility of separating adjacency from precedence in cross-linguistic generalizations, consider the order patterns of the three main sentence constituents Subject (S), Verb (V) and Object (O) in the languages of the world. All six logically possible orders are attested but they vary greatly in frequency.

(5) (a) FREQUENT ORDERS:
   - SVO
     e.g. English: *Bill hit John.*
   - SOV
     e.g. Japanese: *Biru ga   gohan o   tabeta.*
                     Bill SBJ rice   DO ate
                     'Bill ate rice.'
   - VSO
     e.g. Irish: *Bhuail Liam Sean.*
                  hit   Bill John
                  'Bill hit John.'

(b) LESS FREQUENT ORDERS:
   - VOS
     e.g. Fijian (Keenan 1978: 277):

> *A raica   na tagene na yalewa.*
> PAST see the man   the woman
> 'The woman saw the man.'
> • OVS
> e.g. Hixkaryana (Derbyshire 1985: 32):
> *Toto yahoosıye   kamara.*
> man it:grabbed: him jaguar
> 'The jaguar grabbed the man.'

(c)   RARE ORDER:
> • OSV
> e.g. Apurinã (Derbyshire and Pullum 1981: 206):
> *anana   nota apa*
> pineapple I   fetch
> 'I fetch the pineapple.'

If precedence and adjacency were viewed as inseparable Siamese twins, the six orders could only be described as all equally distinct; no generalization would be possible to differentiate frequent, less frequent and rare patterns. But notice that there is a characteristic that is unique to the frequent patterns: S precedes O, whether immediately or non-immediately. Furthermore, there is a feature that sets apart the less frequent orders from the single rare one: in the former, V and O are adjacent, while in the rare pattern, they are separated. The possibility of stating these generalizations about frequent, less frequent and rare orders crucially hinges on our being able to refer to adjacency and precedence as two separate relations.

Thus, the answer that emerges to the question raised above is that in many cases it is useful to formulate adjacency and precedence rules separately. What the separation of the two relations allows is limiting language-internal and cross-linguistic differences in word order to differences in precedence with adjacency invariant, or the other way around.

This argument provides an example of Niels Bohr's point cited in the epigraph at the start of this chapter: that the goal in science is to develop concepts that allow us to talk productively about things in the world. The goal is to arrive at generalizations and create concepts that best support them.

3.1.2 Interlocking

While immediate precedence is the dominant order pattern in syntax, interlocking is also amply documented. As was seen in Section 2.2, interlocking involves immediate precedence where the terms for which this relation holds are parts of the larger constituents whose order is to be determined. In other words, interlocking involves discontinuous constituents: wholes are split into two or more parts by the intrusion of one or more parts of another constituent.

One might expect to find discontinuity in any unit of grammar: words, phrases and clauses. In actuality, larger constituents are more subject to discontinuity than smaller ones. To start with morphological structure: words are rarely discontinuous although the phenomenon is not unattested – English provides examples of interwoven words such as *fan-bloody-tastic, abso-blooming-lutely.*

Much more common is discontinuity in phrases and clauses. English phrasal verbs (= verb plus particle constructions) illustrate split phrases. The (ii) examples below show that the object noun phrase may interrupt this unit:

(1) (a) (i) *The man **called up** the fire department too late.*
          (ii) *The man **called** the fire department **up** too late.*

    (b) (i) *The gorilla **put down** the rock.*
        (ii) *The gorilla **put** the rock **down**.*

Latin poetic language is famous for interlocking phrases, as in the following example (Ovid, *Metamorphoses* VII: 620–1):

(2) *Tiliae   cotermina quercus   collibus est Phrygiis*
    linden.tree adjacent oak.tree in:hills is in:Phrygian
    media   circumdata   muro.
    smallish surrounded by:wall
    'In the Phrygian hills, next to a linden tree there is an oak
    tree surrounded by a smallish wall.'

As the shared inflectional suffixes help to see, the words *collibus Phrygiis* 'in the Phrygian hills' form a phrase which is interrupted by *est* 'is'; *media* and *muro* also make a single phrase ('by a smallish wall') but this phrase is interrupted by *circumdata* 'surrounded'. This word in turn belongs with *quercus* 'oak tree', which is four words away.

The interruption of clauses by parenthetical expressions is even more common than that of phrases. The (ii) sentences of (3) are examples:

(3) (a) (i) ***As I told you many times***, *vipers are very dangerous.*
          (ii) *Vipers,* ***as I told you many times***, *are very dangerous.*

    (b) (i) *Diamond rings are of great value.* ***I wish I had one!***
        (ii) *Diamond rings –* ***I wish I had one!*** *– are of great value.*

In most cases, if two constituents occur in interlocking order, we find that this ordering pattern is only one of two options in the language: the constituents can also occur in immediate precedence. This was already shown by the (i) sentences of the English examples in (1) and (3); and it is also true for the Latin example in (2) where the non-discontinuous alternative would be *Quercus cotermina tiliae circumdata media muro in collis Phrygiis est.*

Nonetheless, in some cases discontinuity is the only order pattern for two constituents. For example, while in English, verbal particles and full noun

phrases may occur in either order, one involving discontinuity of the verb &
particle phrase, and the other not, if the object is a pronoun, the particle
must be split off its verb:

(4) (a) *John **called up** Jill.*
     *John **called** Jill **up**.*

(b) *John **called** her **up**.*
    John **called up her.*

Another example of obligatory interlocking comes from French, where the
negative marker consists of two words separated by the verb that is being
negated:

(5) *Je **ne** sais   **pas**.*
   I **not-** I:know **-not**
   'I do not know.'

   Je **ne pas sais.*
   Je sais **ne pas.*

In addition to the fact that syntactic interlocking order patterns mostly alter-
nate with non-discontinuous expressions, there is also another limitation on
them: they tend to involve only a single constituent split by another, rather
than several constituents intertwined. This is to be noted all the more since
examples of multiple interlocking of morphemes do occur within words.
See, for example, Arabic *katab* 'he wrote', *kaatib* 'writer', *kitaab* 'book', where
the word root is the discontinuous *k–t–b* and the affixes are similarly discontinuous pairs of vowels.

In sum, let us formulate some generalizations about linear relations in
syntax. These generalizations show that the facts part ways with the logical
possibilities surveyed in Section 2. Although both logically possible syntactic order relations – immediate precedence and interlocking – do occur in
languages, the two differ in frequency and each operates under some
constraints.

(6) 1. Of the two temporal relations that can hold between words,
immediate precedence is more frequent than interlocking
both within and across languages.
2. The two component relations of immediate precedence –
adjacency and precedence – can vary independently both
within and across languages.
3. For two constituents, interlocking generally alternates with
immediate precedence but in some cases it is the only
alternative.

4. Interlocking commonly involves splitting clauses, less commonly, splitting phrases, and least commonly, splitting words.
5. Interlocking is generally minimal in that it involves one constituent split by one other constituent.

3.2 TERMS

3.2.1 *Tokens and types*

In the preceding section, some of the actually occurring syntactic temporal relations were surveyed. We will now turn to how the terms of syntactic order statements are defined.

At the end of Section 2.6 (see (2)), we exemplified the six logically possible ways in which ordering rules may refer to the two words *new* and *puppy*. Here is another set of (partly hypothetical) examples employing *sleep* and *late*. Here and throughout the book, the modality marking MUST will be omitted from obligatory rules since this is the most common, default modality.

(1) (a) TOKENS ORDERED AS TOKENS
       (*sleep, late*) → *sleep* & *late*

    (b) TOKENS ORDERED BY THEIR TYPES
       (Verb, Adverb) → Verb & Adverb

    (c) PARTS ORDERED BY THEIR WHOLES
       (Verb Phrase, Adverb Phrase) → Verb Phrase & Adverb Phrase

    (d) WHOLES ORDERED BY THEIR PARTS
       ([*sl*. . .], [*l*. . .]) → [*sl*. . .] & [*l*. . .]

    (e) NUMERICAL ORDER
       (*sleep*, X) → *sleep* & X

    (f) FREE ORDER
       (X, Y) → X & Y

Let us now see which of these patterns actually occur in languages.

In the overwhelming majority of cases, words do not need to be fully identified in the rules that put them in order. That is, there are few words in any language that stand out from all others by obeying an order rule that is unique to them. Instead, as we saw in the beginning of Chapter 1 in connection with the Turkish sentence, words belong to classes according to their order characteristics. Thus, for example, there is no specific rule needed to order *about* before *Jack* in the phrase *about Jack*, one that would specifically mention the two words; instead, there is a general rule that orders adpositions before nouns. The rule holds for many other pairs of words as well, such as *from Jack* and *about lions*. Additional examples of ordering words by word classes are as follows:

(2) (Determiner, Noun) → Determiner & Noun
   Examples: *the letters*
      apig
      these papers

(3) (Numeral, Noun) → Numeral & Noun
   Examples: *five owls*
      three plums
      five solutions

Nonetheless, there are cases where order rules need to refer to individual words. One example comes from English. The overwhelming majority of English adpositions is preposed to the noun phrase. Thus, there is *under the bed* and *in the room* and not **the bed under* and **the room in*. But there is one adposition – *ago* – which must be postposed: *a week ago* (and not **ago a week*). The rule assigning obligatory postpositional order to *ago* must make reference to this particular word.

Another example of token-based ordering comes from Tagalog (Schachter and Otanes 1972: 414).

(4) *Nagtatrabaho nga   rin daw   kayo roon.*
   work   indeed also they:say you there
   'They say it is true that you are working there too.'

The ordering of some of these words follows from general rules mentioning word classes. *Nagtatrabaho* 'work', for example, stands in the beginning of the sentence since it is a verb and verbs in Tagalog are generally sentence-initial. Similarly, the order of the words *kayo* 'you' and *roon* 'there' follows from the generalization that subjects precede adverbs. However, there is no generalization from which the order of *nga* 'indeed', *rin* 'also' and *daw* 'they' would follow: their ordering can be stated only in reference to these very items. The rule is as follows:

(5) (*nga, rin, daw*) → *nga* & *rin* & *daw*

In sum, with few exceptions, words are ordered as types rather than as individual items in languages. This is a good thing: the extreme alternative – every word having its own order constraint – would clearly make language learning an even more formidable task than it already is.

In (1) are illustrated six ways in which terms of order rules may be defined. So far we have explored the first two: words ordered as tokens and words ordered as types. We now turn to the remaining four.

3.2.2 *Parts and wholes*

If you position a whole, you cannot help positioning its parts at the same time. For example, if I raise my hand, all five fingers will also be raised; and if an entire family moves from Kansas to Nebraska, that means every member of the family will move.

This simple fact about how parts and wholes relate to each other can be exploited in formulating rules of word order. For one thing, this is how the ordering of morphemes and words brings about the ordering of phonetic segments (cf. Section 1). Thus, in order to get the /d/ to precede the /ɪ/ in the word *reading*, we construct a rule that orders the verb stem, along with all its phonetic segments, to precede the affix along with all its sounds. Similarly, to get the final /n/ of *learn* to precede the initial /r/ of *rules* in the expression *learn rules*, we formulate a rule that puts the word *learn* in front of the word *rules* by reference to the fact that learn is a verb and *rules* is its object: verbs must precede their objects in English.

While words can serve as wholes whose ordering results in the ordering of their constituent morphemes and sounds, words can in turn be parts themselves that are ordered in terms of the larger wholes that they belong to. Consider the following sentences:

(1) (a) **The heavy rain** *destroyed several villages.*
     (b) *Several villages were destroyed by* **the heavy rain.**

(2) (a) **The five squirrels** *ate all the acorns.*
     (b) *All the acorns were eaten by* **the five squirrels.**

What is responsible for the word sequence *the heavy rain* preceding the verb in the first sentence of (1a)? It cannot be a characteristic of any of these three words since, as (1b) shows, the very same three words can also follow the verb. Rather, the pre-verbal position of these three words is the result of the fact that they form a larger unit: the subject of the sentence, which must precede the verb. In (1b), the three words do not form a subject and this is why they are not sentence-initial. Similarly, *several villages* follows the verb in (1a) because these words make an object in (1a) (but not in (1b)) and objects must follow verbs. The same argument applies to the ordering of the word sequences the *five squirrels* and *all the acorns* in (2). The rule for (1a) and (2a) may be formulated as follows:

(3) (Subject, Object, Verb) → Subject & Verb & Object

In this rule, words are ordered by virtue of the wholes (subject, object) that they are parts of.

Another example of words ordered by their superordinate wholes is what is known in the literature as the 'heavy NP shift'. The (a) and (b) sentences in (4–7) differ in the order of the direct object (DO) and the prepositional phrase (PP).

(4) (a) **DO** & PP: *We discussed **the problem** in class.*
     (b) PP & **DO**: **We discussed in class **the problem**.*

(5) (a) **DO** & PP: *We discussed **the problem that Sue raised** in class.*
     (b) PP & **DO**: *We discussed in class **the problem that Sue raised**.*

(6) (a) **DO** & PP: **We discussed **the problem that Sue raised and that hit the front page last Tuesday night** in class.*
     (b) PP & **DO**: *We discussed **the problem** in class **that Sue raised and that hit the front page last Tuesday**.*

(7) (a) **DO** & PP: **We discussed **the problem that Sue raised and that hit the front page last Tuesday even before I ever heard of it** in class.*
     (b) PP & **DO**: *We discussed in class **the problem that Sue raised and that hit the front page last Tuesday even before I ever heard of it**.*

What these examples show is that the direct object phrase, which is normally right after the verb in English, may be or must be shifted to the end of the sentence depending on the 'weight' of the phrase. 'Weight' does not mean phonological length: a single-word object that consists of many syllables still tends to follow the verb directly. Rather, it has to do with syntactic complexity: whether the object does or does not include a relative clause and how complex the relative clause is. But complexity is not a property of any one part of the phrase; just like the combined age of a married couple in our example in Section 2.3, it is a property of the whole. Thus, the ordering of a heavy noun phrase at the end of the sentence is another example of the ordering of parts through ordering the whole.

The inverse possibility is for wholes to be ordered by their parts. To change our earlier examples to fit this possibility: if I raise my forefinger high above the table, my entire hand cannot but follow suit; and if the head of a close-knit family is relocated to Nebraska, the whole family will ordinarily move with him. For a syntactic example, consider English adjectives. They generally precede their nouns:

(8) ***big** problems*
     ***easy** solutions*
     ***delightful** cookies*

Consider now the following:

(9) ***very big** problems*
     ***deceptively easy** solutions*
     ***such delightful** cookies*

In these examples, the adjective is modified by an adverb and it is now the whole complex – adverb and adjective – that precedes the noun.

One might try to account for this by saying that the entire whole – the adjectival phrase – is ordered. This would then be a case of parts: the adverb and the adjective being ordered by their wholes – a pattern exemplified above by subject–verb–object order. But notice that there is a difference. The labels 'subject' and 'object' apply to entire phrases: there is no particular element within the phrase that is the primary carrier of subjecthood and objecthood. But in (9), what we see is that any phrase that contains an adjective with or without adverbs is ordered in the same way as an adjective is all by itself. The ordering of subjects has nothing to do with the ordering properties of the words that make them up; but the ordering of adjectival phrases follows the ordering of one of the parts: the adjective itself. Thus, while the subject phrase is best thought of as a whole with various parts, the adjective phrase is best thought of as consisting of a 'head' – the adjective – and its dependents. In terms of this analysis, a single ordering pattern holds for both (8) and (9):

(10) (Adjective, X), Noun → (Adjective, X) & Noun
      (where X may be an adverb or may be 0)

When applied to (9), this rule orders wholes by virtue of one of their parts – just as when a couple gets to see the doctor because of the age of one of them (see Section 2.3).

In sum: in this section, we have seen that two of the logically possible ordering rules – parts ordered by virtue of their wholes and wholes ordered by virtue of their parts – do indeed occur in natural human languages.

Note that in order for such rules to be formulated, we cannot just think of sentences as strings of words all on the same level. To be able to formulate whole-based rules, we need to view sentences as containing several larger-than-word units of which words are parts; and in order to state type-based rules (see Section 3.2.1), words and the phrases and clauses that they are parts of must be representable as types rather than tokens. We will call the relation between a whole and a part **partonomy** (such as the relation between the hand and a finger); and the relation between a type and a token will be called **taxonomy** (such as the relation between hand and right hand).

On the next page, the partonomic structure of the categories making up *very furry cats* is given. Partonomic relations are represented by branches; taxonomic categories are shown by the labels assigned to the nodes.

Such tree diagrams are well known from traditional grammar. What is important to realize, however, is that they are not somehow 'given' to begin with nor does their creation represent a goal in and of themselves. The rationale for positing tree diagrams is that they make explicit the assumptions that are needed to support generalizations about the ordering of constituents (and, as we will see in Chapter 3, their selection). Although

(11)

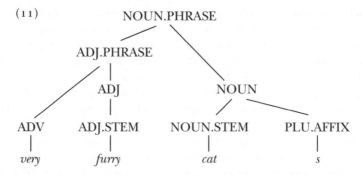

partonomic and taxonomic analyses are presupposed in the formulations of such generalizations, they are heuristically posterior to them: we know what whole-part and type-token relations would be useful to assume only when we begin to discover patterns of order and selection. Tree diagrams are thus conceptual tools that we deploy in our attempt to formulate maximally simple generalizations about syntactic structure. This bears out once again Niels Bohr's point in the epigram at the start of this chapter. More will be said about creating concepts in Section 3 of Chapter 4.

3.2.3 Unrestricted terms

So far we have seen examples where terms of syntactic ordering rules are represented as tokens, or as wholes and parts, and/or as types. We will now turn to a further logical possibility: where one – or both – of the terms is not specified at all.

An example comes from Tagalog. As discussed in Section 3.2.1, Tagalog orders some words as individual tokens. In addition, this language also provides an example of **numerical ordering**. Consider the position of the word *siya* 'he' in the sentences in (4) (Schachter and Otanes 1972: 183–93).

(1) (a) *Masaya **siya** ngayon.*
     happy **he** today
     'He is happy today.'

   (b) *Hindi **siya** masaya ngayon.*
     not **he** happy today
     'He is not happy today.'

   (c) *Bakit **siya** hindi masaya ngayon?*
     why **he** not happy today
     'Why is he not happy today?'

What rule is responsible for the position of *siya* 'he'? In (1a), *siya* follows *masaya* 'happy'; but it would not do to conclude that *siya* must always follow *masaya* 'happy' or that it must follow adjectives in general since in (1b), *siya* precedes *masaya*. Similarly, even though in (1b), *siya* follows a negative word *hindi* 'not', this cannot be a general rule either since in (1c) *siya* precedes *hindi*. What this shows is that *siya* is not ordered relative to any particular word or word class. The generalization is that *siya* immediately follows the first word of the sentence whatever it is – an adjective as in (1a), a negative word as in (1b), or a question word as in (1c). The rule is given in (2)(where #X is the first word of the sentence):

(2) (*siya*, #X) → #X & *siya* / Tagalog

For a similar example, consider the following sentences in Serbo-Croatian (Javarek and Sudjic 1963: 71).

(3) (a) *Ja **ga** vidim.*
 I **him** I:see
 'I see him.'

 (b) *Sada **ga** vidim.*
 now **him** I:see
 'Now I see him.'

 (c) *Vidim **ga**.*
 I:see **him**
 'I see him.'

The pronoun *ga* 'him' follows the pattern of Tagalog *siya* 'him': its position is not fixed relative to any particular word or word class. Rather, *ga* follows the first word of the sentence regardless of whether it is a subject pronoun as in (3a), or an adverb as in (3b), or the verb as in (3c). The rule is stated in (4):

(4) (*ga*, #X) → #X & *ga* / Serbo-Croatian

Although it might look as if Tagalog *siya* and Serbo-Croatian *ga* are placed in the second position of the sentence, this is not so because *siya* and *ga* are not 'real words': they do not have their own stress. Such elements are called clitics. The numerical position that they occupy is therefore not 'second' but 'first' since these elements are stuck – 'encliticized' – to the first word of the sentence. To illustrate true second-position ordering, consider the order of major sentence constituents in German. In the sentences of (5), the verb consistently follows the first phrase of the sentence, no matter what it is. The sentences all mean 'John saw a wolf yesterday in the forest', with emphasis on whichever constituent is directly pre-verbal.

(5) (a) *Hannes **sah** gestern einen Wolf im Wald.*
 John **saw** yesterday a wolf in:the forest

(b) *Gestern* **sah** *Hannes einen Wolf* *im* *Wald.*
yesterday **saw** John a wolf in.the forest

(c) *Einen Wolf* **sah** *Hannes gestern* *im* *Wald.*
a wolf **saw** John yesterday in.the forest

(d) *Im* *Wald* **sah** *Hannes einen Wolf gestern.*
in.the forest **saw** John a wolf yesterday

(e) **Hannes einen Wolf* **sah** *gestern* *im* *Wald.*
John a wolf **saw** yesterday in.the forest

(f) **Einen Wolf gestern* **sah** *Hannes im* *Wald.*
a wolf yesterday **saw** John in.the forest

(g) **Sah Hannes einen Wolf gestern* *im* *Wald.*
saw John a wolf yesterday in.the forest

Numerical ordering of the kind seen in the Tagalog, Serbo-Croatian, and German data is not a frequent pattern across languages and its actual instances do not begin to exhaust the range of logical possibilities. In principle, constituents could be ordered into first, second, third, fourth, fifth positions and so on. They could also be ordered into initial, final, medial, penultimate, antepenultimate and so on places. Of these, first position, second position and final position may be the only ones that ever figure in syntactic order rules.

While numerical ordering involves one of the two terms left unspecified, Tagalog also provides an example of free order, where both terms of the order pattern are unspecified. Consider the following sentence (Schachter and Otanes 1972: 83):

(6) *Nagbigay ng libro sa babae ang lalaki.*
gave DO book IO woman SUBJ man
'The man gave the woman a book.'

In (6) is shown the order Verb & Direct Object & Indirect Object & Subject. While this sentence is grammatical as it stands, there are five additional versions of it that are all equally good and mean the same thing. All six versions have the verb in initial position but they differ in the ordering of the post-verbal noun phrase constituents.

(7) (a) V DO SBJ IO
Nagbigay ng libro ang lalaki sa babae.
gave DO book SBJ man IO woman

(b) V IO DO SBJ
Nagbigay sa babae   ng   libro ang lalaki.
gave   IO woman DO book SBJ man

(c) V IO SBJ DO
Nagbigay sa babae   ang lalaki ng   libro.
gave   IO woman SBJ man DO book

(d) V SBJ DO IO
Nagbigay ang lalaki ng   libro sa   babae.
gave   SBJ man DO book IO woman

(e) V SBJ IO DO
Nagbigay ang lalaki sa babae   ng   libro.
gave   SBJ man IO woman DO book

The text in (8) states this pattern: it says that post-verbal noun phrases can be freely ordered.

(8) (X, Y) → X & Y / Verb___
(where X and Y are noun phrases of any kind)

Although free word order does occur, there are stringent limits to this freedom. First of all, as already observed above, no language allows all words to occur in any conceivable position in the sentence: all languages observe some adjacency and some precedence constraints. This is interesting because there is no reason why languages should not be able to do without either or even without both. Latin poetic language (exemplified in (2) in Section 3.1.2), where affixes are the sole formal indicators of which words belong together, shows what all languages could be like; and the question is why they are not all like that.

A second constraint on the occurrence of free word order is that in many cases, if alternative orders are available, the alternative turns out to be not freely selectable: the two order patterns are not completely equivalent. The alternative orders may be differentiated by the lexical choice of the terms, by their structural make-up, or by their meanings.

One example of lexical constraints on alternative orders was already referred to above: English adpositions. Based on a hasty inspection of phrases such as *about the book, under the table*, and *two years ago*, one might formulate a general rule that states free order for adpositions: they may precede or follow the noun phrase. But in fact, as mentioned above, most English adpositions are strictly ordered: *about, under* and so on must all be preposed while *ago* must be postposed. Thus, what might appear to be free order for the category of adpositions is actually strict order for the particular lexical tokens of the class.

A similar example is numerals that, in some languages, show two kinds of orders: standing before and standing after the noun. While this may appear as free order, the ordering depends on the particular numeral. In Igbo, for example, most numerals follow the noun but 'one', '20' and '400' precede it (Greenberg 1978: 285).

A second way in which what might appear to be free order is actually constrained has to do with the structural composition of the terms. A case in point is English bare adjectives and adjectives with a complement:

(9) (a) *angry children*
          *children angry

     (b) **angry with their parents children*
          children angry with their parents

(10) (a) *beloved teachers*
          *teachers beloved

     (b) *beloved by students teacher
          teachers beloved by students

These examples show that adjectives are not free to occur either before or after the noun. Rather, adjectives that lack complements precede the noun and adjectives with complements follow it.

Regarding order variation of this kind accompanied by structural differences, there are two generalizations to make. First, if two constituents can occur either adjacent or non-adjacent and there is a structural difference between the two constructions, non-adjacency favours the explicit marking of at least one of the two constituents. This extra marking shows the semantic relationship between the two.

Here is an illustration from Hungarian. In (11) the possessor immediately precedes the possessum and it may or may not be marked with the genitive suffix *-nak* (if it is, the possessum takes the definite article).

(11) (a) A   *fiú-**nak**   a   kávéját   öntsd ki.
          the boy-**GEN the** his:coffee:ACC pour out
          'Pour out the boy's coffee.'

     (b) A   *fiú* kávéját   öntsd ki.
          the **boy** his:coffee:ACC pour out
          'Pour out the boy's coffee.'

However, the immediate precedence of possessor relative to the possessum is not the only available order: possessor and possessum may be separated from each other with either of them preceding the other, as in (12):

(12) (a) *A fiú-nak   öntsd ki a kávéját.*
      the boy-GEN pour out **the his:coffee:ACC**

   (b) *A kávéját   öntsd ki a fiú-nak.*
      the his:coffee:ACC pour out **the boy-GEN**

What is interesting is that non-adjacent ordering is possible only if the genitive case marker is present; otherwise, it is ungrammatical:

(13) (a) **A fiú öntsd ki (a) kávéját.*
      the boy pour out **(the) his:coffee:ACC**

   (b) **A kávéját   (a) fiú öntsd ki.*
      the his:coffee:ACC (the) boy pour out

A similar example showing the need for explicit marking on non-adjacent constituents comes from Warlpiri, an Australian language with fairly free word order. If the noun and the adjective are adjacent, only the adjective is case-marked; if the two are separated, both have to be case-marked (Hale 1973: 314). The sentences of (14) both mean 'The big dog bit me.'

(14) (a) *tjaṇtu wiri-ŋki tji yalkuṇu*
      dog   big-ERG me bit

   (b) *tjaṇtu-ŋku tju yalkuṇu wiṛi-ŋki*
      dog-ERG me bit   **big-ERG**

A second generalization about alternative orderings paralleled by structural differences, possibly related to the first, is that 'larger' constituents have more linear freedom than 'smaller' ones. This generalization holds across phonology, morphology, syntax and discourse structure. Affixes are almost always strictly ordered within a word; single words are less subject to alternative ordering than phrases are; and phrases are more fixed in position than clauses. Add to this the relative ease with which paragraphs of a discourse may be switched around and, at the other end, the infrequency with which the phonetic segments of a morpheme may be freely scrambled and we end up with the scale in (15), where terms on the left tend to have more freedom of order than terms on the right:

(15) paragraph sentence clause phrase word morpheme sound

This observation parallels the generalization offered in Section 3.1.2, according to which interlocking order most commonly involves splitting clauses, less commonly splitting phrases, and least commonly splitting words. Thus, in comparison to larger constituents, smaller ones are more resistant both to internal discontinuity and to alternative ordering.

The examples above show that seemingly free word order is often not free: it may be constrained either by the lexical choice of the terms involved or by their structural complexity. As already mentioned, there is also a third constraining factor on seemingly free order: alternative orders of the same items may be correlated with semantic differences. In Russian, if a numeral precedes the noun, it expresses a precise number but if the same item follows – as it may in colloquial style if there is a round number involved – the number is approximate (Vladimir Nedjalkov, personal communication; Greenberg 1978: 284):

(16) (a) *pjat' čelov'ek*
       five man:GEN
       'five men'

(b) *čelov'ek   pjat'*
     man:GEN five
     'about five men (perhaps four or six)'

Another example of alternative precedence correlated with a meaning difference is French adjectives, as illustrated in (17) and (18) (Waugh 1977: 87–8).

(17) (a) *l'homme   pauvre*
       the man poor
       'the poor (=impecunious) man'

(b) *le pauvre   homme*
     the poor man
     'the poor (=pitiable) man'

(18) (a) *un mangeur furieux*
       an eater   angry
       'an angry eater'

(b) *un furieux mangeur*
     an angry   eater
     'a compulsive eater'

The post-nominal adjectives of these examples modify the referent of the noun; the pre-nominal adjectives pertain to the particular description of the referent that the noun provides. Thus, (18a) means 'an angry person, who is an eater' while (18b) means 'a person who eats ferociously'.

In sum, we have seen that all six logically possible patterns of term specification in order rules actually occur in languages although not with equal frequency and not without constraints. The following cross-linguistic generalizations emerge:

(19) 1. Words are rarely ordered as individual tokens.
2. Words are frequently ordered by reference to the types they belong to.
3. Words may be ordered by reference to the wholes – phrases or clauses – that they belong to.
4. Phrases and clauses may be ordered by reference to the parts that belong to them.
5. Of the various numerically definable positions, only a few – such as first and second – actually occur.
6. All known languages observe some constraints on both adjacency and precedence.
7. Alternative orders within a language often differ from each other by the lexical choice of the terms, or by their structural complexity, or by meaning.
8. Syntactically more complex constituents are more prone to alternative ordering than less complex ones.

3.3 CONTEXT

As was seen in Section 2.4, the ordering of any two events may depend on surrounding context. This is true for the ordering of words as well. First of all, many order rules apply in one language but not in others. Thus, as we have just seen, adjectives that would precede the noun in English will follow it in French. Another example is the ordering of adpositions (ADP) relative to the noun phrase (NP) in English and in Japanese:

(1) (a) (ADP, NP) → ADP & NP /English
example: *of John*

(b) (ADP, NP) → NP & ADP /Japanese
example: *John no* 'of John'

In addition to the choice of language, structural characteristics of sentences may also limit the applicability of a rule. This is illustrated in (2).

(2) (a) **The plane should** *arrive at 6 pm.*
When **should the plane** *arrive?*

(b) **All papers must** *be in by Friday.*
When **must all papers** *be in?*

These sentences show that the order of subject and auxiliary varies in English depending on whether the sentence is a statement or a question. In declarative sentences, the order is subject before auxiliary; in (certain) interrogative sentences, it is auxiliary before subject. The choice between the two orders is conditioned by the presence and absence of the question words *when* or *where*. Certain additional restrictions aside, the relevant rule, with both intra-sentential and language context specified, is given in (3).

(3) $(AUX, SBJ) \rightarrow AUX \ \& \ SBJ \ /\#WH_Q\_\_$
                                      English

3.4 MODALITIES

As our general discussion in Section 2.5 showed, there are three modalities: requirement ('must'), permission ('may') and exclusion ('must not' or, equivalently, 'may not'). Do all three modalities apply in syntactic order rules in languages? As noted in Section 3.1.1, there certainly are obligatory order rules in languages. Since every rule that states a required order pattern implies the exclusion of the opposite order, rules of the prohibitive kind also hold.

Furthermore, our discussion of degrees of freedom in word order may also be taken to show that order rules can be optional. For example, the Tagalog free word order rule given in (8) above – $(X, Y) \rightarrow X \ \& \ Y \ / \ Verb\_\_$ (where X and Y are noun phrases of any kind) – which states precedence between any two post-verbal noun phrases, can also be formulated by identifying the particular noun phrases and stating two optional precedence relations for each pair.

Thus, we conclude that syntactic order rules do manifest all three possible modalities.

4 Conclusions

This chapter focused on two issues: how COULD the order of words be specified in natural language sentences; and how is it defined in ACTUAL FACT? In (1) is a summary of the main points that have emerged about the syntactic order relations that occur in languages, and the terms, contexts and modalities involved in ordering rules.

(1) (a) RELATIONS:
    1. Of the two temporal relations that can hold between words, immediate precedence is more frequent than interlocking both within and across languages.
    2. The two component relations of immediate precedence – adjacency and precedence – can vary independently both within and across languages.
    3. For two constituents, interlocking generally alternates with immediate precedence but in some cases it is the only alternative.
    4. Interlocking commonly involves splitting clauses, less commonly splitting phrases, and least commonly splitting words.
    5. Interlocking is generally minimal in that it involves one constituent split by one other constituent.

(b) TERMS:
1. Words are rarely ordered as individual tokens.
2. Words are frequently ordered by reference to the types they belong to.
3. Words may be ordered by reference to the wholes – phrases or clauses – that they belong to.
4. Phrases and clauses may in turn be ordered by reference to the parts that belong to them.
5. Of the various numerically definable positions, only a few – such as first and second – actually occur.
6. All known languages observe some constraints on both adjacency and precedence.
7. Alternative orders within a language often differ from each other either in the lexical choice of the terms, or the structural complexity of the terms, or the meaning of the construction.
8. Syntactically more complex constituents are more prone to alternative ordering than less complex ones.

(c) CONTEXT:
Syntactic order rules may vary with context, such as sentence type or language.

(d) MODALITIES:
Both obligatory and optional order rules occur in languages.

These points call for explanations: each point is an empirical observation in the sense that it could be otherwise. The question is therefore: why are they not otherwise?

The generalizations above reveal two kinds of gaps between expectation and reality. First, the occurring patterns do not exhaust all the logical possibilities: some conceivable patterns do not occur. For example, as noted above, it is easy to imagine a language where adjacency and precedence do not vary independently; that is, where all pairs of adjacent words and phrases appear only in one order. Similarly, there is nothing in the mere concept of language that would bar complex interlocking patterns with multiply-interlaced constituents. And why should numerical orders be restricted to only a few positions, such as first and second? Rules that assign stress to words can 'count' farther than that: there are patterns of penultimate and antepenultimate stress positions. So why are there no words that stand in penultimate or antepenultimate position in the sentence?

The other gap between expectation and observation is that some order patterns are more frequent than others even though they all appear equally plausible. What are the reasons for the distributional differences? For example, why is numerical order infrequent within and across languages?

An explanatory account would therefore need to address two basic questions about syntactic order:

(a) Why don't all logically possible patterns occur in human languages?
(b) Of those patterns that do occur, why are some more frequent than others?

One obvious answer to both questions might be that some logically possible orders are more complex than others and that therefore some patterns do not occur or are rare because of their complexity. This seems to be true to an extent; for example, as we saw, words are rarely ordered as individual tokens and, as suggested in Section 3.2.1, the reason might be that it would be very difficult to learn a language if the ordering of each word needed to be memorized separately. But how does the difficulty of a pattern lead to that pattern not occurring or occurring only infrequently? Languages are not designed; they evolve. Thus, there is a missing link here: if complexity is indeed a factor, we still need to explain how it comes into play in linguistic evolution. Besides, we would also need to explain why some of the complex patterns nonetheless do occur.

We have to leave these difficult questions unanswered at this point. The issue of explaining syntactic patterns will be taken up in more detail in Chapter 7; here it will suffice to describe one attempt to explain the existence of a complex linear pattern: verb negation in French. This account demonstrates how a complex construction can evolve historically.

As noted in Section 3.1.2. verb negation in French involves interlocking. In (2) is a repeat of example (5) from Section 3.1.2.

(2) *Je **ne** sais   **pas.***
    I **not-** I:know **-not**
    'I do not know.'

    Je **ne pas sais.*
    Je sais **ne pas.*

Interlocking is a complex order pattern that, as we saw above, is less frequent than immediate precedence; yet it occurs. How did this particular pattern in French arise? Margaret E. Winters (1987) proposes that the original Old French construction was similar to the English expressions in (3).

(3) (a) *I shall **not** go **one step** further.*
    (b) *He **doesn't** know **diddly squat**.*
    (c) *I **haven't** heard **a peep** from her.*

In such sentences, the negated verb is followed by a noun phrase: *one step, diddly squat, a peep*. Winters calls these 'expressive reinforcements'. They refer to the smallest amount of a category and thus, by conveying the meaning 'not even an X', they serve to emphasize the complete and unnegotiable force of the negation. In Old French, negation was expressed by *ne* but negative sentences optionally included such negative reinforcements as well; the nouns that served this purpose included *pas* 'step'. In the course of time, *pas* lost its original meaning and nominal character and was reduced to a mere grammatical marker that became an obligatory part of the negative construction.

This kind of change, called grammaticalization, is common. Another instance of it is the verb *going to* being reduced to the future marker *gonna* in today's English. Thus, the interlocking order of the negator *ne . . . pas* and the verb is explained by the fact that earlier, *ne* was the negator all by itself; *pas* was an object and since it occupied the usual post-verbal position, it was separated from the pre-verbal *ne* by the verb. When *pas* changed from a noun to a negator, it continued to keep its original post-verbal position.

This much explains how the interlocking order of verb and negator arose in French. But the story is not over: the historical change from *ne* as the sole negative marker to *ne . . . pas* becoming first an optional and later an obligatory marker of negation is currently reaching a new stage, leading to the elimination of the interlocking order pattern. This is shown by the fact that in today's colloquial French, *ne* is frequently omitted with the task of negation fully left to *pas*. In (4) are shown a '*ne*-full' and a '*ne*-less' sentence, both grammatical and both meaning 'I am not saying it.'

(4) (a) *Je **ne** le **dis** pas.*
      I **no** it say **no**

(b) *Je le dis **pas**.*
    I it say **no**

As noted by Winters, the dropping of *ne* may be precipitated by a phonetic factor: a general tendency to omit the schwa (the vowel of *ne*) in Colloquial Modern French.

Thus, the complex, discontinuous negative marking *ne . . . pas* turns out to have been just an intermediate stage between an earlier simple, non-interlocking pattern where pre-verbal *ne* was the sole marker of negation, and the more recent non-interlocking, equally simple pattern where post-verbal *pas* is the sole carrier of the negative meaning. The complex interlocking pattern came about through the re-interpretation of *pas* from a post-verbal object to being part of the negator; the return to a non-interlocking pattern may be facilitated by phonetic change which erodes *ne* but leaves *pas* alone.

Winters' analysis appeals to general historical processes to explain both the origin and the demise of a complex interlocking order pattern. It thus provides the link between the complexity and the lack of frequency of a pattern: the interlocking order appears as a transition between two stages, each free of interlocking.

Notes

Section 2.2   Relations

While words cannot be simultaneous, morphemes can since they are not defined as independently pronounceable. A suprasegmental feature, such as a tone, may be a morpheme by itself and may thus be superimposed on segmental material. While this is not a frequent phenomenon, there are examples of it, such as in Lango, where, for some verbs, tone change on the last vowel makes the difference between perfective and habitual aspect (Noonan 1992: 92). The difference between nominal and verbal meaning is signalled by alternative stress position in English, as in *tormént* versus *tórment, addréss* versus *áddress.*

Section 3.1.1   Immediate precedence

Information on the frequency of the various order types comes from Tomlin (1986: 22) and Derbyshire and Pullum (1981). Tomlin does not report any OSV languages and mentions only five OVS languages, but Derbyshire and Pullum provide data on eight languages with OVS and four with OSV, all in South America.

Section 3.1.2   Interlocking

- Morphemes can also interrupt morphemes: the stem may be split in two by an infix (infixing in Tagalog will be discussed in Chapter 5, Section 3.2), or an affix may be split by the stem (such an affix is called ambifix or circumfix; e.g. the progressive marker *pe-an* in Malay: *rasa* 'feel' *pe-rasa-an* 'be feeling' (Lewis 1956: 208); or the German past participle marker *ge-t* in *ge-lieb-t* 'beloved'. Neither is a common pattern. For a cross-linguistic overview of infixation, see for example Moravcsik (2000).
- On discontinuity in syntax, see Huck and Ojeda (1987) and Bunt and van Horck (1996).

Section 3.2.3   Unrestricted terms

- On clitics in general, see Dainora *et al.* 1995.
- On the verb-second phenomenon, see Haider and Prinzhorn (1986). For a unified account of second-position clitics and second-position verbs, see Anderson (1993).
- The terms subject and direct object are not quite appropriate for Tagalog: they are used here only for convenience. See Schachter (1976).
- For a detailed analysis of the ordering of French adjectives, see Waugh (1977).

Section 4   Conclusions

The historical change exemplified by the French data, called grammatical-ization, will be further documented in Chapter 3 (Section 4), Chapter 6 (Section 4.1), and Chapter 7 (Section 4.2).

Exercises

1. Consider the sentence *The porcupines scurried away* in phonetic transcription: [ðə porkjupaynz skərɪd əwey]. For each pair of adjacent phonetic segments, determine the reason for their order: is it phonetic, lexical, morphological or syntactic? Formulate the rules.

2. In Section 3.2.2, it was noted that English direct objects are 'extraposed' to the back of the sentence if they are syntactically complex. Construct examples to find out whether it is indeed syntactic complexity and not phonological length that favours extraposition.

3. As noted in Section 3.2.3, alternative ordering is sometimes related to other aspects of sentence structure. State order rules for the following sentences from Lebanese Arabic. Can you detect a relationship between the position of the direct object and the rest of sentence structure?

    (a) *huwwe šaaf l   bint*
            he   saw the girl
            'He saw the girl.'

    (b) *l   bint huwwe šaaf-ha*
            the girl he   saw-her
            'He saw the girl.'

    (c) *huwwe šaaf l   walad*
            he   saw the boy
            'He saw the boy.'

    (d) *l   walad huwwe šaaf-u*
            the boy   he   saw-him
            'He saw the boy.'

4. Consider the following orderings of determiner, numeral, adjective and noun in English, Kikuyu and Swahili. Formulate the rules and determine how they differ in terms of precedence and adjacency.

    English: *these two good men*
    Kikuyu: *andũ acio er ɪ ega*
                man those two good
                'those two good men'

Swahili: *watu wazuri watatu wale*
        men good three these

5. Find extralinguistic examples of immediate precedence, adjacency, precedence and numerical ordering.

6. Consider the following Indonesian sentences (Sanders 1982). All four mean 'The girl believed that I am a student.' Compare them with their English equivalents. What is the shared Indonesian and English pattern and what might explain it?

(a) *Perempuan ita menanggap* **bahwa** *saja murit.*
    girl   the believed **that** I   student

(b) *Perempuan ita menanggap saja murit.*
    girl   the believed I   student

(c) **Bahwa** *saja murit   perempuan ita menanggap.*
    that I   student girl   the believed

(d) **Saja murit   perempuan ita menanggap.*
    I   student girl   the believed

Chapter Three

Selection

The word **real** does not seem to be a descriptive term. It seems to be an honorific term that we bestow on our most cherished beliefs – our most treasured ways of speaking. The lesson we can draw from the history of physics is that as far as we are concerned, **what is real is what we regularly talk about**. For better or for worse, there is little evidence that we have any idea of what reality looks like from some absolute point of view.

(Gregory 1988: 184, emphasis original)

1 Preliminaries

One of the ways in which a sentence can be syntactically ill-formed is if the words are not placed in the right order. Thus, the sentence *The seagull alighted the mast on* is ungrammatical because *on* should precede *the mast* rather than follow it. The word order rule violated is that adpositions must precede noun phrases in English.

But, as seen in the beginning of Chapter 1 in connection with the Turkish sentence, word order errors are not the only source of ungrammaticality. Consider the sentence *The seagull alighted the mast.* This sentence is also ungrammatical even though no word order rule is violated. The rule placing adpositions before noun phrases, not observed in *The seagull alighted the mast on,* is not infringed upon in this sentence since it does not include an adposition at all. And this is exactly the problem: the sentence is missing a word. The verb *alight* must occur with the adposition *on.*

Syntactic ungrammaticality thus has two sources: the wrong order of words and the wrong choice of words. Accordingly, a grammar must include both rules of word order and rules of word choice. Word order rules were discussed in Chapter 2; we now turn to rules of word selection.

What does choosing the words for constructing a sentence depend on? The answer would seem simple: it depends on what we want to say. There is indeed much truth to this statement. For example, if I want to say that the peppers I am eating are hot, I have to mention the word *peppers* in the sentence and not the word *apples* or *bananas* instead. Much of Chapter 5 will be devoted to exploring the role of meaning in word selection.

However, while meaning plays a large role in the choice of words, it does not fully determine it. Recall the example in the beginning of Chapter 1 of a traveller trying to construct a Turkish sentence based on the intended meaning and how he failed. For the meaning 'Where are my two suitcases?', he came up with (1a) while the correct version would have been (1b).

(1) (a) *Nerede var benim iki bavullar?*
         where are my   two suitcases

    (b) *İki bavul-ım   nerede?*
         two suitcase-my where

Besides not getting the order of some of the words right, he made two kinds of error: he picked words that did not belong to the sentence (*var* 'are' and *benim* 'my') and for one of the words chosen correctly, he did not get the right form (he chose the form *bavullar* 'suitcases' rather than *bavulım* 'my suitcase').

Parallel examples for these two kinds of mistakes in word selection can be constructed in English. Consider (2).

(2) (a) *I feel myself sick.*
    (b) *I feel sick.*

In (2a), there is an extra word that does not belong: the reflexive pronoun *myself.* On the basis of the intended meaning, one might expect this word to be part of the sentence since 'feeling' is a self-directed action. In fact, the German equivalent of the sentence would include the reflexive pronoun.

Thus, *myself* in (2a) is like *var* in (1a): both are semantically plausible words whose choice nonetheless results in syntactic ungrammaticality.

The other kind of problem with the Turkish sentence in (1a) – the choice of the wrong word form – is illustrated for English in (3a).

(3) (a) *The seagulls flies high.*
     (b) *The seagulls fly high.*

The sentence in (3a) is ill-formed because an inappropriate word form is used: *flies* rather than *fly*. This is similar to the use of *bavullar* in (1a) as opposed to *bavulım*: right word but wrong word form. Once again, meaning does not provide guidance: it does not tell us that the verb *fly* has to be in plural form. It is true that the subject – *the seagulls* – is a plural expression; but why should the verb re-iterate this fact? In Korean, for example, verbs do not show the number of their subjects.

Note that this is not a morphological problem: it is not due to an ill-formed word. The English word *flies* is well-formed, as is the Turkish word *bavullar* 'suitcases'. It is just that these word forms are not the right ones for these sentences.

Based on the examples considered so far, we see two ways in which a sentence may be ungrammatical on account of incorrect word choice: a word is chosen which should not be in the sentence, or a form of a word is chosen that does not fit. A third possible word selection error is the inverse of the first: not using a word that should have been chosen. This was the case in *The seagull alighted **the mast*** and it is further illustrated in (4a).

(4) (a) *Is raining.*
     (b) ***It** is raining.*

There is nothing about the meaning of the sentence that would call for the presence of the word *it*; in fact, in Hungarian and in many other languages, no corresponding word would be used in the equivalent sentence. Yet, in English, the sentence is ungrammatical without *it*.

In sum: meaning does not fully determine the choice of the words in a sentence. The intended meaning might mislead one

(a) to include words that render the sentence ungrammatical; or
(b) not to include words that are needed for grammaticality; or
(c) to include right words in wrong forms.

But if meaning does not fully determine the choice of words and word forms in a sentence, then what does? This is the topic of this chapter.

Just as in our discussion of linear order, we will follow the overall logic of inquiry adopted in this book by asking three questions: what could word-selection patterns be like? what are they actually like? and to what extent do actual and possible match? Sections 2, 3 and 4 will take up these issues in turn.

2 Selection: some possibilities

Imagine that you are constructing a toy building out of Lego pieces. The instructions enclosed with the game will tell you which are the right pieces for the structure you are building: a house, a school or a tower.

All instructions dictating the selection of elements for constructing complex objects of any kind must follow the same logic: based on what you intend to build, they tell you what components to select from what is available. Thus, the basic schema of all selection rules – whether for constructing buildings, sentences or anything else – is this:

(1) **(M) If A, then B /W**
In prose: In context W, if A has been selected, B must (or may, or must not) also be selected.

Here are some additional extralinguistic examples:

(2) (a) In American cuisine, for making a cake, flour and sugar must be selected.
(A = cake; B = flour, sugar; W = American cuisine; M = must)

(b) For making a cake and given that flour has already been selected, eggs may also be selected provided the prospective consumers are not allergic to eggs.
(A = cake, flour; B = eggs; W = prospective consumers not allergic to eggs; M = may)

(c) In a cold climate, for constructing a building and given that a roof has already been selected, walls must also be selected.
(A = building, roof; B = walls; W = cold climate; M = must)

(d) Everywhere on earth, for constructing an animal body and given that feathers have been selected, four legs must not be selected.
(A = animal body, feathers; B = four legs; W = everywhere on earth; M = must not)

These examples highlight the four components that all selection rules must include. There are two terms. One is the item to be selected (B above), which we will call the **selectee**. The other term (A above) is the constituent or constituents that have already been selected and that call for (or allow for, or bar) the selectee. We will refer to this term as the **selector**. The relation between selector and selectee will be called **selectional dependency**; the selectee is the dependent term and the selector is the independent one. For example, in (2d), the selectional dependency relation holds between a feathered animal body (the selector) and four legs (the selectee).

The remaining two components are familiar from ordering rules (Chapter 2, Section 2.1). **Context** (W above) is the overall conditions under which the selectional pattern is said to hold; **modality** (M) specifies whether something must or may or may not be selected. For example, in (2d), the context is 'everywhere on earth' and modality is 'must not'.

Let us now explore how selector and selectee may vary. As we saw in Chapter 2, the terms of ordering rules may differ in their partonomic and taxonomic status. The same is true for the terms of selectional rules: selector and selectee may vary partonomically and taxonomically. In addition, they may vary by complexity.

Let us first consider the taxonomic parameter. The selector may select either the type of an object or a particular subtype of an object. For example, all multi-storey buildings require a staircase; but narrow towers require a specific one: a spiral staircase.

In addition to whether a rule specifies the type or subtype of the selectee, a second way in which selection statements may differ is the **partonomic relation** that selector and selectee have relative to each other. Both selector and selectee may be parts of a whole; the selector may be a whole and the selectee a part, or the selector may be a part and the selectee a whole. Cooking provides examples:

(3)	SELECTOR	SELECTEE	EXAMPLE
	part	part	If a recipe includes flour, then it also must include a liquid.
	whole	part	If the recipe is for a cake, then there must be sugar in it.
	part	whole	If the recipe includes yeast, then the result must be bread or pastry.

In addition to their taxonomic and partonomic status, selectors and selectees may differ in complexity: whether they involve one or more entity. In (2a), for example, the selectee was complex: both flour and sugar; and in (2d), the selector was complex: both animal body and feathers. Here are the logical possibilities.

(4) complex selectors:
    (a) conjoined selector:
        If both A1 and A2, then also B.
    (b) disjoined selector:
        If either A1 or A2, then also B.

(5) complex selectees:
    (a) conjoined selectee:
        If A, then also both B1 and B2.
    (b) disjoined selectee:
        If A, then also either B1 or B2.

Three of these four statement types (all except (4a)) are conflations of simple statements. This means that they abbreviate two statements each with only one selector and one selectee, with the two statements sharing either selector or selectee. This is shown in (6); shared terms are in bold.

(6) (4b) broken down into simple statements:
        If A1, then also **B**, AND
        If A2, then also **B**
    (5a) broken down into simple statements:
        If **A**, then also B1, AND
        If **A**, then also B2
    (5b) broken down into simple statements:
        If **A**, then also B1, OR
        If **A**, then also B2

There are two additional types of statement pairs with shared terms which have conflated alternatives with complex terms. These are chained dependencies, where the selectee of one statement is the same as the selector of another, and bidirectional dependencies, where both the selector and the selectee of one statement figure in the other but in reverse roles. An instance of chained dependencies comes from business: if production costs go up, sales prices go up too; and if sales prices go up, sales go down. Bidirectional (mutual) dependency holds between lightning and thunder.

(7) chained selectional dependencies:
    • conjunction of simple statements:
    If A, then also **B**, AND
    If **B**, then also C
    • conflated into a complex statement:
    If A, then also B and then also C.

(8) bidirectional selectional dependency:
    • conjunction of simple statements:
    If **A**, then also **B**, AND
    If **B**, then also **A**.
    • conflated into a complex statement:
    If A, then also B and vice versa.

In sum: the components of all selectional statements are a selector, a selectee, a context and modality. Selector and selectee can vary in their taxonomic and partonomic status as well as in their complexity. As rules of any kind, selection rules may also vary in context and in modality.

In the next section, we will look at some real facts of syntactic selection; but first, the question of the independence of selectional patterns from order patterns will be taken up.

3 Selection in syntax: some facts

3.1 ORDER AND SELECTION

So far, two basic types of syntactic rules have been proposed: ordering and selection. Here are the two rule schemata (temporal order is represented here by immediate precedence):

(1) GENERAL SCHEMA FOR SELECTION
(M) If A, then B /W
In prose: In context W, if A has been selected, B must (or may, or must not) also be selected.

(2) GENERAL SCHEMA FOR IMMEDIATE PRECEDENCE
(M) If (A, B), then A & B /W
In prose: In context W, if A and B have been selected, A must (or may, or must not) immediately precede B.

The concept of selecting items is logically separable from ordering them with respect to each other: one can select items without ordering them. For example, one can pick people to invite to a dinner party without saying how they should be seated around the table; and it is one thing to be selected for the shortlist when applying for a position and it is another thing to be rank-ordered within that list. Ordering, however, presupposes selection.

Since only words that have been selected can be ordered, an ordered set of words necessarily reveals what words have been selected. But if word selection can be 'read off' the ordered string of words, why should syntactic selection rules be stated separately from rules of order? Why not formulate rules that select and order words in a single step?

This quandary is somewhat similar to the one discussed in Chapter 2, Section 3.1.1: whether adjacency and precedence should be construed as two separate relations or as a single atomic relation: immediate precedence. In both cases, the question is whether a complex relation should be analysed into components or whether it should be taken as one monolithic entity. The answer in both cases is an empirical one: it depends on what the facts are. If an account of the facts based on separation is more general, we separate the two relations but if separation does not result in more generality, we do not. As the epigraph at the start of this chapter implies, scientists create their own concepts.

In the case of adjacency and linear order, the data argued for the utility of specifying the two relations separately. This was so because we found that the two relations did not always go hand-in-hand in syntax. We saw cases where terms occurred either as A & B or B & A while remaining adjacent; and also examples where the two stood in the same precedence relation but were alternatively adjacent or distant. With the two statement types separated, adjacency statements provide a common denominator for constituents that vary by precedence while remaining adjacent; and precedence statements provide a common denominator for constituents that vary by their adjacency relations but not by precedence.

Similar reasoning applies to the issue of selection and ordering. If two selected elements always occur in the same order, we might as well specify selection and order together. If, however, there are constructions where the same elements occur in different orders, then we do need to be able to talk about selection independently of order. In such cases, selection provides a level on which the similarity of the two structures can be captured in spite of their different temporal arrangement.

Evidence emerges from data considered in Chapter 1 (Section 1) and especially in Chapter 2 (Section 3.2.3): there are indeed constructions that contain the same items in different orders. For an additional example, consider the basic sentence constituents S(ubject), O(bject) and V(erb). As was shown in Section 3.1.1 of Chapter 2, all six logically possible orderings of these sentence parts occur across languages: SOV, SVO, VSO, VOS, OVS, OSV. By formulating separate adjacency and precedence statements, we created a conceptual tool that allowed us to highlight common properties of the more frequent orders as opposed to the less frequent ones. Thus, in the three most frequent orders – SOV, SVO, VSO – there is a shared precedence relation although adjacency varies: the subject precedes but is not necessarily adjacent to the object. In the less frequent patterns (VOS and OVS), there is a shared adjacency relation although precedence varies: object and verb are next to each other. The rare order (OSV) differs from the less frequent ones by violating this adjacency relation.

But there is also something common to all six of these orderings: they all include the same constituents: subject, object and verb. To highlight this similarity among all six constructions, we need a rule that says that in all these languages, the three constituents may be selected to occur together. This rule of selection abstracts away from both adjacency and precedence relations among the constituents and captures a selectional similarity underlying all six order patterns.

This example suggests the utility of separate selection rules and order rules for purposes of cross-linguistic generalizations. The same point can also be made on the basis of sentences coming from a single language. Consider the English examples in (3):

(3) (a) **Unfortunately**, *the apples turned out to be wormy.*
(b) *The apples,* **unfortunately**, *turned out to be wormy.*
(c) *The apples turned out to be wormy,* **unfortunately**.

Just by having separate adjacency and precedence statements, the similarity among these sentences would not be made explicit. This is because the word *unfortunately* does not consistently precede nor consistently adjoin any other word. Nonetheless, the sentences are alike in that they consist of the very same words. If there were no way to talk about the occurrence of words without also specifying where they occur, this similarity between the sentences could not be captured.

The same point can be made on the basis of the German sentences in (4). In these sentences all having the same meaning, the phrases *ein Buch* and *von deinem Bruder* have no invariant neighbours nor does one always precede the other. Yet, there is a similarity among the sentences: the presence of the same words.

(4) (a) *Ich möchte*   **ein Buch von**   **deinem**   **Bruder** *kaufen.*
       I   would:like a   book from your$_s$ brother to:buy
       'I would like to buy a book from your$_s$ brother.'

(b) **Ein Buch** *möchte ich* **von deinem Bruder** *kaufen.*

(c) **Von deinem Bruder** *möchte ich* **ein Buch** *kaufen.*

(d) **Von deinem Bruder, ein Buch** *möchte ich kaufen.*

In sum: there are structures both within and across languages that include the same words in different orders. To capture the similarity of selectionally alike but linearly distinct structures, selectional statements need to be stated separately from linear order statements.

Section 3.2. will discuss the selection of words; Section 3.3. will take up the selection of word forms.

3.2 THE SELECTION OF WORDS

3.2.1 *The general schema*

The general schema for word selection is a subtype of the general template for selection given as (1) in Section 2:

(1) **(M) If A, then B /W,**
       where A and B are syntactic constituents.
       In prose: In context W, if syntactic constituent A has been
       selected, syntactic constituent B must (or may, or must not) also
       be selected.

In (2) are given some examples. ((2c) pertains to sentences such as *They don't know nothing.*)

(2) (a) In English, for constructing a sentence, a verb must be selected.
(A = sentence; B = verb; W = English; M = must)

(b) In Slavic languages, for constructing a noun phrase and given that an adjective has already been selected, a noun may also be selected.
(A = noun phrase, adjective; B = noun; W = Slavic languages; M = may)

(c) In African-American English, for constructing a sentence and given that a negative verb has already been selected, a negative indefinite object may also be selected.
(A = sentence and negative verb; B = negative indefinite object; W = African-American English; M = may)

As we saw in Section 1, selectional rules may differ from each other in selector, selectee, context and modality. Do actual word selection rules exemplify all the logically possible options? While a complete exploration of this question cannot be offered here, the following three sections will provide partial answers by highlighting four points:

(a) Terms of syntactic selectional rules may differ by partonomic and taxonomic status.
(b) Syntactic selectional rules may have complex selectors and complex selectees.
(c) There are both unidirectional and mutual selection patterns in syntax.
(d) There are syntactic selection rules exhibiting each of the three modalities.

3.2.2 *The taxonomy and partonomy of terms*

As we saw in Chapter 2, words are not generally ordered as individual lexical items; rather, the terms of order rules are often wholes of which individual words are parts, and categories of which individual words are tokens. The same is true for selectional rules: they, too, may apply to superordinate partonomic and taxonomic units rather than to individual words. (1) and (2) are cases in point.

(1) (a) *Peter fainted.*
(b) **Peter fainted Mary.*

(2) (a) *Peter resembles Mary.*
(b) **Peter resembles.*

In (1b) the sentence is selectionally ill-formed because it has an extra word in it that does not fit: the verb *faint* cannot be followed by *Mary*. In (2b) the sentence fails the opposite way: it has too few words in that the verb *resemble* cannot stand by itself.

That we are not dealing with constraints having to do merely with the number of words in a sentence is proven by (3):

(3) (a) *Peter fainted today.*
    (b) **Peter resembles today.*

In (3a) it is shown that, even though *faint* cannot put up with a directly following noun (cf. (1b)), it can readily co-occur with an adverb. In (3b) it is shown in turn that *resembles'* requirement for something to follow it is also not unqualified: what it needs is a nominal and not an adverb. In other words, the selectional rules for the two verbs *faint* and *resemble* must mention particular categories of words. One rule states that *resemble* must occur with a nominal. Another rule states that *faint* must not occur with a nominal.

The verbs *faint* and *resemble* are not unique among English verbs in their selectional constraints. There are other verbs like *faint* – such as *sit* or *exist* – which do not select nominal complements; and there are other verbs like *resemble* – such as *require* or *convince* – which require a nominal complement. Thus, the selection rules are best stated on subcategories of verbs – labelled intransitive and transitive verbs, respectively – rather than on individual lexical items:

(4) (a) Transitive verbs must co-occur with an object nominal.
    (b) Intransitive verbs must not co-occur with an object nominal.

The rules in (4) illustrate the utility of taxonomic relations in the formulation of selection rules.

While example (3) showed that the verb *resemble* does not just require any word to occur: it requires an object, the examples in (5), (6) and (7) show further that it is not just that transitive verbs require some object; rather, they require a particular kind. Thus, *spill* must take a liquid object; *break* takes something rigid for an object; and *massacre* requires a multitude of people as the referent of its object.

(5) (a) *Peter spilled the milk.*
    (b) **Peter broke the milk.*
    (c) **Peter massacred the milk.*

(6) (a) **Peter spilled the window.*
    (b) *Peter broke the window.*
    (c) **Peter massacred the window.*

(7) (a) **Peter spilled the crowd.*
(b) **Peter broke the crowd.*
(c) *Peter massacred the crowd.*

These examples illustrate the need for word taxonomies with multiple levels for stating syntactic selectional constraints.

The significance of partonomic relations can be similarly illustrated. Take the rule in (4a) stating that transitive verbs require a nominal object. In actuality, the object required by transitive verbs is not necessarily a single noun or pronoun, such as *Mary* or *her*; *resemble* can also take entire noun phrases, as in *Peter resembles his favourite uncle in Portugal.* Thus, a more general formulation of (4a) is (8):

(8) Transitive verbs must co-occur with an object noun phrase.

Another illustration of the fact that the terms of selection rules are not necessarily single words is provided by the English and Hungarian sentences in (9).

(9) (a) *Peter massacred ten people.*

(b) *Péter lemészárolt tíz embert.*
     Peter massacred ten person:ACC
     'Peter massacred ten people.'

In both languages, the verb for 'massacre' requires a plural object. In view of this requirement, it may seem surprising that (9b) is grammatical since the object noun – *embert* 'man:ACC' – is singular. This is because in Hungarian, unlike in English, nouns co-occurring with numerals are in the singular. But, since the object noun phrase includes the plural numeral *tíz* 'ten', the requirement that the verb's selectee be plural is fulfilled on the level of the noun phrase.

Other examples of partonomically variant syntactic selectors and selectees are shown in (10).

(10) SELECTOR	SELECTEE	EXAMPLE
part	part	If a phrase includes a preposition, it must also include a noun phrase.
whole	part	If a phrase is to be a prepositional phrase, it must include a preposition.
part	whole	If a phrase includes a preposition, it will have to be a prepositional phrase.

3.2.3 Complex terms

Complex selectees can be exemplified by English verbs.

(1) (a) *Jill is going.*
  (b) **Is going.*

(2) (a) *Jill wants a house.*
  (b) **Wants a house.*
  (c) **Jill wants.*

(3) (a) *Jill gave a sticker to the child.*
  (b) **Gave a sticker to the child.*
  (c) **Jill gave a sticker.*
  (d) **Jill gave the child.*

These examples show that verbs differ in their valence; that is, in the number of obligatory noun phrases they occur with. While intransitive verbs such as *go* have one valence: they require only a single noun phrase, transitive verbs such as *want* have two valences: they require two noun phrases, and ditransitives such as *give* have three valences: they require three noun phrases.

(4) (a) Intransitive verbs select a subject.
  (b) Transitive verbs select a subject and a direct object.
  (c) Ditransitive verbs select a subject, a direct object and an indirect object.

The rules in (4b) and (4c) involve complex selectees. The general schema that they conform to is 'If A, then B1 and B2 . . . are required.'

Complex selectors also occur. Take the dependency relations within a phrase such as *the long snake that slid out of the cage*. The presence of *snake* is required by the article *the*, by the adjective *long*, and by the relative clause *that slid out of the cage*: none of these three constituents could stand by themselves in the sentence position where the entire phrase can. *Snake* thus figures as a selectee of three selectors. This is stated in (5):

(5) (a) If there is an article in a noun phrase, there must also be a noun.
  (b) If there is an adjective in a noun phrase, there must also be a noun.
  (c) If there is a relative clause in a noun phrase, there must also be a noun.

These statements are examples of the schema 'If A1 and A2 . . ., then B is also required'.

3.2.4 Modality

As was seen in Section 2, there are three modality options for selectional dependency relations: requirement, permission and prohibition. If we map these three options over unidirectional and mutual selectional dependencies, discussed in Section 2, we get four patterns: a constituent may unidirectionally require the other; the two may mutually require each other; they may (mutually) tolerate each other; and they may (mutually) exclude each other. (There are only four rather than six options because tolerance and exclusion are necessarily mutual relations.) All four of these occur in syntax. Here are some examples from English:

(1) (a) unidirectional requirement:
- adjectives require nouns; nouns do not require adjectives
- adverbs require verbs or adjectives; verbs and adjectives do not require adverbs
- auxiliaries require main verbs; main verbs do not require auxiliaries
- the reflexive pronoun *himself* requires the presence of a singular masculine subject; but singular masculine subjects do not require the presence of a reflexive pronoun

(b) bidirectional (=mutual) mutual requirement:
- finite verbs require tense; tense requires finite verbs
- (some) nouns require articles; articles require (some) nouns

(c) (mutual) tolerance:
- the verbs *eat* and *drink* may or may not co-occur with objects
- an anaphoric pronoun such as *she* may or may not have an antecedent (i.e., a full noun phrase that it refers to)

(d) (mutual) prohibition
- articles and proper names of people mutually exclude each other
- the verb *give birth* and masculine subjects mutually exclude each other
- verbs and adjectives mutually exclude each other

In the preceding sections, we have seen evidence for the four generalizations made at the end of Section 3.2.1. The examples of syntactic selection statements illustrated that terms of word selection statements may vary in taxonomic and partonomic status and in their complexity, that their dependency relation may be unidirectional or mutual, and that the relation may differ in modality.

As seen in the Turkish and English examples reviewed in Section 1, having chosen the right words does not yet guarantee the selectional well-formedness of a sentence. We will now turn to the selection of word forms.

3.3 THE SELECTION OF WORD FORMS

3.3.1 Two patterns

Here is another English example to show that syntactic well-formedness requires not only the selection of the right words but also the selection of the right word forms.

(1) **The dog like to runs fastly.*

While the word categories of (1) are all correctly selected, the affixes that the words carry are not. First, *like* can occur without the affix *-s* but not if the subject is third person singular, such as *the dog*. Second, *run* can take *-s* but not when it is preceded by *to*. And third, *fast* cannot take the affix *-ly* at all. These examples show that proper selection requires not only the proper choice of words but also the proper choice of word forms complete with the appropriate affixes.

What determines the correct choice of word forms? Apart from the intended meaning, which – just as in word selection – plays a large role, there are two other factors: the word stem and the syntactic context in which the word appears. To illustrate the first factor: *fastly* is morphologically ungrammatical in any context simply because the word stem *fast* cannot take *-ly*. This is not so in the case of *runs*, which is a possible word form in some contexts but not when preceded by the infinitival marker *to*. This word is like the Turkish word *bavullar* 'suitcases', which is also well-formed by itself but it cannot occur in certain contexts, such as with a numeral.

The interplay of the two factors – word stem and sentential context (morphology and syntax) – can be illustrated in more detail on noun forms and verb forms in Latin. The noun stem *colon-* 'settler' may occur in the forms given in (2). (Nominative is the case of the subject, Accusative is the case of the direct object, Genitive is the case of the possessor, Dative is the case of the indirect object, Ablative is a case used after certain prepositions and Vocative is the case of a name used to address somebody. Vowel length is not marked.)

(2) CASE:

	SINGULAR:	PLURAL:
Nominative	*colon-us*	*colon-i*
Accusative	*colon-um*	*colon-os*
Genitive	*colon-i*	*colon-orum*
Dative	*colon-o*	*colon-is*
Ablative	*colon-o*	*colon-is*
Vocative	*colon-e*	*colon-i*

The verb stem *vide-* 'see' also has different inflected forms shown in (3).

(3) PERSON: NUMBER:

	SINGULAR	PLURAL
First person	*vide-o*	*vide-mus*
Second person	*vide-s*	*vide-tis*
Third person	*vide-t*	*vide-nt*

The choice among these noun forms in (2) is contextually free: it just depends on what one wants to say. Thus both (4a) and (4b) are well-formed, one involving the noun form *colon-um*, the other, *colon-os*: either form can be used without anything else in the sentence structure having to be different.

(4) (a) *Colon-**um***   *vide-o.*
         settler-**SG.ACC** see-S1
         'I see a settler.'

     (b) *Colon-**os***   *vide-o.*
         settler-**PL.ACC** see-S1
         'I see settlers.'

The choice among the six verb forms listed in (3) is free in the same sense: instead of *vide-o*, a singular first person form, the singular third person form *vide-t* could also occur, with the meaning different but grammaticality unimpaired:

(5) (a) *Colon-um*   *vide-**t**.*
         settler-SG.ACC see-**S3**
         'He sees a settler.'

     (b) *Colon-os*   *vide-**t**.*
         settler-PL.ACC see-**S3**
         'He/she sees settlers.'

In other instances, however, the choice of a word form is grammatically restricted, rather than free: it is dictated either by the word stem or by some other word of the sentence or by both. Constraints on inflectional choice imposed by the word stem are illustrated in (6):

(6) (a) *Uxor-**em***   *video.*
         wife-**SG.ACC** see:S1
         'I see the wife.'

     (b) **Uxor-**um***   *video.*
         wife-**SG.ACC** see:S1
         'I see the wife.'

The singular accusative ending of the noun *uxor* 'wife' must be *-em*; unlike *colonus* 'farmer', it cannot take *-um*. As in the case of **fastly* discussed above, the constraint is morphological.

More interesting for our purposes are constraints on inflectional choice imposed by the syntactic context. Consider the combinations of the words *puer* with *videt* and *video*.

(7) (a) *Puer colonum   vide-t.*
       boy settler:SG.ACC see-**S3**
       'The boy sees the settler.'

   (b) **Puer colonum   vide-o.*
       boy settler:SG.ACC see-**S1**

   (c) *Ego colonum   vide-o.*
       I settler:SG.ACC see-**S1**
       'I see the settler.'

   (d) **Ego colonum   vide-t.*
       I settler:ACC   see-**S3**

Puer can go with *videt* but not with *video*: if the subject of the sentence is a noun, the verb affix cannot be *-o*. *Video* in turn requires a first person singular subject. Similarly, as shown in (8), once the numeral *duos* 'two(ACC)' occurs with the noun for 'settler', the form *colonum* is excluded:

(8) (a) *Puer duos   colon-os   videt.*
       boy two:ACC settler-**PL.ACC** see:S3
       'The boy sees two settlers.'

   (b) **Puer duos   colon-um   videt.*
       boy   two:ACC settler-**SG.ACC** see:S3

So far we have seen that the choice of affixes on a word is limited by two grammatical factors: local (morphological) – that is, the stem that the affix goes on – and contextual (syntactic) – that is, other words in the sentence.

As far as the syntactically determined choice of word forms is concerned, there are again two ways in which this can happen. The examples in (7) and (8) instantiate the first, with the pertinent rules stated in (9).

(9) (a) THE USE OF THE THIRD PERSON SINGULAR AFFIX
       If the subject of the sentence is of **a particular grammatical person** (such as first or third), the verb must take an affix that shows **the same person.**

(b)   THE USE OF PLURAL AFFIXES
If a noun is associated with a **plural** numeral (such as 'two'),
the noun must take a **plural** affix.

Compare this with the choice between the accusative case and the dative
case as shown in (10). These examples illustrate a second way in which syntactic context can determine word choice.

(10) (a)   *Puer colon-**um**   videt.*
boy settler-**ACC** see:S3
'The boy sees the settler.'

(b)   *Puer colon-**o**   invidet.*
boy settler-**DAT** envy:S3
'The boy envies the settler.'

The rules are stated in (11):

(11) (a)   THE USE OF THE ACCUSATIVE AFFIX
If the verb is *vide-* **'see'**, the complement noun must take the
accusative affix.

(b)   THE USE OF THE DATIVE AFFIX
If the verb is *invide-* **'envy'**, the complement noun must take
the **dative** affix.

The difference between the rules in (9) and (11) is striking: the former do
make some intuitive sense but the latter do not. In (9), the choice of the
person or number of one constituent calls for the affix of another constituent
to show the same person and number: third person subject requires third
person affix on the verb and plural numeral requires plural affix on the noun.
In (11), this is not so: when the verb 'see' requires an accusative affix on the
complement, this is not a duplication of one of its own characteristics.
Similarly, 'dativity', which the verb *invide-* 'envy' requires on its complement,
is not a feature of the verb itself.

The difference is analogous to the ways in which employee uniforms may
be determined at a work place. Picture two alternatives. In one case, each
supervisor requires that his employees wear the same uniform as he wears.
In another case, each supervisor requires a particular uniform for the
employees that, however, he does not wear himself.

The more 'egalitarian' selectional pattern shown in (9) is called, appropriately enough, **agreement**; the more arbitrary one in (11) is called
government.

Let us now see English examples of agreement and government. In
English, case may be marked by a special form of pronouns or by preposition.

(12) (a) *I like her.*
      (b) *You like her.*
      (c) *John likes her.*
      (d) *They like her.*

(13) (a) *John likes **her**.*
      (b) *John approves **of her**.*
      (c) *John worries **about her**.*
      (d) *John confides **in her**.*

In (12), the person and number marking on the verb depends on the person and number of the subject; in (13), the choice of the preposition depends on the verb. The text in (12) exemplifies the agreement of the verb with its subject in person and number; (13) exemplifies the government of the complement by the verb. Here are the relevant rules:

(14) (a) AGREEMENT:
          A subject of **a given person and number** must select the **the same person and number** marker on the present-tense verb.

      (b) GOVERNMENT:
          • The verb *like* selects the **accusative case** for its complement.
          • The verb *approve* selects *of* for its complement.
          • The verb *worry* selects *about* for its complement.
          • The verb *confide* selects *in* for its complement.

Agreement and government will be discussed in more detail in the next two sections.

3.3.2 Agreement

Like all selection patterns, agreement involves a selector and a selectee. The selectee is the constituent whose affix is to be determined and is called the **(agreement) target**. The selector is the constituent that dictates the choice and is called the **(agreement) controller**. The selectional dependency relation between controller and target is called the **agreement relation**. The characteristic that the controller and the target agree in is called the **agreement feature**. The Russian examples below are parallel to the English examples in (12) of Section 3.3.1: the controller is the subject, the target is the verb, and there are two agreement features: person and number.

(1) (a) ***Ja govor-ju** po ruski.*
          I speak-**S1** by Russian
          'I speak Russian.'

(b) **Ty** *govor-iš* *po ruski.*
you$_s$ speak-**S2** by Russian
'You$_s$ speak Russian.'

(c) **Oni** *govor-jut* *po ruski.*
they speak-**P3** by Russian
'They speak Russian.'

How do we determine which of the two constituents of an agreement relation is the controller and which is the target? The subject–verb agreement
rule, stated in (14a) of the preceding section, says that it is the verb that
agrees with the subject rather than the other way around; in other words, it
designates the subject as the primary locus of the agreement features. How
do we know that it is not the reverse: the subject agreeing with the verb? Or
why not say that the two constituents simply co-vary with neither constituent
chosen independently of the other?

There is proof that the subject calls the shots rather than the verb. If the
person and number properties of pronouns came from the verbs, pronouns
would not have person and number when they occur without a verb. But this
is not so: pronouns have person and number properties in all their occurrences. Verbs, however, have no person and number markings in English
unless a subject is present. Thus, the subject is indeed the controller of
agreement and the verb is the target rather than the other way around.

The agreement relation between controller and target may be signalled
by the phonetic form of the affixes: controller and target may have phonetically identical affixes. This is so in the following examples of Latin adjective
and noun agreement:

(2) (a) *colon-**us***   *Roman-**us*** 'Roman settler (SBJ)'
     settler-**MSC.SG.NOM** Roman-**MSC.SG.NOM**

   (b) *colon-**um***   *Roman-**um*** 'Roman settler (OBJ)'
     settler-**MSC.SG.ACC** Roman-**MSC.SG.GEN**

   (c) *colon-**is***   *Roman-**is*** 'to Roman settlers'
     settler-**MSC.PL.DAT** Roman-**MSC.PL.DAT**

More commonly, however, the two affixes differ in phonetic form – as in our
earlier examples in this section – and the controller may even lack an affix
entirely. These possibilities are further illustrated from Latin in (3):

(3) (a) *colon-**us***   *Roman-**us*** 'Roman settler (SBJ)'
     settler-**MSC.SG.NOM** Roman-**MSC.SG.NOM**

   (b) *colon-**us***   *Atheniens-**is*** 'Athenian settler (SBJ)'
     settler-**MSC.SG.NOM** Athenian-**MSC.SG.NOM**

   (c)   *gen-**us***   *Roman-**um*** 'Roman tribe (SBJ)'
          tribe-**NEUT.SG.NOM** Roman-**NEUT.SG.NOM**

   (d)   *vir*   *Roman-**us*** 'Roman man (SBJ)'
          man-**MSC.NOM.SG** Roman-**MSC.NOM.SG**

In (3a) and (3b), both adjectives – *Romanus* and *Atheniensis* – co-vary with the noun *colonus*, but only *Romanus* shows the same-shape affix as the noun. The irrelevance of the phonetic shape of the controller's affix is further shown by the fact that the *-us* affix on the noun does not always call for *-us* on the adjective: in (3c), where it is the ending of a neuter noun rather than of a masculine one, the adjective must take the neuter ending *-um*. In turn, (3d) shows the irrelevance of the very presence of the controller's affix: the noun *vir* has no affix at all, yet it requires the same affixes on the adjective as the noun *colonus*.

    The following examples from Swahili make the same points. CL1 and CL2 indicate gender classes.

   (4) (a) ***m-*tu**   ***m-*zima**   ***yu-*le**   'that healthy man'
              CL1-man **CL1**-healthy **CL1**-that

       (b) ***m-*ti** ***m-*zima**   ***u-*le**   'that healthy tree'
              CL2-tree **CL2**-healthy **CL2**-that

       (c) *bwana*   ***m-*zima**   ***yu-*le** 'that healthy gentleman'
              CL1-gentleman **CL1**-healthy **CL1**-that

In Swahili, both the adjective and the demonstrative agree with the noun in gender. From just looking at the adjective affix in (4a) and (4b), one might think that agreement involves the adjective copying the *-m* affix of the noun. However, the affix of the demonstrative shows that agreement is not necessarily in terms of phonetic shape: the noun *mtu* 'man' requires a *yu-* prefix on the demonstrative, rather than its own *m-* prefix.

    The irrelevance of the phonetic shape of the noun's affix is further shown by the fact that the nominal *m-* prefix – just as the suffix *-us* in Latin seen in (3) – does not uniquely identify the gender of the noun: 'man' and 'tree', although they both have an *m-* prefix, belong to different gender classes as shown by the different affixes that they require on the demonstrative adjective (*yu-* and *u-*, respectively). Finally, note that, just as in Latin (cf. (3d)), a noun can serve as a controller of agreement even if it has no affix at all: *bwama* 'gentleman', a bare stem without a prefix, controls the same kind of agreement as *m-tu* 'man'.

    To summarize so far, agreement is a selectional pattern that involves two constituents. One (the controller) varies in the value of a feature and the other (the target) co-varies with the first by carrying a marker that expresses that same feature value. The schematic characterization of agreement is given in (5).

(5) AGREEMENT:

(M) If A.Xα and B, then B-xα /W,

where • A and B are co-occurring syntactic constituents,
• A.Xα is a subtype of A defined by a particular value α of the feature X, and
• xα is a marker (an affix or a clitic) associated with B that represents the feature value Xα.

In prose: In context W, if constituents A and B have been selected to co-occur and A shows a given value for the feature X, then B must (or may) have an associated marker representing that same value of X.

In the remainder of this section, we will survey examples of different kinds of controllers, targets and agreement features that occur in various languages.

Agreement targets come in great variety; they may be verbs, adjectives, numerals, demonstratives, possessive pronouns, articles, anaphoric pronouns and others. This is in striking contrast with the uniformity of agreement controllers: apart from a few possible exceptions, they are always nominals (i.e., nouns, pronouns or phrases headed by them). Common agreement features are person, number, gender, case and definiteness. The examples below (taken mostly from Lehmann 1982) provide a sample of these options to complement the ones already seen above.

(6) Controller: noun
Targets: article and adjective
Agreement features: number and gender

ANCIENT GREEK
(a) singular and plural masculine forms (in nominative):
h-o   *sof-os*   *anthrop-os*
the-**MSC.SG**.NOM wise-**MSC.SG**.NOM man-**MSC.SG**.NOM
'the wise man (NOM)'

h-oi   *sof-oi*   *anthrop-oi*
the-**MSC.PL**.NOM wise-**MSC.PL**.NOM man-**MSC.PL**.NOM
'the wise men (NOM)'

(b) singular and plural feminine forms (in nominative):
h-e   *sof-e*   *kor-e*
the-**FEM.SG**.NOM wise-**FEM.SG**.NOM girl-**FEM.SG**.NOM
'the wise girl (NOM)'

h-ai   *sof-ai*   *kor-ai*
the-**FEM.PL**.NOM wise-**FEM.PL**.NOM girl-**FEM.PL**.NOM
'the wise girls (NOM)'

(7) Controller: possessor
Target: possessum
Agreement features: number and person

HUNGARIAN
az **én** *testvér-em* 'my sibling'
the **I** sibling-**my**

a **te** *testvér-ed* 'your$_s$ sibling'
the **you$_s$** sibling-**your$_s$**

a **mi** *testvér-ünk* 'our sibling'
the **we** sibling-**our**

(8) Controller: noun
Target: adposition
Agreement features: number and person

FINNISH
minun kanssani 'with me'
I **with:me**

sinun kansassi 'with you$_s$'
you$_s$ **with:S2**

(9) Controller: direct object
Target: verb
Agreement feature: definiteness

HUNGARIAN
lát-ok ***egy*** *lányt* 'I see a girl.'
see-S1:**INDEF.OBJ a** girl

lát-om *a* *lányt* 'I see the girl.'
see-S1:**DEF.OBJ the** girl

(10) Controller: antecedent noun
Target: anaphoric pronoun
Agreement features: number and gender

ENGLISH
*The **man** called. **He** was happy.*
*The **girl** called. **She** was happy.*
*The **people** called. **They** were happy.*

As was noted in Section 2, the terms of selectional dependency patterns may vary along three parameters: their taxonomic level, their partonomic level and their complexity. Just as in word selection (see example (9) in Section 3.2.2), in agreement, too, controllers and targets may be multi-word phrases. Here follow two cases where the controller is an entire phrase: the agreement features cannot be attributed to any of its parts but only to the entire whole.

The first example is whole-to-part selection: the controller is an entire phrase and the targets are its own parts. The following examples from Latin, Hungarian, German and the Australian language of Duungidjawu in (11) illustrate a pattern also implicit in the Ancient Greek examples of (6): that in some languages, various constituents of a noun phrase will all show the same case. Agreeing terms are in bold.

(11) (a) HUNGARIAN: **DEM** ART ADJ **NOUN**
ez a magas ember 'this tall man (NOM)'
ezt a magas embert 'this tall man (ACC)'

(b) DUUNGIDJAWU: **NOUN ADJ** DEM (Wurm 1976: 108–9)
dʸan-bam-ma   *buːgubu-na man* 'these two short men'
men-DUAL-ACC short-ACC this

(c) GERMAN: **DEM ADJ** NOUN
dieser hoche Mann 'this tall man (NOM)'
diesen hochen Mann 'this tall man (ACC)'

(d) LATIN: **DEM NOUN ADJ**
hic vir magnus 'this large man (NOM)'
hunc virum magnum 'this large man (ACC)'

What is the controller in these phrases? The examples show that languages differ in how case is distributed over parts of the noun phrase and that there is no reason to analyse any one constituent as the primary carrier of case. One might propose that the noun is the controller of case agreement within the noun phrase, just as it is the controller of gender agreement in Swahili and Ancient Greek above ((4), (6)). There is, however, a difference. Gender is inherent to the noun: it is a lexical characteristic that the noun 'carries' with it regardless of where it occurs in a sentence. But case is variable depending on the grammatical role of the noun phrase in the sentence and thus the noun has no primary claim on it. Therefore, case is best viewed as a property of the entire noun phrase rather than initiating with one or the other of its constituents. Case then 'percolates' from the whole rather than 'spreading' from one part to another. Thus in Latin, for example, rather than the demonstrative and the adjective agreeing with the noun in case, the noun, adjective and demonstrative all agree with the noun phrase by partaking of its case. This analysis is further supported by languages where the case marker is simply attached to the last word of the noun phrases whatever that word might be, such as in Western Desert (Dixon 1980: 270) and in some instances of Duungidjawu (Wurm 1976: 109–10).

A second situation where the controller is an entire phrase rather than a single word involves conjoined phrases as controllers. The first example comes from English.

(12) (a) ***I was*** *surprised.*
    (b) ***He was*** *surprised.*
    (c) ***He and I were*** *surprised.*
    (d) ***We were*** *surprised.*

The subject *I* requires the verb form *was*, as in (12a), and so does *he*, as in (12b). But if, as in (12c), the two pronouns form a conjoined subject, they require not *was* but *were* which, as (12d) shows, is a plural form of the verb. In other words, the agreement feature that *he and I* impose upon the verb is not a feature of either of the parts (since both *I* and *he* are singular by themselves); instead, they require the plural form, which is a feature of the whole that the two pronouns make up. Thus, the verb agrees with the entire subject phrase rather than with a part of it.

Conjoined subjects acting as phrasal controller occur in many other languages as well, such as Russian (Corbett 1988: 25):

(13) *prepodava-**li**-s'*   *matematik-**a***   *i*   *fizik-**a***
     teach-PST.**PL**-REFL mathematics-FEM.**SG**.NOM and physics-FEM.
                                                   SG.NOM
     'Mathematics and physics were taught.'

The verb is in the plural. The subject consists of two nouns each singular by itself; but they add up to plural when conjoined.

Interestingly, there is also an alternative way of crafting the above sentence where the verb is in the singular:

(14) *prepodava-**la**-s'*   *matematik-**a***   *i*   *fizik-**a***
     teach-PST.FEM.**SG**-REFL mathematics-FEM.**SG**.NOM and physics-
                                                    FEM.**SG**.NOM

Here, the verb agrees with only one of the two conjuncts of the conjoined subject phrase – the one closest to it – instead of the whole phrase. This example indicates that agreement rules may differ in their modality: while they are obligatory in most cases, they may offer alternative options which, in this case, are agreeing with the entire phrase or only part of it.

In sum: agreement is a pattern of word form selection where the marker of one constituent co-varies with the subtype of another constituent. Apart from the fact that the controller is always a nominal, controllers, targets and agreement features show a range of variation in and across languages.

3.3.3 *Government*

Besides agreement, government is the other selectional pattern responsible for determining correct word forms. The difference, as we saw above in Section 3.3.1, is that in agreement a constituent duplicates a feature value of another constituent; whereas in government, a constituent requires another one to display a property which is not its own. Here is the schema for government:

(1) GOVERNMENT
   (M) If A.X and B, then B-CASE$_n$ /W,
   where
   - A and B are co-occurring syntactic constituents,
   - A.X is a subtype of A, and
   - CASE$_n$ is a particular case marker (an affix or a clitic).
   In prose: In context W, if constituents A and B have been selected to co-occur and A is of subtype X, then B must (or may) have a marker for a particular case.

As agreement and all other selectional patterns, government, too, involves a selector and a selectee. The selector of government is called the **governor**; the selectee – the noun phrase that receives case from the governor – will be called **governee**. Thus, 'governor' corresponds to 'controller' in agreement and 'governee' is parallel to the target of agreement. The selectional dependency relation between governor and governee is called the **government relation**. Both agreement and government assign a marker – an affix or a clitic – to another constituent. The choice of the marker assigned to the selectee is restricted in both agreement and government albeit in different ways: in agreement, the affix represents the same feature value that the selector has; in government, it is always a **case** marker. As in all syntactic rules, there is a choice of modalities and there may be a context.

Just as in the case of agreement, the question arises as to how to determine what selects what. Here is an instance of government in Latin which points at the answer:

(2) (a) *Puer currit e   silv-ā.*
       boy runs **from** forest-**ABL**
       'The boy is running from the forest.'

    (b) *Puer currit **ad** silv-**am.***
       boy runs **to** forest-**ACC**
       'The boy is running to the forest.'

The noun stem *silv-* 'forest' may occur either with the-*ā* suffix indicating the ablative case 'from', or with *-am*, the accusative suffix. The choice does not depend on the noun stem since the stem is the same in both cases. What is different in the two sentences is the preposition: *e(x)* 'from' in one case and *ad* 'to' in the other. The occurrence of the preposition *e(x)* is correlated with the ablative *-ā*; the occurrence of the preposition *ad* is correlated with the accusative *-am*. Thus, prepositions are the governors of the affixal case of their complements.

That the correlation is unidirectional, rather than mutual, can be seen from (3), which shows that the accusative affix can occur without the *ad* 'to' preposition: it can occur with another preposition (*propter* 'because of'), as in (3a), or even without a preposition, as in (3b). *Ad* 'to', however, cannot occur with any case affix – ablative or dative – but the accusative (see (3c)).

(3) (a) *Puer **propter** puell-**am** currit.*
boy **because.of** girl-**ACC** runs
'The boy is running because of the girl.'

(b) *Puer puell-**am** amat.*
boy girl-**ACC** loves
'The boy loves the girl.'

(c) **Puer **ad** silv-**a** currit.*
boy **to** forest-**ABL** runs

Similarly, while the ablative suffix *-ā* in (2a) may or may not occur with the preposition *e(x)* 'from', the preposition *e(x)* does require the ablative. Thus, it is clear that the preposition selects the affixal case form of the complement and the case affix does not select the preposition.

Government in Latin provides an example of chained dependency: verbs govern their complements by requiring a particular preposition in them; and prepositions in turn govern their own complement by requiring a particular affixal case form.

As mentioned above, case may be expressed as an affix or as an adposition. Case affixes are typically suffixes; adpositions may be prepositions or postpositions. For example, the dative case is expressed as a suffix in Hungarian, as a postposition in Japanese, and as a preposition in English:

(4) (a) Hungarian: *Mari-**nak***
Mary-**DAT**
'to Mary'

(b) Japanese: *Mary **ni***
Mary **DAT**
'to Mary'

(c) English: ***to** Mary*

While the governee is always a nominal constituent – since only nominals can have case – the governor can vary. Besides verbs and adpositions, for which we have already seen examples, adjectives, nouns and numerals can also select case and thus serve as governors. Some of these patterns can be illustrated from English. The verb *approve* requires the preposition *of* and *decide* takes *on*. The adjective *worthy* takes *of* and *intent* takes *on*. And while most nouns take *of* for their complements such as *the result of the storm*, some select other propositions such as *to*, as in *supplement to the book;* or *about*, as in *opinion about the artist.*

The text in (5) and (8) provides examples from Turkish, Latin, Hungarian and Russian showing various governors and governees, with the governed case markers in bold.

(5) Governor: verb
Governee: the verb's complements: direct object, indirect
object and locative phrase
TURKISH

  (a) *Mektub-**u***   *profesör-**e***   *gösterdim.*
      letter-**DEF.ACC** professor-**DAT** I:showed
      'I showed the letter to the professor.'

  (b) *Lübnan-**dan***   *ayrıldı .*
      Libanon-**from** he/she:departed
      'He/she departed from Libanon.'

(6) Governor: adjective
Governee: the adjective's complement phrase
LATIN

  (a) *filius patr-**e***   *dignus*
      son   father-**SG.ABL** worthy
      'a son worthy of his father'

  (b) *filius patr-**i***   *similis*
      son   father-**SG.DAT** similar
      'a son resembling his father'

(7) Governor: noun
Governee: the noun's complement phrase
HUNGARIAN

  (a) *szeretet az   apa*   **iránt**
      love   the father **towards**
      'love for the father'

  (b) *vélemény a   könyv-**ről***
      opinion the book-**from.the.top**
      'opinion about the book'

(8) Governor: numeral
Governee: the co-occurring noun
RUSSIAN
(a) *od'in mal'čik*
one boy-**SG:NOM**
'one boy (NOM)'

(b) *dva mal'čik-a*
two boy-**SG:GEN**
'two boys (NOM)'

(c) *pjat' mal'čik-on*
five boy-**PL:GEN**
'five boys (NOM)'

In sum: government is a pattern of word form selection where the case marker of one constituent is determined by another constituent. Apart from the governee always being a nominal, governors, governees and the kinds of cases involved show a range of variation across languages.

3.4 A COMPARISON OF WORD SELECTION AND WORD FORM SELECTION

Schemata for the three syntactic selection patterns are repeated below from the preceding sections.

(1) SELECTION OF WORDS
   (M) If A, then B /W,
      where A and B are syntactic constituents.
      In prose: In context W, if syntactic constituent A has been selected, syntactic constituent B must (or may) also be selected.

(2) SELECTION OF WORD FORMS
   (a) AGREEMENT:
   (M) If A.Xα and B, then B-xα /W,
   - where A and B are co-occurring syntactic constituents,
   - A.Xα is a subtype of A defined by a particular value α of the feature X, and
   - xα is a marker (an affix or a clitic) associated with B that represents the feature value Xα.
      In prose: In context W, if constituents A and B have been selected to co-occur and A shows a given value for the feature X, then B must (or may) have an associated marker representing that same value of X.

(b) GOVERNMENT:
(M) If A.X and B, then B-CASE$_n$ /W,
where

- A and B are co-occurring syntactic constituents,
- A.X is a subtype of A, and
- CASE$_n$ is a particular case marker (an affix or a clitic).
  In prose: In context W, if constituents A and B have been
  selected to co-occur and A is of subtype X, then
  B must (or may) have a marker for a particular case.

Let us assess the similarities and differences among the three syntactic selection patterns from the point of view of the terms involved, the selectional properties involved and the directionality of the selection relation.

(A) SHARED TERMS
In **both agreement and government**, one of the terms is a nominal constituent. This is not necessarily so in word selection.

As noted above, the nominal constituent is the selector in agreement and it is the selectee in government. Word selection patterns may or may not involve nominal constituents.

(B) SELECTIONAL PROPERTIES
(a) In **both agreement and in some instances of word choice**, the basis of selection is **similarity** between the selector and the selectee. This is not so in government.

Both agreement and some cases of word selection manifest the 'similar with similar' principle (also known from phonological assimilation). Take, for example, the selection of objects by their verbs. The verb *eat* takes an object with a solid referent; the verb *drink* takes one with a liquid referent. But *eat* all by itself already implies consuming something solid and *drink* implies consuming something fluid. Thus, the proper choice of the objects requires a kind of matching: the object has to include a property that the verb has. If instead of having separate lexical items for 'eat' and 'drink', we used the generic term 'consume' and affixes for 'solid' and 'liquid' depending on whether the verb occurred with say 'bread' or 'milk', the pattern would be agreement rather than word selection.

(b) In **government**, the assigned property in government **must be case**; **in agreement**, it **may be case**.

As discussed above, government, by definition, assigns case. Case may be an agreement feature as well: as case is assigned to noun phrases, constituents of the noun phrase are targets for case agreement with the noun phrase as controller.

(C) DIRECTIONALITY

If **government and word selection** involve the same terms, the
directionality of selection is the **same**; that is, selector
in one pattern corresponds to selector in the other and
selectee in one corresponds to selectee in the other.
In agreement, the selector and selectee of government and word
selection switch roles.

To illustrate (C), here is first some data to show that selector and selectee of
agreement are the opposite of the selector and selectee in government. The
following Russian data clearly show the differing directionality of agreement
and government. Example (3) shows that the numeral 'one' agrees in
gender with the noun:

(3) (a) *od'in   mal'čik*
          one-**MSC** boy-**MSC**.SG.NOM
          'one boy'

     (b) *odn-a   d'evuška*
          one-**FEM** girl-**FEM**.SG.NOM
          'one girl'

In (4) is shown that the numeral 'three' governs the genitive case on
the noun:

(4) (a) *tri   mal'čik-a*
          three boy-MSC.SG.**GEN**
          'three boys'

     (b) *tri   d'evušk-i*
          three girl:FEM.SG.**GEN**
          'three girls'

In (5) is shown a composite of the agreement and government patterns in
(3) and (4): the numeral for 'two' agrees in gender with the noun and
governs the genitive case on it.

(5) (a) *dv-a   mal'čik-a*
          two-**MSC** boy-**MSC**.SG.**GEN**
          'two boys'

     (b) *dv-e   d'evušk-i*
          two-**FEM** girl-**FEM**.SG.**GEN**
          'two girls'

In these examples, the direction of dependency is clearly opposite in agreement and government: the numeral determines the case form of the noun by government but the noun determines the gender form of the numeral by agreement.

Another example of the opposite directionality in agreement and government comes from Hungarian. In this language, as illustrated above, the verb agrees with the direct object in definiteness.

(6) (a) *Jancsi   csokoládé-t   szeret.*
       Johnny chocolate-ACC like:**INDEF**.OBJ
       'Johnny likes chocolate.'

(b) *Jancsi **a**   csokoládé-t   szeret-**i.***
       Johnny **the** chocolate-ACC like-**DEF**.OBJ
       'Johnny likes the chocolate.'

In these examples, there are two selection patterns holding between the verb and the object: in one, the verb is the selector and, in the other, the object is. In particular, the accusative case is present on the object because the verb governs it; and the verb in turn shows a definite or indefinite suffix in agreement with the object.

These examples illustrate that the directionality of selectional dependency in government and agreement is reversed. That the directionality of word selection and government in turn can be the same is shown by the English verb *assassinate*. This verb both selects and governs its object: it requires a human object of public stature and it requires that, if it is a pronoun, it be in an oblique case form (e.g. *him* and not *he*).

In sum: agreement and government share the property of involving a nominal as one of their terms; agreement and word selection are similar in that they involve selection by similarity between selector and selectee; and government and word selection are alike in that, if they involve the same selectors and selectees, the direction of the selectional dependency relation is the same.

4 Conclusions

In this chapter, a variety of syntactic selection patterns were seen. Are these phenomena surprising? Or are they to be expected? As discussed in the first chapter of this book, the goal of science is to align expectations and facts so that all true facts are expected and no expected ones fail to occur. Let us therefore see if there are any discrepancies between expectations based on the simple logic of selection and the actual facts of how words and word forms are selected. If there are, explanations are called for to bring expectations in line with facts.

Three kinds of mismatches stand out. First, there are patterns that may be seen as possible but not at all likely; yet they do occur. Second, what one might consider likely does not necessarily occur. Third, what one might consider impossible does occur. Let us look at instances of each.

First: why is there agreement and why is there government to begin with? And why do these patterns occur in some languages but not in others? Why do agreement and government work in opposite directions? These phenomena seem conceivable; but why do they actually occur? There is a gap here between what appears possible but not necessary or even probable and what actually occurs.

Second, some forms of selection patterns would seem more plausible than others. Here are two reasonable expectations:

    (a) Selector and selectee should be adjacent.
    (b) Selector should precede selectee.

One might expect (a) to hold because, if two constituents are selectionally related, one would expect that they are linked by other kinds of relations as well, such as adjacency. And, since the selector calls the shots – that is, the speaker needs to know what the selector is before he knows what the selectee should be – one might expect (b): that the selector comes before the selectee.

There is lots of evidence to show that neither expectation holds in all cases. Consider the following English sentences:

(1) (a) **A man who** *was drunk came to the station.*
     (b) **A man** *came to the station* **who** *was drunk.*

(2) (a) **About whom** *was Jill complaining?*
     (b) **Who(m)** *was Jill complaining* **about**?

In (1), the relative pronoun *who* agrees with the head of the relative clause in animacy (the corresponding inanimate form is *which*). While, as (1a) shows, controller and target may be adjacent, (1b) shows that they are not necessarily so.

In (2), the oblique case form of *whom* is governed by the preposition *about* but, as (b) shows, *about* is not necessarily adjacent to *whom* nor does it necessarily precede it. In (b), the case-selecting force of *about* is weaker when it is divided from the target – both *whom* and *who* are grammatical – but it is nonetheless operative.

These examples show that what seems likely is not necessarily what occurs: both more likely and less likely patterns are documented.

Thirdly, there are actual patterns of word and word form selection that would appear to be beyond the realm of what might seem possible. Two such patterns are selectors without selectees and selectees without selectors.

Perhaps the lesser surprise is seeing **selectors without selectees**. An example comes from word selection. One of the rules of English is that verbs select subjects. If this rule were to hold unconditionally, every time there was a verb, there ought to be a subject. Yet, this is not necessarily so:

(3) (a) *The hippo dove into the water and began to swim.*
   (b) *Leave him alone!*

In (3a), the first verb has a subject – *the hippo* – but the second – *began* – does not; yet, the sentence is grammatical. In (b), *leave* also does not have a subject. Both illustrate a selector – the verb – that lacks a selectee.

More suprisingly, the opposite pattern also occurs: **selectees without selectors**:

(4) (a) *Jill lectured **about** butterflies and Jim, **about** rattlesnakes.*
   (b) *This puppy was born **on** the Fourth of July and the other, **on** Labor Day.*

In (4a), the prepositional phrase *about butterflies* is governed by *lectured*; but what governs *about rattlesnakes*? There is no verb in the second clause. Similarly, the *on* of *on the Fourth of July* is selected by *was born* but there is no governor for the second *on*-phrase: *on Labor Day*.

More dramatic examples of case-marked noun phrases without governors in sight are the following:

(5) ENGLISH:
   (a) *Now, **about** your grade.*
   (b) ***With** the lawsuit finally settled, they left town.*

(6) LATIN
   (a) ***Me**   miser-**um**!*
      I.**ACC** miserable-**ACC**
      'Miserable me!'

   (b) *Consul-e   elect-o,   senatus exiit.*
      consul-**ABL** elected-**ABL** senate departed
      'With the consul elected, the senate departed.'

In each instance, there is a case-marked noun without a verb or adposition to govern it.

A further example of selectees that lack selectors comes from agreement. Consider first the Serbo-Croatian sentences in (7):

(7) (a) *Ja čita-m.*
      I read-**S1**
      'I read.'

(b) **Ty**   čita-š.
   you$_s$ read-**S1**
   'You$_s$ read.'

These sentences illustrate the well-known pattern of subject–verb agreement: the verb carries person and number affixes in harmony with the subject pronouns. But now consider the sentences in (8):

(8) (a) *čita-m.*
       read-**S1**
       'I read.'

   (b) *čita-š.*
       read-**S2**
       'You$_s$ read.'

In (8), just as in (7), the verb carries an affix that indicates the subject's person and number. However, while in (7) there is a source for these features – the subject is there to control verb agreement – in the sentences of (8), there is no subject, and yet the verbs still look as if they agreed with a subject. Languages that allow this kind of pattern are referred to in the literature as 'pro-drop languages'. Earlier Latin examples ((4)–(6) in Section 3.3.1) show that Latin, too, is a pro-drop language, as is its daughter language Spanish.

Are there any explanations for any of these facts? Explanations for syntactic phenomena in general will be explored in Chapter 7; here we take up just one why-question and outline an answer for it. The question is: why is there verb agreement at all? That is, why do verbs agree with their subjects and with other noun phrase constituents in some languages?

Generally, verb agreement markers start out historically as independent pronouns. Consider the following:

(9) (a) *His father is a lawyer.*
    (b) *His father, he is a lawyer.*

The differences between the two sentences is that the subject *his father* is topicalized in (9b) – that is, it is set up as the topic, or anchor point, of the sentence. In such constructions, the subject pronoun *he* merely refers back to the topic: it is a stressless element cliticized to the verb and, through frequent use, it can become an affix on the verb with the topic turning into the subject of the sentence. When the rest of the personal pronouns also undergo this change – *I, I was born in Chicago* becomes *I I-was born in Chicago* and so on – the verb develops a full inflectional paradigm for number and person agreement with the subject.

The pronominal force of verb agreement markers is clear in languages where the inflected verb can occur by itself – that is, without the subject controller but implying a pronominal subject. This was already shown by the

Serbo-Croatian examples in (8); (10) exemplifies the pattern for subject agreement and (11) for both subject and object agreement, both from Swahili (Givón 1976: 157):

(10) (a) ***wa-****toto*   ***wa-****li-kuja*
        CL1.PL-child **CL1.PL**-PST-come
        'The children came.'

   (b) ***wa-****li-kuja*
        CL1.PL-PST-come
        'They came.'

(11) (a) ***m-****toto,*   *ni-li-****mw****-ona*
        CL1.SG-child **I**-PST-**him**-saw
        'The child, I saw him.'

   (b) *ni-li-****mw****-ona*
        I-PST-**him**-saw
        'I saw him.'

In the course of history, the pronominal meaning of the verb affixes may further weaken so that the third person singular pronoun becomes an invariant – non-agreeing – marker of a verb. This happened in Tok Pisin, the English-based creole language of New Guinea: the original subject pronoun *he* became the general verb marker *i-* and the original object pronoun *him* became the transitive verb marker *-im* (Givón 1976: 168). These markers now occur not only when the subject and object are singular third person (as in (12a)) but also when they are not: in (12b), the subject is first person plural and the object is third person plural.

(12) (a) *em **i-**har-**im***   *John*
        he **MARKER**-hear-**MARKER** John
        'He heard John.'

   (b) *mipela **i-**lus-**im***   *pinis   sin   bilong ol   man*
        we   **MARKER**-forgive-**MARKER** PERF sins of   all people
        'We forgive the sins of all people.'

Verb agreement can thus arise through the univerbation – that is, the merging into a single word – of a pronoun and a verb. In the course of history, verb agreement may turn out to be an intermediate step between the separate-word pronoun and its semantically generalized and formally reduced version as an invariant, non-agreeing verb marker. The basic process is similar to the one seen at the end of Chapter 2 in connection with the historical origin of the discontinuous negator *ne . . . pas* in French. In both cases, the gradual formal and semantic reduction and automatization of an originally meaningful pattern gave rise to an otherwise puzzling syntactic construction. The general process, called grammaticalization, will be further discussed in connection with the origin of the English definite article (Chapter 6, Section 4.1) and the origin of a Mandarin Chinese preposition (Chapter 7, Section 4.2).

Notes

Section 1   Preliminaries
Dependency is a very general concept manifested in domains outside language. On dependency in a social, cultural, political and psychological sense, see Doi 1973; M. Moravcsik 1981; Day 1992.

Section 2   Selection: some possibilities

- Since the selection schema in (1) makes the selection of one constituent dependent on another one that has already been selected, the question arises how the selector 'got there' to begin with. It is assumed that the 'first selector' is supplied simply by the category of the structure that the analyst intends to build.
- For selection and order as two basic relations in language, see Bloomfield 1933, especially 162–5.

Section 3.3.2   Agreement
In the Swahili example (4), the noun *bwana* 'gentleman' is glossed as belonging to Class 1. Actually, it formally belongs to Class 3 but it controls Class 1 agreement because it refers to a human being, a characteristic of Class 1 nouns (Ashton 1944: 89, 64).

Section 3.3.3   Government

- When case is marked by adpositions rather than affixes, the governor does not seem to select a word form but, rather, a phrase. However, adpositions are generally cliticized and thus the selection of adpositional case is not too distinct from the selection of affixal case.
- For cross-linguistic surveys of agreement see, for example, E. Moravcsik 1978a; Lehmann 1982; Corbett 1983b; Barlow and Ferguson 1988; especially Corbett, forthcoming. For agreement-related materials, check (www.smg.surrey.ac.uk).

Exercises

1. Find all the agreement controllers and agreement targets of English.

2. Compare grammatical agreement with phonological assimilation such as the one involved in the choice among the English prefixes /ɪm/, /ɪn/ and

/ɪŋ/ (cf. *impossible, inability, incongruous*). What are the similarities and differences between the two patterns?

3. There are analogues to grammatical agreement in non-linguistic domains such as animal mimicry. Think of others.

4. Compare the following Turkish and English sentences:
   (a) *Ahmet   Paris-ten   Cleveland-e   gitti.*
       Ahmed Paris-from Cleveland-to went
       'Ahmed went from Paris to Cleveland.'
   (b) *Ahmed went from Paris to Cleveland.*
   Characterize the similarities and differences between the two sentences in terms of:
   (a) word selection
   (b) word form selection
   (c) adjacency
   (d) precedence

5. Characterize the selectional relations between the following phenomena:
   (a) sunshine and shadow
   (b) rain and clouds
   (c) buttons and buttonholes
   (d) nasality and voicing in English
   (e) lip-rounding and back vowels in English
   (f) personal computer and printer
   (g) dogs and fleas

6. The following sentences are ungrammatical. For each, decide whether ungrammaticality is because of an agreement error or a government error and state the rules that are violated:
   (a) *Sue has lived in these city for ten year.*
   (b) *He (i.e., Sue) is good friends of mine.*
   (c) *Sue and I are good friend.*
   (d) *Most people are distrustful for the future.*
   (e) *Most student in the campus are Americans.*
   (f) *Most students in the yard is sitting in the lawn.*
   (g) *Peter and Paul, teacher in the high school, is brothers.*
   (h) *I gave the book for Paul.*
   (i) *The book describes about Italy.*
   (j) *The lecturer talked on Italy.*
   (k) *The little boy view themselves in the lake.*
   (l) *Paul has been accused with cheating.*
   (m) *The theory was based in false facts.*
   (n) *Most kids are respectful for their parents.*
   (o) *I are very satisfied of my exam.*

Chapter Four

Categories

'The Eskimos got thirty different names for snow', I say. I read it in a book. [. . .]

'There ain't thirty different kinds of snow,' Lucy says. 'There are two kinds. The clean kind and the dirty kind, clean and dirty. Only two.'

'There are a million zillion kinds,' says Nenny. 'No two exactly alike. Only how do you remember which one is which?'

(Cisneros 1985: 36)

1 Preliminaries

As discussed in the preceding chapters, syntactic description specifies the selection and linear order of words. But common sense calls for a third component: just as the ordering of words presupposes that the words have been selected to be present in a structure, selecting them presupposes that they have been available for selection. This suggests that, in addition to selection and order rules, syntactic descriptions should also include the inventory of the available elements.

Since selection rules specify the choice of words in sentences, one might think that the inventory on which selection rules draw is nothing else than the dictionary (the 'lexicon') of the language. However, as was seen before, words are generally not selected as individual lexical items; rather, they are selected by reference to the larger units that they are part of – such as phrases – and in terms of the categories that the words and phrases are tokens of. Thus, the list of available terms for selection rules will not show actual words, such as *apple* and *mumble*; instead, it will be a super-list of sorts – one that names **word categories,** such as noun and verb, and **phrasal categories**, such as noun phrase and verb phrase.

In (1) and (2), the descriptions of English adjective–noun and subject–verb constructions are provided, complete with inventory, selection and order statements (where '. . .' stands for additional items in the list):

(1)   NOUN AND ADJECTIVE IN ENGLISH
Inventory: Noun; Adjective; Verb; Adverb . . .
Selection: If a noun is selected, an adjective may also be
   selected.
Order: The adjective must immediately precede the noun.

(2)   VERB PHRASE AND SUBJECT PHRASE IN ENGLISH
Inventory: Subject Noun Phrase; Object Noun Phrase; Verb
   Phrase . . .
Selection: If a verb phrase is selected, a subject noun phrase
   must also be selected.
Order: The subject noun phrase must immediately precede
   the verb phrase.

Inventory statements list items that are available for selection; selection statements specify the proper choice from among them, and order statements specify the proper sequence of the selected elements. Inventory statements are rules of existence; selection rules are rules of coexistence; order rules are rules of arrangement. While rules of selection and rules of order are syntagmatic constraints – constraints on items that co-occur within a structure – rules of inventory are constraints of a paradigmatic sort: they state what is available across structures in a language. The logical dependency relation among the three kinds of statement is made explicit in (3):

(3)   (a)   INVENTORY OF SYNTACTIC CATEGORIES
Schema: **A; B; etc.** /W
In prose: In context W, the categories A, B, etc. are
   available.

(b) SELECTION OF SYNTACTIC CATEGORIES
Schema: **(M) If A, then B /W**
In prose: In context W, given that categories A, B are
available, if A has been selected, B must (or
may, or must not) also be **selected**.

(c) ORDER OF SYNTACTIC CATEGORIES
Schema: **(M) If (A, B), then A & B /W**
In prose: In context W, if categories A, B have been
selected, A must (or may, or must not) be **ordered**
to immediately precede B.

But is it worth actually including the list of available categories in the syntactic description of a language? After all, the inventory can be read off the rules: the total list of the terms mentioned in the selection rules is the inventory of available elements.

In Chapter 3, Section 3.1, we encountered a similar quandary: given the order rules of a language, is it worth spelling out the rules of selection as well? After all, the terms mentioned in the order rules equal the ones that have been selected. Recall our reasoning: if there are structures that show the same selection pattern but different orders, selection should be stated separately to provide us with a level on which order-wise different structures can be shown to be similar.

The same argument applies to the present issue of whether the inventory of the terms of selection rules should be given a separate listing. If each category occurred always with the same other category, the inventory list would make no contribution. If, however, categories vary in which other categories they can be co-selected with, inventory statements will provide a common denominator for sets of structures that have the same categories available but differ in the co-occurrence patterns of those categories.

The point may be illustrated with a phonological example. Consider the phonemes /p/ and /s/ in English. In word-initial position, the order of the two is fixed: there are words that begin with /sp/ – such as *spoon* – but none that begin with /ps/. Standard Eastern Armenian is like English in this regard (e.g. *spitak* 'white' (Bert Vaux, personal communication)). Thus, the two languages are the same with respect to the ordering possibilities of /p/ and /s/ in word-initial position. By implication, they also agree in the co-selectability of the two sounds and, again by implication, that both sounds are available in the phonemic inventories of the two languages.

Let us now take German. German shows a pattern opposite to English: there are words that start with /ps/ (e.g. *Psychologie* 'psychology') but none that start with /sp/. Although the two languages differ in the ordering of these two sounds, they agree in allowing the two sounds to be co-selected word-initially and, by implication, in the availability of both sounds to begin with.

Next, consider Spanish. In this language, there are no words that start either with /sp/ or with /ps/. Thus, English and Spanish differ not only in the ordering possibilities of these two sounds in word-initial position but also in whether they can be co-selected as the onset of a word-initial syllable. But there is still a similarity: both languages have both /p/ and /s/ available in their phonetic inventories.

Finally, let us compare English with Hawaiian. With respect to possible word-initial clusters of /p/ and /s/, Hawaiian is completely different from English: it has /p/ but does not have an /s/ phoneme at all, which means of course that neither /ps/ nor /sp/ is possible.

These similarities and differences among English, Standard Eastern Armenian (S.E. Armenian), German, Spanish and Hawaiian are shown in (4).

(4) WORD-INITIAL /p, s/   THE LANGUAGES ARE
     IN DIFFERENT   SIMILAR IN
     LANGUAGES

		ORDER	SELECTION	INVENTORY
(a) ENGLISH	S.E. ARMENIAN			
/sp/ */ps/	/sp/ */ps/	+	+	+
(b) ENGLISH	GERMAN			
/sp/ */ps/	*/sp/ /ps/	−	+	+
(c) ENGLISH	SPANISH			
/sp/ */ps/	*/sp/ */ps/	−	−	+←
	/p/			
	/s/			
(d) ENGLISH	HAWAIIAN	−	−	−
/sp/ */ps/	*/sp/ */ps/			
	/p/			
	*/s/			

This comparison illustrates the usefulness of inventory statements in the comparative phonological description of languages: as the arrow pointing to English and Spanish shows, two languages may be similar in their phoneme inventories even when they differ in the selection and ordering of the sounds in question.

Note that it is not logically necessary that this should be so: it would be easy to construct a scenario where inventory statements served no purpose. This would be so if the choice of an item would leave no alternatives for the choice of the co-occurring items. For example, two languages could differ in whether they do or do not have a sound – say, /ð/; but if both languages have that sound, it would always occur with the very same other sound in both. Given such a scenario, compiling a separate inventory of sounds would not yield a useful level of generalization. This shows that the utility of inventory statements is an empirical matter and whether in syntactic descriptions inventories are called for or not will have to be decided in terms of empirical evidence.

In sum: we have characterized the notion of syntactic inventory statements as involving word and phrase categories and suggested that they may or may not be useful for purposes of stating generalizations. This is the first of several logically available alternatives against which we will assess actual syntactic patterns in Section 3. But first, Section 2 will explore other logically available options for inventories of syntactic categories.

2 Partonomy and taxonomy: some possibilities

How are the basic elements discovered that figure in our generalizations? There are two conceptual operations involved in creating syntactic categories: segmentation and classification. For example, talking about nouns implies that sentences have been segmented into word-size parts and the parts have been sorted into classes, one of which is the class of nouns. Categories are created by imposing a partonomic structure on sentences and by taxonomizing the parts.

Partonomy – also known as mereology, mereonomy or meronomy – is the relationship between wholes and their parts. The relationship of a part to its whole is the 'is a part of' relation – for example, the liver is a part of the body. Or, starting with the whole, it is said to 'contain' parts – for example, a car contains an engine. Since syntactic units are termed constituents, partonomic structure in grammar is generally referred to as **constituent structure**. Wholes are called 'mothers', parts are 'daughters' relative to their wholes and 'sisters' relative to each other.

Taxonomy – also known as classification or categorization – is the relationship between classes (also called categories or types) and their tokens (i.e., individual items). The relationship of a subtype to its type is the 'is a' relation – for example, the liver is an organ; a type in turn 'may be' a subtype – for example, a car may be a Chevrolet. The terms taxonomy, classification and categorization will be used interchangeably and so will the terms category, class and type.

Part–whole relations and type–subtype relations are fundamental conceptual tools created by the human mind to simplify our view of the world. They are ubiquitous both in scientific analysis and in everyday thought. Saying that something is a whole which has parts, and saying that something is a type with subtypes are not observational statements: they are interpretations of the facts. As the conversation of the little girls about snow cited in the epigraph at the start of this chapter shows, the question of what are same things and what are different things can be a matter of debate: taxonomic claims are highly negotiable as are partonomic claims as well. Much of scientific research consists of attempts to decide among competing parto-nomic and taxonomic views of objects and phenomena in the world – debates about what things do or do not make a single whole and what things do or do not form a single type.

A benefit of thinking in terms of parts and wholes and of tokens and types is that these concepts resolve certain contradictions. Let us first see how partonomy achieves this. The assumption of whole–part relations allows us to conceptualize objects as both single units and assemblages of smaller ones at the same time without incurring a contradiction. Consider a human hand: is it one thing or a collection of several things? If I want my right thumb to move from point A to point B – for example, when turning a door latch – I can either move the thumb itself with the four fingers at rest or I can move the whole hand as I might if the thumb is immobilized by splints. For an observer who is innocent of the intricacies of human conceptual-ization – such as a young child might be – this might seem like a paradox. How can the thumb sometimes be subject to the control of the hand and, at other times, be its own controller? The recognition of part–whole rela-tions dispels the mystery. The thumb is neither fully dependent on the hand nor is it entirely separable from it; rather, it is a part of the hand, which means that it exhibits both a degree of dependence and a degree of independence. It can 'do things' on its own without the 'consent' of the whole; but once the whole 'does something,' the part cannot but follow suit. The hand is thus both one thing and several things at the same time. This statement would appear contradictory and thus impossible; but it is sanctioned by partonomy and is therefore brought into the realm of what is possible.

Just as partonomy resolves contradictions relative to the quantity of objects – one thing or many? – taxonomy resolves contradictions relative to the quality of things. This is because taxonomy lets us say that two things are both the same and not the same. In creating a **whole** out of two or more dis-tinguishable items, we treat them **as if** they were one. In creating a **category** out of two or more distinguishable items, we treat them **as if** they were the same (Mervis and Rosch 1981: 89; Brown 1990: 17). For example, the right hand and the left hand may seem the 'same' thing but also not the same. They are the same in that each is connected to an arm by a wrist, each is elongated in shape and each has five digits with nails; but, except for ambidextrous people, they differ in what they can do. For a conceptual system that can 'think' only in terms of same and different, this is a contra-diction. However, embracing the notion of type–subtype relations resolves the problem: two objects may be the same in that they belong to the same type and yet not the same if they belong to distinct subtypes of that type. Thus, right hand and left hand are subtypes of the type 'hand'. By way of answering the question 'How can A and B be both of the same kind and of different kinds?' taxonomy relativizes the notions 'same' and 'not same' and allows us to say that two things are the same in some ways and not the same in other ways. In taxonomy, the contradictory notions of 'same' and 'different' happily coexist, just as in partonomy, the contradictory notions of 'one' and 'many' do.

Let us now take a closer look at partonomy and taxonomy starting with the former. What are logically possible kinds of partonomic systems? Five parameters of variation come to mind, having to do with the number of parts within wholes, the number of levels, the equality or non-equality of the parts, whether parts are uniquely assigned to wholes, and whether the sum of the parts adds up to the whole. A maximally simple partonomic system would exhibit the following choices along these parameters:

(1) SIMPLE PARTONOMIC SYSTEMS
   (a) ONLY TWO PARTS
       There are two and only two sister parts within each whole.
   (b) ONLY TWO LEVELS
       Parts do not contain further parts.
   (c) PARTS ARE EQUAL
       Parts of a whole are of equal rank.
   (d) PARTS ARE UNIQUELY ASSIGNED TO WHOLES
       Every part belongs to one and only one immediately
       superordinate whole.
   (e) THE WHOLE IS COMPOSITIONAL
       The characteristics of the whole are the sum of the
       characteristics of its parts and their relations.

The available choices for taxonomic systems are similar, with a minimal system obeying constraints that parallel those holding for the simplest partonomic systems:

(2) SIMPLE TAXONOMIC SYSTEMS
   (a) ONLY TWO SUBTYPES
       There are two and only two sister subtypes within each type.
   (b) ONLY TWO LEVELS
       Subtypes do not contain further subtypes.
   (c) SUBTYPES ARE EQUAL
       Subtypes of a type are of equal rank.
   (d) SUBTYPES ARE UNIQUELY ASSIGNED TO TYPES
       Every token belongs to one and only one immediately
       superordinate type.
   (e) THE TYPE IS INTERSECTIONAL
       The characteristics of the type are the intersection
       of the characteristics of the subtypes.

There do exist partonomic and taxonomic systems in the world that exhibit such simple characteristics. Written exams that have a test part and an essay part are an example of a whole that observes the Only-Two-Parts constraint (see (1a)) and the Parts are Uniquely Assigned to Wholes constraint ((1d) above). Similarly, the classification of numbers into integers and fractions is a truly binary one: there is no third category of numbers and any one number clearly falls into one or the other of these two classes as the Only-Two-Subtypes constraint ((2a) above) and the Subtypes are Uniquely Assigned to Types constraint ((2d) above) require. Compositionality (see (1e)) is observed in arithmetic: the sum of two numbers is the sum of the addenda. Intersectionality (see (2e)) holds with respect to the concept 'table' relative to the subtypes 'dining table' and 'coffee table': the properties of 'table' are those that dining tables and coffee tables have in common.

However, more often than not, partonomic and classificatory systems are complex: one or more of the simple properties listed above will not hold. Here are some examples of complex partonomies:

(3) SOME COMPLEX PARTONOMIC SYSTEMS
  (a) MORE THAN TWO PARTS
    Universities generally consist of several schools.
  (b) MORE THAN TWO LEVELS
    Universities consist of schools; schools in turn
    consist of departments; departments may in turn consist of
    various curricular areas.
  (c) PARTS ARE NOT EQUAL
    Entrée and dessert are parts of a meal but not of equal
    significance.
  (d) A PART BELONGS TO MORE THAN ONE WHOLE
    In the USA, for purposes of snow removal, the sidewalk
    in front of a home is counted as part of the property but for
    general maintenance, it is taken to be part of the street.
  (e) THE WHOLE IS NOT COMPOSITIONAL
    The combination of two drugs may have an effect that is
    not the sum of the effect of each drug when taken
    individually.

Similarly, there are many examples of complex taxonomies, such as the following.

(4) SOME COMPLEX TAXONOMIC SYSTEMS
  (a) MORE THAN TWO SUBTYPES
    Animal genera generally include more than two families.
  (b) MORE THAN TWO LEVELS
    Animal genera consist of families; families in turn
    consist of species.
  (c) SUBTYPES ARE NOT EQUAL
    Adults and children are subtypes of humans but
    adults are more prominent members of society than
    children.

(d) A SUBTYPE BELONGS TO MORE THAN ONE TYPE
Uncle Joe is both a member of the class of males and a
member of the class of adults.

(e) THE TYPE IS NOT INTERSECTIONAL
Uncle Joe and nephew Billy may not have any distinctive
physical characteristics in common; yet, they are both
subtypes of the general family type.

Of these ten kinds of partonomic and taxonomic complexities, four will be
singled out for more detailed discussion because of their special relevance to
syntax. These are: unequal parts, unequal subtypes, assignment of parts to
multiple wholes and assignment of subtypes to multiple types.

2.1 Unequal parts and unequal subtypes

Parts of a whole are not necessarily of equal importance. A meat course and
a dessert are both parts of a dinner but the meat course is a more essential
part since it can make up a dinner by itself whereas desserts normally cannot.
Similarly, subclasses of a class may be ranked, with one of them being more
dominant than the other. For example, cakes and cookies are both kinds of
desserts but a cake is a better representative of desserts than cookies.

There is a shared characteristic between unequal parts and unequal subtypes. This shared feature is dominance: the dominant item can stand both
for itself and for its non-dominant counterpart. Meat courses are dominant
parts of a meal; cakes are a dominant subtype of desserts. Thus, if a restaurant displays pictures to indicate that it serves dinner, it will use the picture
of a meat course rather than the picture of a cake. Similarly, if it advertises
desserts, it will use the picture of a cake or ice cream rather than the picture
of cookies.

The dominant part of a whole is called the head. The dominant member
of a type is called the prototype. The **head** is a part of a whole that can stand
for the entire whole by itself. When a congressman speaks for his entire district, he acts as a head of the district. The **prototype** is a subtype of a type
that can stand for the entire type all by itself. A family consisting of a father,
a mother and two children is the prototype of the type 'American family'.

Prototypes are a particularly interesting concept. According to the Greek
philosopher Aristotle (384–322 BC), all members of a class are on a par.
They are assigned to their class by criteria that are both necessary and sufficient for class membership and thus, like people who have passed the admis-
sion criteria of a club, they have the same status. However, the classes that
the human mind constructs in everyday life are more often than not in conflict with this classical class concept. If you ask someone to name a wild
animal, he is more likely to say *lion* than to say *lobster* although, if queried,
he will admit that both are wild animals. This shows that for most of us, lions
are prototypical animals and lobsters are seen as marginal members of the
class. Similarly, the class 'furniture' is better represented by a table than by

a piano; and the class of land vehicles has cars as a more characteristic member than, say, tractors. In other words, tables are a prototypical piece of furniture and cars a prototypical vehicle. Categories that are centred around a prototype, rather than being defined by necessary and sufficient criteria, are known as **natural categories** as opposed to the **classical categories** of Artistotelian logic.

When a class consists of only two opposing members, the dominant, prototypical member is termed **unmarked**; the other member is **marked**. Thus, among greeting cards, birthday cards are unmarked vis-à-vis all others: they are a better representative of greeting cards than, say, graduation cards. Similarly, everyday clothing is unmarked: everyday garb is a better representative of clothes than, say, wedding dresses.

So far we have identified one characteristic of the unmarked member of an opposition: **dominance**. In addition, there are three other properties that tend to converge upon the unmarked member. One is **greater frequency of occurrence**: the unmarked member tends to be encountered more often than the marked one. Greater frequency is plausibly related to dominance: the frequency of an object can easily lead to it being capable of representing the entire class that it is a member of. Thus, birthday cards may be dominant in the category of greeting cards because they are more frequent in our experience than, say, get-well cards or sympathy cards.

A further property of unmarked members is **greater taxonomic complexity** – that is, having more subtypes. Birthday cards or Christmas cards come in many more kinds than get-well cards or sympathy cards. Artifacts in everyday use – such as everyday clothing or everyday foods – come in more varieties than artifacts that have special designations, such as wedding dresses and Christmas Day food.

Just as it makes sense for dominance to be correlated with frequency, frequency's correlation with taxonomic complexity also stands to reason: the more often we encounter things, the better we know them and thus the more we are able to detect – or create – secondary characteristics which assign them to subclasses. For example, Chinese and Japanese tourists often find it hard to discern differences among Caucasian faces while they see Chinese and Japanese people as having a rich variety of facial features. Similarly, people who have never studied bird songs will hear most birds as sounding the same even though their ears are able to differentiate many kinds of more familiar sounds. Temporal and spatial distance also blurs differences. Thus, events that are long past in one's life may lose their special characteristics: all childhood friends may later be recalled as more or less indistinct members of a general class, just as different kinds of trees may all seem alike if viewed from a great distance such as a mountain top.

In addition to dominance, greater frequency and greater taxonomic complexity, there is a fourth characteristic that tends to converge on the unmarked member of an opposition: **partonomic simplicity** – that is, simpler internal composition. The more common an object in our experience, the simpler it tends to be. For example, everyday clothing, everyday food and basic-purpose buildings tend to have a simpler structure than festive clothing, holiday food and special-purpose architecture; and Caucasians often perceive Asian people as having 'added' facial features, such as special skin colour and eye shape, as opposed to the 'simpler' Caucasian physiognomy.

That greater frequency should correlate not only with dominance and taxonomic variability but also with simpler structure is again intuitively reasonable. Just as it makes sense that things that people know better should be more differentiated by subtypes, it is also reasonable that structural simplicity be preferred – and thus more frequent – in human experience. There is thus a four-way correlation involving dominance, frequency, taxonomic complexity and partonomic simplicity. Greater frequency tends to yield dominance and it tends to be paired with simpler structure and greater variability, while less frequent occurrence goes with lack of dominance, increased structural complexity and diminished variability.

Markedness relations hold in all areas of language structure. A phonological example is voiced and voiceless obstruents, with the voiceless ones unmarked and the voiced ones marked. In many languages such as German and Russian, obstruents are always voiceless at the ends of syllables, even if they are voiced when the same word takes a suffix and thus the obstruent occurs in non-syllable-final position (e.g. German *Tag* 'day' pronounced as /tak/; but *Tage* 'days' pronounced /tage/). Thus, voiceless obstruents have a higher frequency than voiced ones and can step in for voiced ones. Also, with voice superimposed, voiced obstruents have an additional component that voiceless ones do not and are thus more complex in structure. Finally, in many languages such as in English, voiceless stops are more differentiated than voiced ones: the former have both aspirated and unaspirated varieties while the latter do not. Thus, by all four criteria of markedness, voiceless obstruents turn out to be unmarked and voiced ones turn out to be marked.

Just as pairs of sound types, pairs of words, too, can be in a markedness relation. For example, English *man* is unmarked and *woman* is marked in that *man* can stand for both males and females – such as in *Man is a two-legged animal* – but *woman* cannot; and while the word *woman* is historically bimorphemic, *man* is monomorphemic. Similarly, antonymic adjectives tend to form marked–unmarked pairs; for example, of the two opposites *old* and *young, old* can be used in an age-neutral sense for the entire dimension of age – such as when we say *How old is the baby?* Another example is the pair *long* and *short: long* is unmarked in that the question *How long have you been in the US?* does not imply that the time period involved must have been long – it refers to the entire dimension of length rather than just one of its poles.

In sum: we have seen that sister terms in both partonomic and taxonomic relations can be asymmetric. Partonomically prominent constituents are called heads; taxonomically prominent constituents are called prototypes and, in the case of binary opposites, the unmarked members of the pair.

Heads, prototypes and unmarked–marked relations exemplify two commonly occurring deviations from the simplest possible kinds of partonomy and taxonomy: the lack of equality of parts and of subtypes. In what follows, we will turn to two additional complex patterns: parts that belong to multiple wholes and tokens that belong to multiple types.

2.2 PARTS THAT BELONG TO MORE THAN ONE WHOLE AND TOKENS THAT BELONG TO MORE THAN ONE TYPE

Parts that belong to more than one whole were exemplified above with sidewalks. In the USA, for some purposes, such as snow removal, the sidewalk counts as part of the property behind it, which means that the owner is responsible for shovelling. For other purposes, however, it counts as part of the street: maintenance will be taken care of by the city along with the street pavement. Another example is teenage years between 17 and 21: these years count as part of adulthood in some ways and as part of childhood in other ways. For example, a 17-year-old, just like an adult, may be able to get a driving licence but, like a child, they may not legally consume alcohol.

Similar instances of 'double allegiance' occur in taxonomy. As noted above, in a simple system no subtype belongs to more than one superordinate type: every subclass is assigned to a single class only (unless the multiple classes that it is assigned to are themselves in a type–subtype relation). In the realm of human thought, however, subtypes or tokens may be seen as belonging to more than one type. There are two such scenarios, which we will label cross-classification and class overlap.

Cross-classification arises when items are subject to classification by two or more criteria. For example, living beings can be classified as animals and plants but also as land-based or water-based. As a result, fish belong to the category of animals that also includes wolves but excludes seaweed; but at the same time it also belongs to the category of water-based beings that includes seaweed but excludes wolves.

How can the multiple taxonomic relations among things be conceptualized, using the examples just discussed? In (1) are shown two alternative representations of the taxonomy of living beings.

In (1a) plants and animals are the basic cut and water-based plants, land-based plants, water-based animals and land-based animals are regarded as the subclasses. This classification captures the similarity among plants and among animals by having a single class label for each life form but it fails to capture the similarity between land-based plants and land-based animals and that between water-based plants and water-based animals since it does not show a single class for 'land-based beings' and one for 'water-based beings'. In (1b) the first cut is made in terms of land-based and aquatic life forms, which results in bringing out the relatedness of wheat and wolf and that of seaweed and fish but it misses the relatedness of wheat and seaweed and that of wolf and fish.

Given that there are generalizations to be made about each of the four classes – all animals, all plants, all water-based life forms and all land-based

(1) (a) SPLIT BY LIFE FORM FIRST:

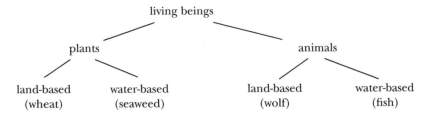

(b) SPLIT BY HABITAT FIRST:

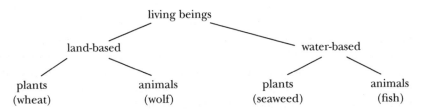

life forms – we need a non-hierarchical classificatory system that makes all four classes readily available. The solution lies in a different concept of categorization: rather than visualizing classes as slots so that once an item is placed in a slot, it cannot be anywhere else, we need to think of categorization as marking objects with strokes of paint so that an object may receive several strokes of different paints indicating its simultaneous assignment to more than one class.

Let us apply this idea to the example above. Rather than designating one or the other of the two classificatory criteria – life form and habitat – as primary and the other as secondary, we will take the two criteria to be on a par: any form of life may be tagged for animal or plant and at the same time, for land-based or water-based. This gives us the following taxonomy:

(2)

I	II	III	IV
+ANIMAL	+ANIMAL	−ANIMAL	−ANIMAL
+LAND-BASED	−LAND-BASED	+LAND-BASED	−LAND-BASED
(wolf)	(fish)	(wheat)	(seaweed)

The diagram in (2) provides us with the conceptual apparatus needed to pick out any of the four classes: all animals are +ANIMAL regardless of whether land-based or water-based; all plants are −ANIMAL regardless of whether land-based or aquatic; all land-based life forms are +LAND-BASED regardless of life form; and all water-based life forms are −LAND-BASED whether animal or plant. Rather than 'slotting', we applied 'paint-marking'. Slotting allows only one category for each item, while paint-marking allows more than one. The 'paint-marks', or 'tags', are called **features**. Feature notation lets us say that wolves are both classmates of wheat and classmates of fish even though wheat and fish are not classmates of each other.

In addition to cross-classification, there is a second scenario where items belong to more than one type: **class overlap**. Let us consider again the dichotomy of animals and plants. As it turns out, not every living being can be put into one or the other of these two classes: the tiny creature euglena straddles the line between the two. Euglenae are one-cell beings that move around in water using their whip-like organs and produce chlorophyll. But locomotion is a property of animals, not plants; and chlorophyll production is otherwise found only in plants, not in animals. Thus, euglenae represent an overlap between plants and animals.

Note that this example is different from the one considered above. In cross-classification, items belong to more than one category because they can be classified along different parameters, such as life form and habitat of living beings. But here, an item – euglena – belongs to two categories that contrast along the same parameter: life form. In (3) the two patterns are compared. In (3a), the vertical boxes indicate categorization by life form; the horizontal ones indicate categorization by habitat.

(3) (a) CROSS-CLASSIFICATION   (b) CLASS OVERLAP

wheat	wolf
seaweed	fish

wheat	euglena	wolf
seaweed		fish

Cross-classification – the overlap of classes defined by different criteria – is complex but not contradictory; but overlap between two classes that are opposed by the same criterion poses a contradiction.

However, just as in the case of cross-classification, there is a way to re-conceptualize the facts. As long as we consider the classes 'animal' and 'plant' as mutually exclusive categories, their overlap is indeed contradictory: something cannot be both ANIMAL and NOT-ANIMAL. But if we view the two as independent properties – ANIMAL and PLANT – they can overlap: something being both ANIMAL and PLANT is not contradictory any more. In (4) are shown both taxonomies. In (4a), euglenae are represented as self-contradictory (hence the asterisk) but in (4b) they are a logically legitimate class.

(4) (a) THE DIFFERENCE BETWEEN ANIMALS AND PLANTS IS REPRESENTED IN TERMS OF **OPPOSITE VALUES OF A SINGLE FEATURE**

I	II	*III
+ANIMAL	−ANIMAL	**+ANIMAL**
		−ANIMAL
(wolf, fish)	(wheat, seaweed)	**(euglena)**

(b) THE DIFFERENCE BETWEEN ANIMALS AND PLANTS IS
     REPRESENTED IN TERMS OF **TWO FEATURES**

I	II	**III**
+ANIMAL	−ANIMAL	**+ANIMAL**
−PLANT	+PLANT	**+PLANT**
(wolf, fish)	(wheat, seaweed)	**(euglena)**

Note that the two-feature-based system in (4b) allows for a fourth category: life forms that are neither animal nor plant. This might be a convenient niche for humans.

Here is a summary of this section. We characterized simple systems of partonomies and taxonomies and then discussed four common types of complexities: unequal parts, unequal subtypes, more than one whole to a part and more than one type to a subtype. Of this last pattern, we have seen two varieties: cross-classification and class overlap. We have invoked four concepts that accommodate these complexities: head, prototype, markedness and classificatory features.

Classificatory features revolutionize taxonomies: they represent instances of complex cross-classifications and eliminate the contradictory nature of class overlap. The train of thought we pursued above is an example of how, in the face of newly observed phenomena in the world, we can keep broadening our conceptual apparatus to capture the facts.

After this brief survey of general properties of partonomic and taxonomic systems, we turn to some actual facts of syntax. We will see that syntactic partonomies and taxonomies can also deviate from maximally simple systems and thus the conceptual tools invoked above will find their application. But first, let us consider the very rationale of inventory statements in syntax.

3 Partonomy and taxonomy in syntax: some facts

3.1 SELECTION AND INVENTORY

Is it important to construct an inventory of syntactic categories as part of the syntactic account of a language? As was noted in Section 1, the question of whether inventory statements do or do not provide a useful level of generalization is an empirical one: it depends on whether members of a category can or cannot differ in their selection patterns. If syntactic categories are invariant in and across languages with respect to what they can occur with, inventory statements are superfluous since there will be no generalization to make about categories independently of their selection. If, on the other hand, categories vary in their selection patterns, inventory statements will be useful. They will show sets of constructions as similar if they draw upon the same list of categories even though the categories differ in what they occur with.

Cross-linguistic evidence indicates that there is indeed selectional variability over the same set of categories. For an example, consider definite articles and adnominal demonstratives (i.e., demonstratives that occur with a noun rather than by themselves: ***This*** *book is old* as opposed to ***This*** *is old*). In Hungarian, the adnominal demonstrative must occur with the definite article.

(1) *ez   a   könyv*   'this book'
    this the book

   a   könyv   'the book'
   the book

   *ez könyv   'this book'
   this book

There are also other languages where the adnominal demonstrative must occur with the definite article but the ordering of the two may or may not be the same as in Hungarian. Maltese shows the same order, Piro shows the opposite order:

(2) MALTESE
   (a) *dan il-ktieb*   'this book'
        this the-book

        il-ktieb   'the book'
        the-book

        *dan ktieb   'this book'

   (b) PIRO (cf. Matteson 1965: 67; simplified example)
        wa nyi   xexine   'these men'
        the these men

        wa xexine   'the men'
        the men

        *nyi   xexine   'these men'
        these men

Thus, Hungarian and Maltese have a common pattern in terms of both selection and order, while Hungarian and Piro are similar in selection but not in order. What about English? In English, the adnominal demonstrative does not occur with the definite article. Thus, English is different both from Hungarian and Maltese and from Piro in the very selection of categories. Nonetheless, it is not as different as Russian: while English does have both adnominal demonstratives and a definite article, Russian has no definite article at all:

(3) RUSSIAN
   eta kn'iga   'this book'
   this book

   kniga   'the book' OR 'a book'
   book

The varying degrees to which these four languages differ from Hungarian are summarized in (4).

(4)

DEM, ADJ AND NOUN IN DIFFERENT LANGUAGES		THE LANGUAGES ARE SIMILAR IN		
		ORDER	SELECTION	INVENTORY
(a) HUNGARIAN Dem & Art & N	MALTESE Dem & Art & N	+	+	+
(b) HUNGARIAN Dem & Art & N	PIRO Art & Dem & N	−	+	+
(c) HUNGARIAN Dem & Art & N	ENGLISH Dem & N Art	−	−	+←
(d) HUNGARIAN Dem & Art & N	RUSSIAN Dem & N *Art	−	−	−

This chart shows that, just as in phonology, in syntax, too, it is useful to present inventories of categories separately from their selectional patterns. The chart in (4) is similar to the chart in (4) of Section 1, where the ordering, selection and availability of the phonemes /p/ and /s/ were compared across languages. Both comparisons show that a separate statement of inventory highlights cross-linguistic similarities that would otherwise go unstated. As the arrow indicates, Hungarian and English are different in selection and order but the same in that both definite articles and demonstratives are part of their syntactic inventories.

This is an empirical finding: there is no logical reason why this should be so. As seen in Section 1, it would be logically possible for the choice of an inventory item to leave no alternative regarding what categories it could occur with. Thus, the fact that languages show similarities in the inventories of their categories says something about the way languages are as opposed to the way they could be.

Syntactic inventories are lists of categories. How do we 'discover' these categories in the first place? This will be illustrated next.

3.2 THE BIRTH OF A SYNTACTIC CATEGORY

Here are some categories that are frequently drawn upon in syntactic analysis.

(1) (a) **word-level categories:**
noun, verb, adjective, adverb, pronoun, auxiliary
(b) **partonomically superordinate categories:**
noun phrase, verb phrase, adjective phrase, relative
clause, interrogative sentence
(c) **partonomically subordinate categories:**
stem, affix
(d) **taxonomically superordinate categories:**
nominal, verbal
(e) **taxonomically subordinate categories:** count noun, mass
noun, common noun, proper noun; transitive verb,
intransitive verb

We will begin with a word-level class: noun. What justifies the assumption of this category? In order to answer this question, we do not need to go back to the writings of ancient grammarians: it is not in deference to descriptive tradition that this category is employed in the grammars of most languages. Just like basic societal institutions such as schools and churches, or moral values such as sincerity and loyalty, it is so useful a concept that, were there no transmission of knowledge between generations of linguists, practising grammarians would keep re-inventing it again and again. So let us take a careful look at how syntactic facts lead us to posit the category noun for English.

As was shown in Chapter 1 (Section 3.2), if we want to construct a general account of syntactic well-formedness, it is necessary to analyse linguistic utterances into parts and to assign the parts to general types. For an illustration, consider (2).

(2) (a) *The red apple is on the table.*
(b) *She likes the red apple.*
(c) *The red apple on the table is sweeter than the red apple in the basket.*

If sentences were not segmented into parts, the rules describing these sentences would have to be as in (3).

(3) (a) *The red apple is on the table* is a grammatical sentence in English.
(b) *She likes the red apple* is a grammatical sentence in English.
(c) *The red apple on the table is sweeter than the red apple in the basket* is a grammatical sentence in English.

However, as also discussed in Section 3.2 of Chapter 1, such enumerative descriptions would be not only undesirable but also non-viable. They would not be viable since they would require an infinite number of descriptive statements to account for the infinite number of sentences in the language. They would also not be desirable since such descriptions would be entirely void of generality and thus of explanatory and predictive force.

The most obvious point that such an enumerative account would leave unexpressed is that sentences contain recurrent parts – items that occur more than once within and across sentences. Thus, the expression *the red apple* occurs in all three sentences in (2) and twice within (2c). If we do not make this fact explicit in our description, the grammaticality of the first occurrence of *the red apple* in (2c) remains unrelated to its second occurrence in the same sentence. Also, the grammaticality of each of its four occurrences in (2) would remain entirely unrelated to the grammaticality of the others. If, on the other hand, we note the recurrence of *the red apple* in and across sentences, we can give a partial reason why all three sentences are grammatical: all three include the grammatical sub-sequence *the red apple*. The same argument holds for other recurrent sentence parts such as *on the table*, which occurs both in (2a) and in (2c).

The new description has rules such as in (4).

(4) (a) Sentences that include *the red apple* are grammatical to that extent.
   (b) Sentences that include *on the table* are grammatical to that extent.
   And so on.

Phrases like *the red apple* and *on the table* can be further dissected. Consider (5).

(5) (a) *The pink apple is on a table.*
   (b) *The yellow apple is on the table.*
   (c) *The yellow pear is on the chair.*

These sentences show that *red, apple, on, the,* and *table* may occur in combination with elements other than in (2) and thus they are units of their own right, just as *pink, yellow, pear* and *a* are. Thus, we may further revise (4) as in (6):

(6) (a) Sentences that include *the* followed by *red, pink* or *yellow* are grammatical to that extent.
   (b) Sentences that include *red, pink* or *yellow* followed by *apple* or *pear* are grammatical to that extent.
   (c) Sentences that include *on* followed by *the* or *a* are grammatical to that extent.

Note that by saying that the sentence has parts we are not denying that these parts make a single whole together. By dividing a sentence into parts, we manage to do justice to two seemingly contradictory characteristics: that the sentence is both one thing and many things at the same time. By maintaining both claims, we are making it possible to refer to a sentence as a whole when we focus on its unity and also as something that consists of parts when we focus on the parts' independence.

However, the description in (6) is still far from being maximally general because the rules involve lists of words without stating the similarities between the words. *Apple* and *pear* are similar in that both can occur with *red, yellow* and *pink*; and *red, yellow* and *pink* are similar in that they can all occur with *apple* and *pear*, but *red, yellow* and *pink* cannot occur with each other and *apple* and *pear* cannot, either. From the point of view of their selectability, *apple* and *pear* form a class and so do *red, yellow* and *pink*. From the examples above, the following classes begin to emerge:

(7)	I	II	III	IV
	on	*the*	*red*	*apple*
		a	*yellow*	*pear*
			pink	*table*

These classes have traditional labels. *On* in column I and its likes are called prepositions, the words in column II are articles, those in column III are adjectives, those in column IV are nouns. This classification now allows us to simplify and generalize the statements of (6) as in (8):

(8) (a) Sentences that include articles followed by adjectives are grammatical to that extent.
(b) Sentences that include adjectives followed by nouns are grammatical to that extent.
(c) Sentences that include prepositions followed by articles are grammatical to that extent.

These statements, unlike those in (6), make predictions for the like behaviour of all other members of the classes they mention.

There are many other selectional and order rules in which these categories figure prominently. In addition to occurring with articles, adjectives and prepositions, nouns can also be co-selected with demonstratives (e.g. *this, that*), numerals (e.g. *one, two* and so on), quantifiers (e.g. *some, few*), relative clauses (e.g. *which has just been picked*), possessive determiners (e.g. *Jill's, my*) and other sentence parts. For describing the obligatory or optional co-selectability of nouns and other constituents and their respective orderings in a general way, the class label noun is thus indispensable, as are labels for the other classes of words.

In sum: categories such as article, adjective or noun are nothing other than handy abbreviations for lists of elements that have some of their selectional and linear properties in common. Although the existence of categories is logically prior to the formulation of selection rules just as selection rules are logically prior to order rules, from a heuristic point of view – that is, how we discover them – the relationship is reversed: it is in order to support statements of co-occurrence and order patterns that we posit categories. Thus, we need to have an idea of the selectional and order regularities that we want to state before defining the categories that would be needed for these statements.

3.3 THE PARTONOMIC AND TAXONOMIC STATUS OF NOUNS

What we have seen so far is that word-level categories such as noun, verb or article come to being through segmenting a sentence into word-size parts and then classifying these parts in terms of their distribution. Let us now see the utility of the partonomic and taxonomic hierarchies that the category noun is embedded in.

As shown in (1), the category noun is an intermediate-level term both partonomically and taxonomically.

(1) (a) THE PARTONOMIC POSITION   (b) THE TAXONOMIC POSITION
        OF NOUNS   OF NOUNS

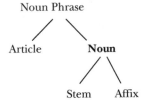
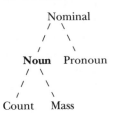

Here are questions that naturally arise about these structures.

    (a) Regarding the place of nouns in partonomy:
- Why is it useful to say that Noun **is part** of a larger whole: the **Noun Phrase**?
- Why is it useful to say that Noun **has parts,** such as **Stem** and **Affix**?

    (b) Regarding the place of nouns in taxonomy:
- Why is it useful to say that Noun **is a subtype** of the broader type labelled **Nominal**?
- Why is it useful to say that Noun **has subtypes,** such as **Count Nouns** and **Mass Nouns**?

The questions about partonomic relations ((a)) will be taken up in Section 3.3.1 and those about taxonomic relations ((b)), in Section 3.3.2.

3.3.1 *The partonomic status of nouns*

As shown in (1a) above, nouns have a middle-level position in grammatical partonomy: they are parts of noun phrases and they in turn include stems and affixes as their parts. What is the rationale for this analysis?

Let us start with the partonomically subordinate notions **stem** and **affix**. Their existence is justified by the fact that they support certain morphological generalizations. If we did not analyse nouns such as *apples* into stem and affix, a similarity among forms such as *apple-s, book-s, read-s, read-ing, walk-ed* would be missed, namely, that all these words consist of a free and a bound morpheme, with the former preceding the latter.

Second, let us look 'upwards' in the partonomy and consider the claim that the three words *the red apples* in the sentence *The red apples are on the table* belong to a superordinate unit: a **phrase**. Syntactic constituents – whether single words or phrases – have a legitimate existence only to the extent that they facilitate the statement of syntactic generalizations. Thus, a set of words can be claimed to form a phrase only if this phrase is a helpful term in a rule of selection or in a rule of order. Some of the relevant syntactic evidence for the phrasehood of a string of words falls into the following broad types:

(1) (a) selection:
- joint recurrence in and across sentences
- joint non-occurrence in a sentence
- joint occurrence as a sentence

(b) order:
- joint adjacency

Examples of joint recurrence in and across sentences were given in (2) of Section 3.2 and are repeated here.

(2) (a) **The red apple** *is on the table.*
(b) *She likes* **the red apple***.*
(c) **The red apple** *on the table is sweeter than* **the red apple** *in the basket.*

What (2) shows is that the selection and ordering of the main constituents of these sentences can be stated more simply if the rules can refer to *the red apple* 'in a single breath', that is, as a unit.

Second, note that in some instances where *the red apple* would occur more than once in a sentence, one of its mentions can be left out without loss of grammaticality. In (3b), the three words are jointly replaced by a pronoun and in (3c), they are jointly omitted without replacement.

(3) (a) **The red apple** *rolled towards the edge of the table and the red apple fell down.*

(b) ***The red apple*** *rolled towards the edge of the table and it fell down.*

(c) ***The red apple*** *rolled towards the edge of the table and* ___ *fell down.*

Rules describing the selection and order of pronouns like *it* and the optional non-selection of *the red apple* can be stated best if they can refer to the three words as a single unit. One rule will say pronouns may replace noun phrases. The other will say given two occurrences of a noun phrase in a sentence, one of them may be left out. Note that the pronoun *it* could not replace just part of the unit: **the red it*, and **the it* are both ungrammatical; and one could not leave out some parts of the phrase while leaving in others, such as * . . . and the* ___ *fell down*, or * . . . and the red* ___ *fell down.*

Further, note that *the red apple* can make a sentence by itself as in answer to a question:

(4) Question: *What is rolling under the sofa?*
Answer: ***The red apple.***

The selection rule that specifies what can be an answer to a question is simpler if it can make reference to phrases rather than individual word types by stating that sets of words can make answers if they form a phrase. Note that some subparts of the phrase, such as *the* or *the red*, could not stand as an answer.

As a fourth source of justification of phrasehood, let us now consider the ordering of the three words. Note that when they occur in a sentence, they must be adjacent, forming a continuous sequence:

(5) (a) ***The red apples*** *probably came from Michigan.*
(b) *****The*** *probably* ***red apples*** *came from Michigan.*
(c) *****The red*** *probably* ***apples*** *came from Michigan.*

This can be stated most simply by a general rule which says members of a phrase must be adjacent; but this is possible only if *the red apple* is analysed as a phrase.

These considerations so far justify the partonomic claim that the three words – *the*, *red* and *apple* – form a single phrase. The next question is taxonomic: whether this phrase needs to be labelled as a particular category of phrases. Are there different kinds of phrases or just one kind?

There are many other sequences of words that exhibit similar selectional and order properties as *the red apple*; they have similar internal composition and similar distribution. Examples are given in (6):

(6) (a) ***The red apples*** *are on the table.*
(b) ***The blue hats*** *are on the table.*
(c) ***The big statues in front of the museum*** *are new.*
(d) ***The three little lion cubs born in the zoo yesterday*** *are doing well.*

But there are also other word sequences that act as phrases even though they are different from those seen in (6) both in internal composition and in distribution. Examples are in (7):

(7) (a) *The red apples are* **on the table.**
    (b) *The car is* **behind the garage.**
    (c) *The clouds* **over the mountain** *are pink.*

This observation indicates that there are different kinds of phrases, not just a single kind. Since the obligatory part of the phrases in (6) is the noun, the mnemonic taxonomic label assigned to them is **noun phrase**. The phrases in (7) have a preposition as their obligatory part and thus they are called **prepositional phrases**. Other phrase types in English are the adjectival phrase (e.g. *very bright*), and the verb phrase (e.g. *hit the target*). In each case, similar internal structure and similar distribution justify the category.

In this section, we addressed the questions under (a) in the beginning of Section 3.3 by seeking evidence for the position of nouns in a grammatical partonomy. Let us now turn to the questions in (b) having to do with the taxonomic status of nouns.

3.3.2 *The taxonomic status of nouns*

As in grammatical partonomy, nouns occupy an intermediate position in grammatical taxonomy as well: as shown in (1b) in the beginning of Section 3.3, a noun is a subtype of nominals and it in turn has count nouns, mass nouns (and others) as its subtypes. But why is it useful to say that nouns are a subtype of nominals, with pronouns constituting another subtype? And why distinguish subtypes of nouns such as count and mass?

To start with the second question: the utility of the subcategories count noun and mass noun is easy to demonstrate by selectional evidence. Count nouns may select numerals but mass nouns may not (e.g. *five suggestions* versus **five advices*). Similarly, count nouns may select the quantifier *many* but not *much*; mass nouns may in turn select *much* but not *many* (e.g. *many pencils, much cotton, *much pencil, *many cottons*). Thus, in order to formulate a rule about the distribution of numerals and quantifiers, we need to make reference to count nouns as distinct from mass nouns. Count and mass nouns are similar in some ways and this is what is reflected in calling both nouns; but they are also different in other ways and it is for the statements of their differences that we need the distinguishing labels 'count' and 'mass'.

Let us now probe into the justification of the supercategory nominal, which includes nouns and pronouns. If nouns and pronouns were exactly the same, a supercategory including both would be justified but the categories noun and pronoun themselves would not. If, on the other hand, the two were distinct in all their properties, the categories noun and pronoun would be useful but the category nominal would be superfluous. For all three categories – noun, pronoun and nominal – to be justified, nouns and pronouns must be both similar in some ways and different in other ways.

Let us first consider relevant evidence from French (cf. Dik 1978: 189). The sentences in (1) all include a subject (SBJ), a direct object (DO) and an indirect object (IO). Some subjects, direct objects and indirect objects are nouns, others, printed in bold, are pronouns.

(1) (a) SBJ: noun, DO: noun, IO: noun
  Le garçon a donné le livre à son frère.
  the boy has given the book to his brother
  'The boy has given the book to his brother.'

(b) **SBJ: pronoun**, DO: noun, IO: noun
  ***Il** a donné le livre à son frère.*
  he has given the book to his brother
  'He has has given the book to his brother.'

(c) SBJ: noun, **DO: pronoun**, IO: noun
  *Le garçon **l'**a donné à son frère.*
  the boy **it**:has given to his brother
  'The boy has given it to his brother.'

  Le garçon a donné **l' à son frère.*
  the boy has given **it** to his brother

(d) SBJ: noun, DO: noun, **IO: pronoun**
  *Le garçon **lui** a donné le livre.*
  the boy **to:him** has given the book
  'The boy has given him the book.'

  Le garçon a donné le livre **lui.*
  the boy has given the book **to:him**

(e) SBJ: noun, **DO: pronoun, IO: pronoun**
  *Le garçon **le lui** a donné.*
  the boy **it to:him** has given
  'The boy has given it to him.'

  Le garçon a donné **le lui.*
  the boy has given **it to:him**

Here are some observations about the order of constituents in these sentences:

(2) (a) When serving as subjects, **both nouns and pronouns** must precede the verb.

(b) When serving as objects whether direct or indirect, **nouns** must follow the verb and **pronouns** must precede the verb.

(c) When serving as direct or indirect objects and occurring on the same side of the verb, **both nouns and pronouns** must be ordered with the direct object preceding the indirect object.

Note the classes that these generalizations call for. That noun objects and pronoun objects are distinct categories is clear: as stated in (2b), noun objects follow the verb and pronoun objects precede it. But nouns and pronouns also have some things in common. First, the distinction disappears in how subjects are ordered: whether noun or pronoun, the subject precedes the verb (cf. (2a)). Second, the noun–pronoun distinction is also irrelevant for the ordering of direct and indirect objects relative to each other: whether pronoun or noun, the direct object precedes the indirect object when they are on the same side of the verb (see (2c)).

To do justice both to their similarities and their differences, nouns and pronouns must be viewed as distinct categories but at the same time, they must be recognized as subtypes of a single supercategory. This taxonomy allows for simplified versions of rules (2a) and (2c): instead of 'both nouns and pronouns', the rule can refer to 'nominals':

(3) (a) When serving as subjects, **nominals** must precede the verb.

(b) When serving as direct or indirect objects and occurring on the same side of the verb, **nominals** must be ordered with the direct object preceding the indirect object.

English evidence, too, supports the supercategory nominal. Note first that, just as in French, there is evidence that nouns and pronouns are distinct classes:

(4) (a) Some **pronouns** show a morphological distinction for Nominative and Accusative (eg. *I, me; he, him*) but no **nouns** do.

(b) Most **nouns** may co-occur with articles, numerals and adjectives but **pronouns** do not.

(c) In phrases that involve both a **noun** and a **pronoun**, the order of the two is fixed: depending on the subtype of the pronoun, it must precede the noun (e.g. *I the teacher . . .*) or it must follow the noun (e.g. *The teacher himself . . .*).

While these differences call for distinguishing nouns and pronouns, there are also similarities between them:

(5) (a) **Both nouns and pronouns** may occur as subjects and objects; e.g. *Jill found a bird, She found a bird, Jill found it.*

(b) **Both some nouns and some pronouns** have number – that is, they may be singular or plural; for example, *bird, birds; he, they.*

(c) **Both some nouns and some pronouns** have gender – that is, they may be masculine or feminine or neuter; for example, *actor, actress; he, she.*

These regularities can be stated more simply if the term 'both (some) nouns and pronouns' can be replaced with '(some) nominals'.

These considerations lend support for the taxonomic status of nouns as intermediate between count and mass nouns on the one hand and nominals, on the other.

The goal of this section was to evaluate the position of nouns in grammatical partonomy and taxonomy. In addition, a general point also emerges from our discussion: grammatical partonomies and taxonomies can be complex in the sense that they may involve multiple levels rather than just two. In the following section, we will take up this and other complex patterns of syntactic taxonomies and partonomies.

3.4 COMPLEX PATTERNS OF SYNTACTIC PARTONOMY AND TAXONOMY

Section 2 listed the characteristics of maximally simple partonomic and taxonomic systems in general and some commonly occurring deviations from them. In this section, our goal is to examine some actual syntactic categories to see which, if any, of these deviations they show.

There are partonomic and taxonomic systems in syntax that are simple. Some partonomies are binary: sentences may usefully be analysed into a subject and a predicate and some predicates in turn into verb and complement. Similarly, taxonomies may involve a single split: sentences may be active or passive, nouns can be definite or indefinite.

More often than not, however, syntactic categories are more complex.

(1) (a) MORE THAN TWO SUBPARTS
A co-ordinate phrase may include more than two conjuncts (for example in **Sue and Bill and Mary and John and Larry arrived late**).

(b) MORE THAN TWO SUBTYPES
Verbs may be intransitive (e.g. *go*), transitive (e.g. *resemble*) and ditransitive (e.g. *give*).

(c) MULTI-LEVEL PARTONOMY
Verb phrase may consist of verb and noun phrase; noun phrase in turn may consist of article and noun.

(d) MULTI-LEVEL TAXONOMY
- Nominals may be nouns and pronouns; nouns in turn may be count and mass.
- Sentences may be simple or complex; complex sentences may in turn be conjoined or may involve subordination; subordinate clauses may be relative clauses or complement clauses.

In what follows, we will analyse examples of four additional complex patterns in some detail. These patterns, discussed in general terms in Section 2, are unequal parts, unequal subtypes and multiple terms for parts and for tokens.

3.4.1 *Unequal subparts*

Verbs and adverbs, verbs and objects, nouns and adjectives, and adjectives and complements are all examples of this pattern. In each instance, one of the two items forming a phrase is distributionally dominant over the other in that it itself can also stand for the entire phrase. Thus, verb and adverb form a phrase but the verb can occur by itself in that context while the adverb cannot; for example, *John runs (fast)*. In other words, the verb is the head of the phrase as defined in Section 2.1. Similarly, the verb is the head of a verb–object phrase (e.g. *John ate (bread)*); the noun is the head of the noun–adjective phrase (e.g. *John has a (bright) smile)*, and the adjective is in turn the head of the adjective–complement phrase (e.g. *John is angry (with his neighbour)*).

3.4.2 *Unequal subtypes*

Two kinds of asymmetries among members of a class will be discussed: prototypical versus marginal members, and unmarked versus marked members. Let us start with the **prototype-based classes**.

English subjects have unequal subtypes: not all English subjects are equally richly endowed with subject characteristics. Nominal subjects are shown in (1):

(1) (a) *The foxes have caught their prey in the garden.*
    **The foxes* has caught their prey in the garden.*
  (b) *The foxes catch their prey in the garden, don't they?*
    **The foxes* catch their prey in the garden, doesn't he?*
  (c) *Do the foxes catch their prey in the garden?*
  (d) *My dad believes the foxes to have caught their prey in the garden.*

These sentences illustrate the following characteristics of English subjects:

(2) RULES OF SELECTION:

    (a)   SUBJECT–VERB AGREEMENT
          Subjects must control verb agreement in number. (See all examples in (1).)

    (b)   MAIN SUBJECT – TAG SUBJECT AGREEMENT
          Subjects must control agreement in person, number and gender for the pronoun in tag-questions person. (See (1b).)

    (c)   'SUBJECT RAISING'
          If a clause is understood as the object of main verbs such as *believe* or *expect*, the subject of that clause may be expressed as the syntactic object of the main verb. (See (1d).)

RULES OF ORDER:

    (d)   SUBJECT–AUXILIARY ORDER IN STATEMENTS
          Subjects must directly precede the auxiliary in declarative sentences. (See (1a).)

    (e)   AUXILIARY–SUBJECT ORDER IN QUESTIONS
          Subjects must directly follow the auxiliary in yes–no questions. (See (1c).)

While nominal subjects exhibit all five of these properties, other kinds of subjects – *there*-subjects and clausal ones – fall short of a perfect record. *There*-subjects are illustrated in (3):

(3) (a) ***There** are foxes in the garden.*
     (b) *Are **there** foxes in the garden?*
     (c) ***There** are foxes in the garden, aren't there?*
     (d) *My dad believes **there** to be foxes in the garden.*

Most – but not all – criteria select *there* as the subject in these sentences. In (3c), the subject of the tag is *there*, rather than *they*, as would be expected if *foxes* were the subject of the main verb. In (3d), *there* acts like the subject of the subordinate clause in that it, rather than *foxes*, is the object of *believe*. In terms of linear order, *there* is in subject position in (3a) and (3b). But verb agreement opts against *there* as the subject: it is *foxes*, not *there*, that controls the person and number of the main verb. Thus, *there* has only four of the five criteria of subjecthood that nominal subjects show.

    Clausal subjects are even poorer in subject properties. Examples are in (4):

(4) (a) ***That foxes live in the garden** is surprising.*
         *It is surprising **that foxes live in the garden.***
     (b) *Is **that foxes live in the garden** surprising?*
         *Is it surprising **that foxes live in the garden?***
     (c) ***That foxes live in the garden** is surprising, isn't it?*

(d) *My dad believes **that foxes live in the garden**
to be surprising.*

As (4a) and (4c) show, clausal subjects do control verb agreement and the
agreement of pronouns in tags ((2a), (2b)); but with respect to the other
three subject characteristics, they fail. Thus, while they may directly precede
the auxiliary in declarative sentences as (2d) requires, they may also be
extraposed to the end of the sentence ((4a)); in yes–no questions, they are
uncomfortable in post-auxiliary position ((4b)); and they cannot stand as
the object of *believe* in sentence (4d).

The chart in (5) summarizes the properties of the three kinds of subjects.
The symbol + means the criterion holds, – means the criterion does not
hold, +/− means there are alternative constructions.

(5) SUBJECT CRITERIA	NOMINAL SUBJECTS	THERE-SUBJECTS	CLAUSAL SUBJECTS
1. Subject–verb agreement	+	–	+
2. Main subject – tag subject agreement	+	+	+
3. 'Subject raising'	+	+	–
4. Subject–auxiliary order in statements	+	+	+/−
5. Subject–auxiliary order in questions	+	+	+/−

The final conclusion we arrive at is that, among subjects, nominal subjects
are prototypical, as opposed to *there*-subjects and clausal subjects, which are
marginal members of the category.

Let us now turn to a more specific kind of unequality among members of
a class: **markedness** oppositions.

As noted in Section 2.1, markedness is abundantly represented in phonology and in the lexicon. Markedness is also a morphological and syntactic
pattern. Take, for example, grammatical number with two values: singular
and plural. Are they on a par? Note the use of the singular and plural in the
following sentences.

(6) (a) *The length is **two feet**.
I need a **two-foot**-long cord.*
(b) ***Lions** are fierce.
The lion is a fierce animal.*
(c) *There **are** two **tables** in the room.
There's two **tables** in the room.*

As the examples in (6) show, the terms of the singular–plural opposition
are not of equal rank. When the formal contrast between singular and

plural nouns is suspended (neutralized), it is the singular whose use is extended to the plural, rather than the other way around. Thus, (6a) shows that the singular form *foot* may function as a plural; (6b) shows that one can refer to more than one lion by using the singular; and (6c) shows that, when the verb disagrees with the noun, it is the singular that takes over for the plural rather than the other way around. The singular is thus the dominant member of the opposition. This is stated in (7):

(7) DOMINANCE
If the distinction between singular and plural is neutralized, it is **neutralized to the singular**, not the plural.

As we saw on phonological and semantic examples in Section 2.1, distributional dominance tends to correlate with greater text frequency, partonomic simplicity and taxonomic complexity, the four properties jointly characterizing the unmarked term of an opposition. Let us test these correlations for singular and plural. Here are the predictions.

(8) (a) FREQUENCY
If the singular and the plural differ in text frequency, **the singular will be more frequent**.
   (b) PARTONOMIC SIMPLICITY
If the singular and plural differ in the complexity of their expression, **the singular will be simpler**.
   (c) TAXONOMIC COMPLEXITY
If the singular and the plural differ in the number of their subdistinctions, **the singular will have more subdistinctions**.

The greater frequency of the singular over the plural as predicted in (8a) is documented by text counts (Greenberg 1966: 37). The point in (8b) is certainly true for English where the singular is expressed by an unmarked stem while the nominal plural is expressed through a stem and an affix, as in *machine* and *machines*. Regarding (8c), take English verb inflection. Verbs differ in person forms in the singular such as *I drink, he drinks*, or *I am, you are, he is*; but there are no person distinctions in the plural: *we drink, you drink, they drink; we are, you are, they are*.

Another syntactic opposition that also shows at least some of the symptoms of markedness relations is active and passive sentences. That passives are more complex than actives is shown in (9) and (10): passive sentences consist of more words than the corresponding active ones.

(9) (a) *The dolphin attacked the diver.*
   (b) *The diver was attacked by the dolphin.*

(10) (a) *The flood swept away the cottage.*
    (b) *The cottage was swept away by the flood.*

Correlated with the simpler structure of the active is its greater frequency: according to some counts in English as well as in some other languages, actives are more common than passives (Greenberg 1966: 46; Givón 1990: 573).

In sum: based on the evidence presented, within the number opposition, singular is unmarked, plural is marked; within the voice opposition, active is unmarked and passive is marked.

In the preceding two sections, we saw syntactic examples of two complex partonomic and taxonomic structures: unequal parts and unequal subtypes. We will now turn to two other complex patterns in syntax: more than one whole for a part and more than one type for a subtype.

3.4.3 More than one whole for a subpart

Consider the following sentences:

(1) (a) *The crowd believed **the thief** to have been arrested.*
   (b) *John expects **us** to come to dinner.*
   (c) *I consider **myself** to have been ripped off.*
   (d) *The lawyer takes **the issue** to have been tabled.*

Each of these sentences includes two verbs: the first is inflected, the second is an infinitive. At issue is the status of the noun phrases in bold: do they form a whole with the preceding inflected verb as its object, or with the following infinitive as its subject?

Linear order provides contradictory evidence: these noun phrases immediately precede the (infinitive) verb as English subjects generally do but they also immediately follow the main verb as direct objects are wont to.

Selectional evidence also turns out to be conflicting. Lexical selection points at these elements being subjects of the infinitive: they obey the selectional constraints of the infinitival verb. Thus, it is only humans such as thieves that can get arrested; only animate entities, such as *we*, may come to dinner or be ripped off; and only things such as issues may be tabled. But other selectional evidence suggests that these items form a constituent with the preceding verb. One is case. As shown by (1b), these items show object forms when they are pronouns and thus seem to be governed by the main verb. Also, as shown by (1c), they may be reflexive pronouns referring back to the subject of the main verb. In general, it is only complements of the verb – and not items outside the main verb's clause – that can be reflexive pronouns (cf. *I talked to John about myself*, **I told John that myself would leave town*).

Thus, it seems that the constituents in question are both subjects of the infinitive and thus parts of the infinitival clause and also objects of the main verb and thus parts of the main verb phrase. They are like the sidewalk in front of a residence that is a part of both the garden and the street; or the teenage years belonging both to childhood and to adulthood (cf. Section 2.2). In (2) this is shown in terms of a (simplified) partonomic tree representation of the sentence (a 'phrase structure tree') with *myself* having two mothers: the verb phrase of the main clause and the sentence node of the subordinate clause.

(2)

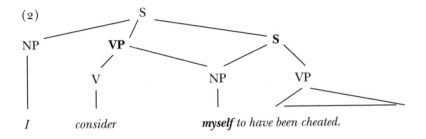

| I | consider | ***myself*** *to have been cheated.* |

3.4.4 *More than one type for a subtype*

As we saw in Section 2.2, there are two ways in which a token may end up belonging to more than one superordinate type: by cross-classification and by class overlap. Both scenarios crop up in syntax. Let us start by looking at **cross-classification.**

In (1) of Section 3.3.2, French data were presented to illustrate the justification for the taxonomic supercategory nominal that includes both nouns and pronouns. The same data set also provides an example of cross-classification. Consider the following generalizations about the French data:

(1) (a) **Noun objects**, both direct and indirect, must follow the verb while **pronoun objects**, both direct and indirect, must precede it.

(b) **Direct objects**, both noun and pronoun, must precede **indirect objects**, whether noun and pronominal, if they occur on the same side of the verb.

These generalizations call for a classification of objects by two different criteria: their function in the sentence – direct versus indirect object – and their word class – noun versus pronoun. This is parallel to the case discussed in Section 2.2: that of classifying living beings by two criteria: life form (animal or plant) and habitat (land-based or aquatic). As we saw there, in 'slotting' taxonomies, all four classes cannot be made available at the same time because one classification disables the other. If we first make the cut between direct and indirect objects (as in (2a) below), we have to give up the classes of nouns and pronouns. Conversely, if the first cut is between nouns and pronouns as in (2b), the other two classes – direct objects and indirect objects – become fragmented. (Compare (1) in Section 2.2.)

As also seen in Section 22, the solution lies in replacing the hierarchical taxonomy with a feature-based one. Features allow for multiple classificatory criteria applying to items at the same time: items are not rigidly slotted but simply 'tagged'. This is shown in (3) (compare (2) in Section 2.2).

(2) (a) SPLIT BY SYNTACTIC ROLE FIRST:

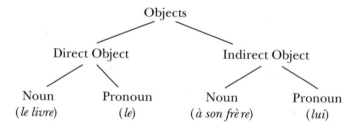

(b) SPLIT BY WORD TYPE FIRST:

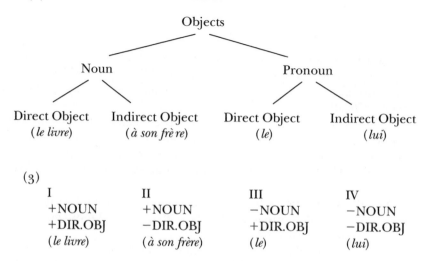

(3)

I	II	III	IV
+NOUN	+NOUN	−NOUN	−NOUN
+DIR.OBJ	−DIR.OBJ	+DIR.OBJ	−DIR.OBJ
(*le livre*)	(*à son frère*)	(*le*)	(*lui*)

This taxonomy makes all four classes available: all noun objects whether direct or indirect are +NOUN, all pronoun objects whether direct or indirect are −NOUN, all direct objects whether noun or pronoun are +DIR.OBJ, and all indirect objects whether noun or pronoun are −DIR.OBJ.

Let us consider the second way in which an item can belong to two types: **class overlap**.

A syntactic analogue to euglenae – the creatures that we found to be at the overlap of the classes of animals and plants in Section 2.2 – is adjectives when considered cross-linguistically. Traditionally, adjectives have been regarded as a category separate from all other categories and thus distinct from both nouns and verbs. This classification has some utility: in some languages, adjectives do have characteristics that are unique to them and thus we must have a way of referring to them exclusively. For example, English adjectives have degrees (*pretty, prettier, prettiest; more beautiful, most beautiful*); nouns and verbs do not. Also, in English, the presence of the nominalizing suffix *-ness*, as in *goodness* or *blackness*, is specific to adjectival stems: neither nouns nor verbs can take it.

On the other hand, representing adjectives as a class unrelated to other word classes is not satisfactory: adjectives do have properties in common with other kinds of words. Take adjectives and nouns. One thing they have in common in English is that they can both occur in so-called cleft constructions. In (4a) and (4b) is shown the grammaticality of clefted adjective phrases and clefted noun phrases; in (4c) it is shown that the same pattern is ungrammatical when it involves verb phrases:

(4) (a) *It is **red** that I want the roof to be painted.*
       *It is **somewhat delicate** that I would call the situation.*
    (b) *It is **the Dutch lady** who brought us this wine.*
       *It is **them** who will find the solution.*
    (c) **It is **drive** that he will.*
       It is **driven a car that he has.*

Additional evidence showing the relatedness of adjectives to nouns is available in other languages. In German, adjectives and nouns have number and gender while verbs have number but no gender. In Tagalog, adjectives and nouns – but not verbs – are pluralizable through the use of the morpheme *mga* (Schachter and Otanes 1972: 111, 229).

This would so far argue that, instead of conceptualizing adjectives as a class of their own (as in (5a)), we should lump them together with nouns to form a single superordinate class (as in (5b)).

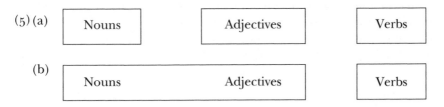

(5) (a) Nouns — Adjectives — Verbs

(b) Nouns Adjectives — Verbs

This, however, still would not do since there are also characteristics that adjectives share with verbs but not with nouns. In Russian both predicative adjectives and past-tense verbs agree with the subject both in number and in gender, while predicate nouns may agree with it in number only. This calls for a classificatory schema where adjectives form a class both with nouns and with verbs, without nouns and verbs sharing class membership with each other, as shown in (6).

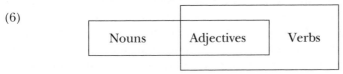

(6) Nouns Adjectives Verbs

This means that adjectives have to be declared both nouns and verbs. But as long as nounhood and verbhood are regarded as mutually exclusive properties, this is a contradiction.

The problem is thus similar to that of euglenae discussed in Section 2.2 (compare (2) with (3b) in Section 2.2) and so is the solution. Rather than considering nounhood and verbhood as two mutually exclusive categories or mutually exclusive values of a single feature (as in (7a)), we will re-analyse them as two distinct and mutually compatible features (as in (3b)). (Compare (3) with (4) in Section 2.2.)

(7) (a) THE DIFFERENCE BETWEEN NOUNS AND VERBS IS REPRESENTED IN TERMS OF **OPPOSITE VALUES OF A SINGLE FEATURE**

I	II	*III
+NOUN	−NOUN	**+NOUN**
		−NOUN
(*bird*)	(*speak*)	(*slow*)

(b) THE DIFFERENCE BETWEEN NOUNS AND VERBS IS REPRESENTED IN TERMS OF **TWO FEATURES**

I	II	III
+NOUN	−NOUN	**+NOUN**
−VERB	+Verb	**+VERB**
(*bird*)	(*speak*)	(*slow*)

Both (7a) and (7b) manage to express the fact that adjectives form a class both with nouns and with verbs: in both, there is one feature value available to call up adjectives and nouns but not verbs, and adjectives and verbs but not nouns. But the big difference is that (7a) accomplishes this by representing adjectives as self-contradictory, while (7b) avoids the contradiction.

4 Conclusions

A syntactic description needs to state what categories a language has available (inventory), how it employs these categories (selection) and how it arranges them (order). This chapter discussed the inventory of the terms that are available for syntactic selection and order statements: syntactic categories. Establishing a category happens through segmentation, whereby we delimit recurrent parts of utterances, and through classification, whereby we assign these parts to classes based on their shared behaviour. Labels assigned to these classes will then function as handy abbreviations for the entire category. Segmentation implies the claim that something is both a unit and a collection of smaller units; classification implies the claim that an element is both the same as another and distinct from it. Thus, partonomy and taxonomy both resolve paradoxes: that something can be both one and many and that two things can be both the same and not the same.

We assessed the position of nouns in partonomic and taxonomic hierarchies. Some simple and complex patterns of category systems were identified and then exemplified from syntax. Conceptual tools that have been found useful in characterizing partonomic and taxonomic structures in syntax are heads, prototypes, markedness and syntactic features.

Notes

Section 2   Partonomy and taxonomy: some possibilities

- On partonomic structures outside language, see for example Hailman *et al.* 1985 (in bird song); Dawkins 1976. In language, see Tversky 1990.
- Compositionality was briefly mentioned in Section 2.3 of Chapter 1.
- On natural categories, see Wittgenstein 1963: sections 64–71; Rosch and Mervis 1975; Rosch 1984; Lakoff 1987.
- For markedness relations between antonymic adjectives, see Wirth 1983. Markedness will be further discussed in section 3.1.2 of Chapter 5.

Section 3.1   Selection and inventory
For a cross-linguistic survey of demonstrative constructions, see Diessel 1999.

Section 3.2   The birth of a syntactic category
In addition to their distribution, word classes also have distinctive characteristics related to their internal structure: their morphological and phonological make-up, as well as related to their meanings. Thus, word classes that are useful for syntactic description may – or may not – also be useful for purposes of morphological, phonological and semantic descriptions. See Gil 2000 for a clear discussion; on whether all languages have nouns and verbs as separate categories, see Gil 1994; Baker 2003.

Section 3.3.1   The partonomic status of nouns
For arguments for phrasehood, see Radford 1988: 64–84; Siewierska 1988: 149–74; Jacobson 1996.

Section 3.4 Complex patterns of syntactic partonomy and taxonomy
For further discussion on the intermediate nature of adjectives, see Wierzbicka 1988; Thompson 1989; Bhat 1994; Stassen 1997. For another example of in-between categories – Russian numerals falling between nouns and adjectives – see Comrie 1989: 106–10.

Exercises

1. Describe the partonomy and the taxonomy of human bodies.

2. Find examples of heads and dependents outside language.

3. In a segment of CBS's '60 minutes' (2 May 2004), Andy Rooney quipped: 'We don't have a filing system here because everything belongs to a different category.' Interpret this statement.

4. At the end of Section 3.3.1, several phrase types were mentioned without providing detailed justification for their phrasehood. Using the four types of evidence for phrasehood given under (1) in this section, show the utility of positing prepositional phrases and adjectival phrases.

5. In Section 3.3.2, arguments were presented to show the need to differentiate count and mass nouns as subtypes of nouns. Is there syntactic evidence for the subtypes common noun and proper noun?

6. Consider the following sentences:

   (a) *Sheila wants a big green apple and Mary wants a small one.*
       (i.e., either 'Mary wants a small green apple' or 'Mary wants a small apple (regardless of colour)')
   (b) *That red apple is sweeter than this one.*
       (i.e., either 'than this red apple' or 'than this apple')
   (c) *I recommended this large round melon to him but he took that one.*
       (i.e., either 'he took that large round melon' or 'he took that round melon' or 'he took that melon')

   Formulate a rule about the distribution of the pronoun *one*. What would be the best representation of the internal constituent structure of noun phrases to support the rule?

7. Here is a set of sentences without translations (adapted from Koutsoudas 1966: 326–7). Construct a lexicon by listing the morphemes and a syntactic description in three parts: inventory of categories, rules of selection and rules of order.

GRAMMATICAL SENTENCES: UNGRAMMATICAL SENTENCES:

1. *man amadam*   **amadam man*
                     *man amad
                     *amadam
                     *man

2. *mahmud amad*   **amad mahmud*
                     *mahmud amadam
                     *mahmud
                     *amad

3. *u amad*   **amad u*
                     *u amadam

          *mahmud u amad
          *man u amad`

4. *man mahmud ra didam*   **man ra mahmud didam*
               *mahmud ra man didam
               *didam man mahmud ra
               *man mahmud ra amadam
               *man mahmud didam
               *man didam

5. *mahmud man ra did*   **man ra mahmud did*
               *did mahmud man ra
               *mahmud man ra didam
               *mahmud man did

6. *man u ra didam*   **man ra u didam*
               *didam man u ra
               *man u ra did

7. *u man ra did*   **did u man ra*
               *u man did
               *u
               *did
               *man ra

8. *u ræft*   **ræft u*
               *u ræftam
               *ræft did
               *did ræft
               *u mahmud ra ræft

9. *man ræftam*   **ræftam man*
               *ræftam
               *man u ra ræftam

10. *u man ra šænid*   **šænid u man ra*
               *u šænid

11. *man u ra šænidam*   **šænidam man u ra*
               *man šænidam
               *šænidam

12. *mahmud man ra šænid*   **šænid mahmud man ra*
               *mahmud man šænid

Chapter Five

Syntax, Meaning and Sound Form

[T]here is something in our mind that is more than the sum of the individual neurons that make up the brain. This something is the self . . . [J]ust as the sea has many properties that cannot be imagined from mere knowledge of the discrete molecules of water – such as tides, waves, whales, icebergs, gulls, boats, and beautiful sunsets – so the self has its own features that cannot be predicted from the discrete bits of information that make it up.

(Csikszentmihalyi 1993: 217)

1 Preliminaries

The three statement types that we have found instrumental in describing syntactic structure – inventory of categories, rules of selection and rules of order – can be employed to describe any other complex one-dimensional object as well, such as strings of beads, dinner menus, line-ups of courses required for a study programme, animal bodies, DNA structures and constellations of stars. That language can be analysed in such terms suggests a fundamental similarity between it and all other complex phenomena in the world.

However, sentences are not just **complex** objects; they are **semiotic** objects, which means they have meaning and sound form. Rather than an ordinary string of beads, a sentence is more like a rosary where beads stand for prayers; and rather than an ordinary dinner, it is more like a ritual meal where each food ingredient has a meaning and each contributes to the overall symbolic nature of the entire event. Syntactic structure is merely the scaffolding to be fleshed out with meaning and pronunciation (cf. Jackendoff 1997: 18). Accordingly, the characterization of syntactic form is not an end in itself; as was noted in Chapter 1 (Section 3.2) it is part of the larger goal of accounting for the relationship between meanings and sound forms.

So far in this book, scant attention has been paid to meaning: our focus has been **structural syntax**. In labelling word and phrase classes we did use terms that hinted at meanings, such as singular, plural, subject or adjective; but nothing hinged on the semantic content choice of these terms. As the last exercise at the end of Chapter 4 showed, the syntactic analysis of sentences is possible even if their meanings are not known. This chapter now turns to **correspondence syntax**: we will take up the question of how syntactic structure conveys meaning and is realized by sound form.

As a first example, consider the sentence *Don't write to me*. Syntax accounts for its well-formedness by licensing the following sequence of word and phrase categories:

(1) [Auxiliary & Negator & [Verb & [Preposition & Pronoun]$_{PP}$]$_{VP}$]$_S$

But this much does not yet tell us what the sentence means and how it is pronounced.

One might respond to this by saying: 'Well, that's what the dictionary is for!' A dictionary explicitly represents the symbolic nature of language in that, for each word, it specifies what that word means and how it is pronounced. The syntactic skeleton of a sentence can thus be made meaningful and 'soundful' if we replace the category labels with words.

There are indeed sentences whose syntactic structure, when supplemented with lexical information, comes close to yielding both the meaning and the sound form of the entire sentence. Consider the sentence *John is a doctor*. Given its syntactic skeleton 'Noun & Copula & Article & Noun', you can more or less arrive at the meaning by putting a word into each category slot and summing up their meanings. Similarly, you can construct a more or less proper pronunciation of this sentence by adding up the sound forms of the words. In this instance, the whole equals the sum of the parts: the sentence is (near-)compositional both semantically and phonetically.

However, as seen in Chapter 1 (Section 1) in connection with a Turkish sentence, more often than not, sentences are not compositional. Let us continue to analyse the sentence given above: *Don't write to me*. In (2) are listed the relevant lexical entries for this sentence along with their meanings and phonetic forms as they would occur outside a sentence in isolation. For each word, pronunciation is given first, followed by an English gloss in all caps that stands for the meaning, followed by the syntactic category of the word.

(2) /dú/ DO auxiliary
/nát/ NOT negator
/ráyt/ WRITE verb
/tú/ TO preposition
/mí/ ME pronoun

When augmented with this lexical information, the fleshed-out version of the syntactic structure (1) looks like (3):

(3) [Auxiliary & Negator & [Verb & [Preposition & Pronoun]$_{PP}$]$_{VP}$]$_S$
/dú/ /nát/ /ráyt/ /tú/ /mí/
DO NOT WRITE TO ME

Let us first compare the sum of the word meanings with the actual meaning of the entire sentence. (In (4b), comma stands for the conceptual association of semantic constituents; parentheses delimit groups of semantic constituents.)

(4) (a) SUM OF WORD MEANINGS:
DO & NOT & WRITE & TO & ME

(b) SENTENCE MEANING:
(COMMAND, (PREDICATE, NOT, WRITE), (AGENT, YOU), (RECIPIENT, I))

It is easy to see that (4a) and (4b) differ in several ways: the sum of the word meanings is not the same as the meaning of the entire sentence. We can take the preposition *to* as the expression of the semantic role RECIPIENT and intonation to convey COMMAND; but this still leaves the following differences:

(5) (a) CONSTITUENTS:
• present in meaning, not in syntax:
• (AGENT, YOU)
• present in syntax, not in meaning:
• DO

(b) RELATIONS AMONG CONSTITUENTS:
• present in meaning, not in syntax: conceptual grouping
• present in syntax, not in meaning: linear order

Second, just as the sum of isolated word meanings does not completely match the total meaning of this sentence, discrepancies exist also between the sum of isolated word pronunciations and the total pronunciation of the sentence. This is shown in (6).

(6) (a) SUM OF WORD PRONUNCIATIONS:
dú & nát & ráyt & tú & mí

(b) SENTENCE PRONUNCIATION:
/dóntraytəmí/

The discrepancies come from the reduction of isolated word pronunciations in sentence context:

(7) (a) In syntactic form, *do* and *not* are separate words; in the pronunciation of this sentence, they make a single word /dónt/.
(b) In syntactic form, /ráyt/ and /tú/ both have stress; in the pronunciation of this sentence, they are stressless.
(c) In syntactic form, /ráyt/ ends in a /t/ and /tú/ begins with a /t/; in sentence pronunciation, the two adjacent /t/-s are merged into a single /t/.
(d) In syntactic form, /tú/ ends in a /u/; in sentence pronunciation, the /u/ is reduced to /ə/.

To summarize so far, (5) and (7) show that the meaning side of syntactically well-formed sequences of words does not always equal the meaning of the entire sentence; and that, similarly, the sound side of syntactically well-formed word sequences does not necessarily add up to the pronunciation of the sentence.

For an analogy, consider a jigsaw puzzle where the pieces are printed on both sides and are laid out in a shallow clear plastic box with a matching lid. When the lid is closed, the box can be flipped so that both the upside and the downside of the completed puzzle can be viewed. If the puzzle is designed perfectly, fitting the pieces together by shape guarantees that both the top and the bottom picture come out as perfect pictures. But if the puzzle is less than ideal, the picture on one side, or perhaps the pictures on both sides, are distorted. In this analogy, the pieces stand for words and the double-sidedness of the pieces symbolizes their bi-facial nature: each word has a sound form and a meaning. The string of words fitted together by 'shape' – that is, by the rules of syntax – may turn out to be both phonetically and semantically well-formed; but it may also be semantically or phonetically ill-formed or ill-formed in both ways.

Evidence abounds to indicate that more often than not, sentences are not 'perfect puzzles'. Given the discrepancies between syntactic and semantic structures, on the one hand, and between syntactic and phonetic structures, on the other hand, a complete account of meaning–form relations in language will have to include not only syntactic well-formedness constraints on strings of words of the sort discussed in the preceding three chapters, but also rules about how syntactic structures are related to sentence meanings and to sentence pronunciations. The two questions are formulated in (8):

(8) (a)   How does syntactic structure supplemented by word
              meanings compare with the meaning of the entire sentence?
       (b)   How does syntactic structure supplemented by word
              pronunciations compare with the pronunciation of the
              entire sentence?

As is the case throughout this book, we are interested not only in how
things are but also in how things could be because it is only by comparing
the two that we can ask meaningful why-questions (see Chapter 1 (Section
2.1.1)). Thus, before exploring some of the actual facts of the syntax-
meaning and syntax-sound interface in Sections 3.1 and 3.2, we will, in
Section 2, take a look at the logical possibilities of these relations.

2 Symbolic correspondence: some possibilities

The relationship between meaning and form will be termed symbolic correspondence. While meaning and form are clearly not the same thing, they
can be said to correspond in the sense that each evokes the other. For
example, the sound sequence of *The milk spilled* brings up a particular
meaning in the mind of an English speaker and, in turn, the intended
message calls for this particular sound form. Statements about symbolic correspondence relations may be schematized as follows:

(1) **(M) If SYN and SEM, then SYN = SEM**
       In prose: Given a **syntactic** representation SYN and a **semantic**
              representation SEM, the two must (or may, or must not) be
              in a **symbolic correspondence relation**.

(2) **(M) If SYN and PHON, then SYN = PHON**
       In prose: Given a **syntactic** representation SYN and a
              phonological representation PHON, the two must (or may, or
              must not) be in a **symbolic correspondence relation**.

As noted above, symbolic correspondence is not a unique characteristic of
natural language: it is the defining feature of all symbol systems (also called
semiotic systems). It is this relation that links colour signals and their messages in the system of traffic lights; hand signals and their meanings in the
gesture system of airport ground controllers guiding planes to the gates; and
national flags and the countries that have chosen them as their symbols. It is
symbolic correspondence that explains why devout Christians are struck by
a sense of awe in the presence of a cross even if it is made of cheap plastic;
why a person familiar with the events of World War II may cringe at the sight
of the swastika even if it is artfully studded with diamonds; why a box of
chocolates presented to a person can bring a happy smile to his lips even if
he is a chocolate-hater; and why the smile will in turn make the gift-giver feel
good. In each case, it is not the mere material properties of the object that

have an effect on people but the ideas that the objects stand for. Recognizing that sentences, too, are symbols amounts to recognizing the similarity between them and all the countless other symbols that figure in the lives of human individuals and societies.

The term for the form of a symbol is **signans** (Latin for 'signaller'; the plural is *signantia*); the meaning that it represents is called the **signatum** ('signalled'; the plural is *signata*). For example, a gift is a signans for the signatum of gratitude or love. In language, semantic structure is the signatum relative to which both syntactic and phonetic structures are signantia.

Symbol systems vary in how closely form traces meaning. The closeness of fit between meaning and form can vary along four parameters: **isomorphism**, **markedness**, **compositionality** and **iconicity**.

The first parameter, **isomorphism**, has to do with how many alternative meanings a symbol's form can have and, conversely, in how many alternative ways a meaning can be expressed. A symbol system is isomorphic if the relationship between the meanings and the forms of the symbols is bi-unique: any one meaning is associated with one and only one distinctive form within the system and, in turn, any one form conveys one and only one unique meaning. In other words, in a isomorphic symbolic system, the relationship between meaning and form – signatum and signans – is one to one. Violations of isomorphism in turn involve one-to-zero or one-to-many relations between meanings and forms.

A **one-to-zero relation** between meanings and forms in a system of symbols would mean one of two things: either there is a symbol whose form is void of meaning, or there is a meaning which has no expression in the system. An example of one-form-zero-meaning is a road sign announcing a garage sale: within the system of traffic signs, it is meaningless. An example of one-meaning-zero-form is that in the system of traffic lights, the message 'proceed slowly' is not expressed by a special colour.

The other departure from bi-uniqueness is **one-to-many relations** between signans and signatum: either one form alternatively expresses more than one meaning, or one meaning is alternatively expressed by more than one form. If there is more than one possible meaning to a symbol, it is said to be **ambiguous**; if there is more than one alternative expression for a meaning, the different symbols expressing the same meaning are said to be **synonymous**. US traffic sign systems involve synonymy: the same message 'Stop, look, and go!' is at times signalled with an octagonal red shield with the word STOP written on it and in other cases with a flashing red light. A flashing red light is in turn ambiguous depending on the context where it is used: as a traffic sign, it means 'Stop, look, and go' while in front of a hospital room or a nuclear plant, it means 'Don't enter'.

A second way in which the fit between meaning and form may be looser or tighter depends on whether **markedness** relations between symbols do or do not hold.

Markedness can apply to forms by themselves, to meanings by themselves, or to entire symbols complete with meaning and form. As seen in Chapter 4

(Section 2.1), the unmarked member of an opposition is more frequent, distributionally dominant, structurally less complex and taxonomically more complex. For symbols, markedness would require that these characteristics hold for both the meanings and the associated forms.

Let us take two symbols A and B, such that the meaning of B properly includes the meaning of A – that is, B's meaning is all of A's meaning plus some. What can the forms of A and B be expected to be like? If form is true to meaning, we would expect the form of B, which has the additional meaning, to include all the form of A plus a bit more to carry the extra semantics.

This is so with some traffic signs. Take the 'No parking' sign: a crossed-out P. The negative meaning 'NO PARKING' includes the positive meaning 'PARKING' plus the added meaning component of negation. Correspondingly, the form of the sign includes the form of the 'Park' sign – a big P – plus an additional form component: the strike-through. The example thus illustrates one characteristic of the unmarked: its structural simplicity relative to the marked. The 'Parking' sign is both semantically and formally less than the 'No parking' sign and thus it is the unmarked member of the opposition.

One might think that if there is added meaning, the form could not help but be larger; but this is by no means so. For example, if the 'No parking' sign were symbolized by a shield with the letters NP (for No Parking) and the 'Parking allowed' sign were a shield with the letters PA (for Parking Allowed), no markedness relationship would hold between the two since the additional negative meaning would be represented by the same amount of form: two letters in each case. And if the 'No parking' sign were NP and the 'Parking allowed' sign were, say, PAD (for 'Parking AlloweD'), an anti-markedness relationship would hold between the two signs since now the form of the less complex meaning properly includes the form of the more complex meaning rather than, as markedness requires, the other way around. Thus, just like isomorphism, adherence to or deviation from markedness is a parameter that symbol systems may vary on.

Isomorphism and markedness apply to meaning–form relations across pairs of symbols. The remaining two parameters of meaning–form relations – compositionality and iconicity – have to do with meaning–form relations within individual symbols.

The third parameter of the ways in which meaning and form relate to each other is **compositionality**. If form is to trace meaning closely, a strict one-to-one relationship between meaning and form needs to hold not only across the entire meanings and entire forms of different symbols (isomorphism) but also between parts of the meaning and parts of the form of any one symbol. In such a system, form and meaning show a strict part-to-part correspondence: for every bit of meaning, there is one and only one bit of form in the structure; and for every bit of form, there is one and only one bit of meaning. A symbol for which this holds true is said to be **compositional**. The label speaks for itself: it suggests that the form is composed of all and only the relevant meaning units.

Traffic signs once again provide examples. Stop signs as we know them are not fully compositional. First, the red colour of a stop sign is a form element that is void of meaning: the intended message could be communicated regardless of the colour of the shield. Second, the meaning is not made quite explicit in the form since the fact that the stop command is intended for vehicles but not for pedestrians is not indicated. Stop signs would be closer to compositionality if the shield included a picture of a vehicle and if the colour carried some part of the message – say, blue signs for 'stop between 8 am and 6 pm only' and red signs for 'stop at all times of the day'.

The match between parts of the form and parts of the meaning of a symbol can manifest itself in two ways. A symbol may be **selectionally compositional** if, for every constituent in the meaning, there is a corresponding constituent in the form and, for every bit of form, there is a corresponding portion in meaning. If, in addition, there is also a one-to-one match between semantic and formal relations, the sentence shows both selectional and **relational compositionality**. The drawing of a person is selectionally compositional if each part of the body – the head, the trunk, the two arms and the two legs – is present in the quantities required – for example, one head rather than two – and there are no other things mixed into the picture – such as, say, a dog's tail and a seagull's beak. Such a drawing is selectionally compositional even if the arrangement of the body parts is random, with, say, arms coming out of the head and legs detached from the trunk. But if all body parts are both present and shown in their true-to-life arrangement, the picture is both selectionally and relationally compositional.

Another example is a plan of a house to be built. If it shows all and only those rooms that a house is to include but in random arrangement, the sketch is selectionally compositional only. But if the plan for the house is an actual blueprint indicating where each room will be relative to the others, the sketch is both selectionally and relationally compositional.

As the fourth and last component of our survey of the ways in which meaning and form may be related to each other, let us focus on a single bit of form and a single bit of meaning in a symbol. What is the nature of the symbolic relation between the two? Their symbolic correspondence may be merely conventional or it may be based on similarity: a common characteristic between form and meaning. For example, the presence of a pine forest may be symbolized on the map by a green dot or by a red one. In the latter case, the choice of the symbol is arbitrary since the colour red does not match the colour of a forest whereas, in the former case, the choice is non-arbitrary: the colour green is shared by the referent and the form of the symbol. And if the symbol is a tree-shaped green triangle rather than a green dot, it depicts the meaning even more closely. Similarly, if a road sign standing for 'deer crossing' depicts a deer, it conveys the meaning more patently than if the sign consists of, say, two concentric circles. A symbol whose form contains at least one characteristic of its message is called **iconic**.

In sum, we have seen that the forms of symbols may trace meaning in different ways and to varying degrees. Variation holds along four parameters:

isomorphism, markedness, compositionality and iconicity. Isomorphism and markedness have to do with the relationship across symbols within a symbolic system: they are paradigmatic patterns. Compositionality and iconicity are syntagmatic relations: they apply to meanings and forms co-occurring within a single symbol. Isomorphism, markedness and compositionality have to do with quantitative similarities between meaning and form; iconicity has to do with qualitative and/or quantitative similarity between the two.

In (3)–(6) are diagrams for the observance and violation of the four patterns with examples from outside syntax. F_A and M_A are the form and meaning of symbol A; F_B and M_B are the form and meaning of symbol B; F1, F2 and so on are form constituents; M1, M2 and so on are meaning constituents; 0 indicates missing form or missing meaning. In (5) and (6), I connects corresponding bits of meaning and form; in (6), II shows similarity between meaning and form and H shows the lack of such similarity.

(3) ISOMORPHISM

    (a) Isomorphism OBSERVED:

                    Symbol A: Symbol B:

        FORM: I_F_A_I   I_F_B_I

        MEANING: I_M_A_I   I_M_B_I

        Example: A: *spinach*

                  B: *lettuce*

    (b) Isomorphism VIOLATED:

        (i) one form, zero meaning:

            FORM: I_F_I

            MEANING: **0**

            Example: *cribbly*

        (ii) one meaning, zero form:

            FORM: **0**

            MEANING: I_M_I

            Example: the special colour of a red rose in shade

        (iii) one form, more than one meaning (ambiguity):

                            Symbol A: Symbol B:

            FORM: I_$F_{A,B}$_I

            MEANING: I_M_A_I   I_M_B_I

            Example: $F_{A,B}$: *fine* (adjective or noun)

        (iv) one meaning, more than one form (synonymy)

                            Symbol A: Symbol B:

            FORM: I_F_A_I   I_F_B_I

            MEANING: I_$M_{A,B}$_I

            Example: A: *shout*

                      B: *yell*

(4) MARKEDNESS
    (a) Markedness OBSERVED:

	Symbol A:	Symbol B:
FORM:	I__I	I__I__I
MEANING:	I__I	I__I__I

    Example: Latin: A: *puer* 'boy'
                      B: *puer-i* 'boys'
                      boy-**PL**

    (b) Markedness VIOLATED:
        more meaning, less form:

	Symbol A:	Symbol B:
FORM:	I__I__I	I__I
MEANING:	I__I	I__I__I

    Example: Southern Barasano (Merrifield *et al.* 1987: #3):
            A: *kahe-**a***   'eye'
                eye-**SG**
            B: *kahe*   'eyes'

    (c) Markedness neither observed nor violated:
        more meaning, no difference in amount of form:

	Symbol A:	Symbol B:
FORM:	I__I	I__I__I
MEANING:	I__I	I__I__I

    Example: Swahili: A: ***ki**-su*   'knife'
                      SG-knife
                  B: ***vi**-su*   'knives'
                      PL-knife

(5) COMPOSITIONALITY
    (a) compositionality OBSERVED:

$$\text{FORM:} \begin{bmatrix} F_1 & F_2 & F_3 & \cdots \\ | & | & | & \\ M_1 & M_2 & M_3 & \cdots \end{bmatrix}_{\text{symbol}}$$
      MEANING:

    Example: *good-ness*

    (b) compositionality VIOLATED:
        (i) a bit of meaning has no corresponding form:

$$\text{FORM:} \begin{bmatrix} F_1 & F_2 & 0 & \cdots \\ | & | & | & \\ M_3 & M_2 & \mathbf{M_3} & \cdots \end{bmatrix}_{\text{symbol}}$$
      MEANING:

    Example: *heart condition* (when used in the sense of
                 'pathological heart condition': the meaning
                 element 'pathological' is not expressed)

(ii) a bit of form has no corresponding meaning:

FORM: $\begin{bmatrix} F_1 & F_2 & \mathbf{F_3} & \ldots \\ | & | & | & \\ M_1 & M_2 & \mathbf{0} & \ldots \end{bmatrix}_{\text{symbol}}$

MEANING:

Example: German *Handel-s-vertrag* 'trading contract' trade-
             0-contract

(iii) a single bit of meaning is expressed more than once in
       form:

FORM: $\begin{bmatrix} F_1 & F_2 & \mathbf{F_3} & \mathbf{F_3} & \ldots \\ | & | & \backslash & / & \\ M_1 & M_2 & & \mathbf{M_3} & \ldots \end{bmatrix}_{\text{symbol}}$

MEANING:

Example: *pizza pie* ('piehood' is both stated by *pie* and
             included in the meaning of *pizza*)

(iv) a single bit of form expresses more than one occurrence
      of a bit of meaning:

FORM: $\begin{bmatrix} F_1 & \mathbf{F_2} & \ldots \\ | & / \quad \backslash & \\ M_1 & \mathbf{M_2} \quad \mathbf{M_2} & \ldots \end{bmatrix}_{\text{symbol}}$

MEANING:

Example: the conductor greeting every member of
             an orchestra by shaking hands with only one
             member

(6) ICONICITY
   (a) iconicity OBSERVED:

   FORM: $\begin{bmatrix} F1 & \ldots \\ \| & \\ M1 & \ldots \end{bmatrix}_{\text{symbol}}$

   MEANING:

   Example: *boom*

   (b) iconicity VIOLATED:

   FORM: $\begin{bmatrix} F1 & \ldots \\ \text{\#} & \\ M1 & \ldots \end{bmatrix}_{\text{symbol}}$

   MEANING:

   Example: *yell*

Let us recapitulate. Sentences are symbolic objects consisting of a signatum and the ultimate signans: phonetic form. Syntactic structure is an in-
between signans mediating between sentence meaning and sentence sound
form. There are four ways in which the meaning–form relationship may be
matched: if syntactic structures are isomorphic, if they show markedness relations, if they are compositional, and if they are iconic. Meaningless form,
formless meaning, ambiguity, synonymy, and lack of markedness relations,

lack of compositionality, and lack of iconic relations in turn show a rift between syntactic structure and meaning.

So far we have seen what symbolic relations can be in principle. We will now turn to what symbolic relations are actually like in syntax. Section 3 will first provide examples of mismatches between syntactic structure and meaning (Section 3.1) and, second, examples of discrepancies between syntactic structure and sound form (Section 3.2).

3 Symbolic correspondence in syntax: some facts

3.1 SYNTACTIC STRUCTURE AND MEANING

3.1.1 Isomorphism

As seen in Section 2, isomorphism requires that the form of every symbol should have one and only one meaning in the system and that the meaning of every symbol should have one and only one expression. It thus excludes one-to-zero and one-to-many relations between the forms and meanings of symbols.

Do syntactic forms and their associated meanings comply with these requirements? Let us first take one-to-zero relations. Are there any syntactic forms without meanings and meanings that cannot be expressed in syntactic form? Consider the following:

(1) *yamana kita siyanayasi*
     yamana kita siyanayasi
     anakiyana tiyasanaya anakiyatana, siyanayasi

The text in (1) is from a glossolalic prayer – a sample of the religious rite known as 'speaking in tongues', or glossolalia, commonly practised in Pentecostal congregations (Samarin 1972: 104). It consists of a sequence of units which shows a pattern: some units are repeated. Thus it qualifies for having syntactic structure – yet, it has no meaning.

The converse relation – a meaning with no syntactic structure – is exemplified in cases where a speaker is at a loss to say something: language fails him in his attempt to express a thought.

Let us now consider one-to-many relations between meanings and forms. Examples are plentiful: both ambiguity and synonymy are more the rule than the exception in language. They have two alternative sources: the lexicon and syntax. Examples of lexical ambiguity and synonymy were given in (3) of Section 2: *fine* (the adjective and the noun) and *shout-yell*, respectively. For additional examples, consider the following less than felicitous newspaper headlines (taken from Lederer 1993).

(2) (a) *Dentist receives **plaque***
     (b) *Some pieces **of** Rock Hudson sold at auction*

    (c) *Kids **make** nutritious snacks*
    (d) *Steals clock, faces **time***

The expressions in (2) are all ambiguous and the ambiguity in each case is because of the double meaning of a word. The culprits are the words *plaque, of, make* and *time*. Thus, *plaque* can mean an award or a deposit on teeth; *of* can mean 'owned by' or 'part of'; *make* is ambiguous between 'prepare' and 'constitute'; and *time* can refer to a progression measured by clocks or to a period spent in prison. The examples in (2) are lexically ambiguous.

    The ambiguity of the sentences in (3) is different: it is not localizable to a single word.

    (3) (a) *Carolina inn loses licence for racism.*
          (b) *Enraged cow injures farmer with axe.*
          (c) *If the baby doesn't thrive on raw milk, boil it.*
          (d) *Jill likes to wear red hats and gloves.*

The ambiguity of (3a) is due to the fact that the prepositional phrase *for racism* can be understood as pertaining either to the verb phrase *loses licence* giving the reason for the loss or to the noun *licence* specifying the purpose of the licence. (3b) is ambiguous in a similar way: the prepositional phrase *with axe* may be understood as describing the cow's action or as modifying the man. In (3c), *it* may be interpreted as referring to the milk – or to the baby. And in (3d), *red* can be construed as a modifier of the entire noun phrase *hats and gloves* or only of its first constituent *hats*. Thus, (3) exemplifies syntactic ambiguity.

    Synonymy may similarly be lexical or syntactic.

    (4) lexical synonymy:
          (a) *The Warriors **defeated** the Bears.*
               *The Warriors **outplussed** the Bears.*
          (b) *Peter went to see an **eye doctor**.*
               *Peter went to see an **ophthalmologist**.*

    (5) syntactic synonymy:
          (a) ***A proof that Bill was wrong** was never found.*
               *A proof was never found **that Bill was wrong**.*
          (b) ***The wine that we drank last night** was delicious.*
               *The wine was delicious **that we drank last night**.*
          (c) *Peter called me and **he** cancelled our date.*
               Peter called me and __ cancelled our date.
          (b) *Fred will go to the bar but I will not **go to the bar**.*
               *Fred will go to the bar but I will not go **there**.*
               Fred will go to the bar but I will not go __.
               Fred will go to the bar but I will not __.

Syntactic synonymy can be described by optional ordering rules or optional selection rules. In (5a) and (5b), synonymy is the result of alternative ordering, in (5c) and (5d), it is the result of alternative selection.

These examples show that syntactic structures may lack isomorphism: the same choice and sequence of words may express alternative meanings and the same meaning may be expressed by different word choices and word orders.

3.1.2 *Markedness*

As we have just seen, there are sentences that depart from a strict one-to-one relationship between meaning and form either because they have identical form but different meanings, or identical meaning but different forms.

Let us now take two sentences whose meanings are not identical but similar in a particular way: the meaning of one sentence includes the meaning of the other sentence plus a bit more. Were the forms of the two sentences to reflect the meaning difference, the sentence with the additional bit of meaning should have an additional bit of form. If so, the two sentences would exhibit a non-arbitrary pattern of symbolization: markedness. Following the discussion in Section 2, the sentence with the less meaning and less form is termed the **unmarked** member of the opposition and the sentence with the additional meaning and additional form is termed **marked**.

Markedness relations are common in morphology and syntax. Two examples presented in Chapter 4 (Section 3.4.2) were the form of singular versus plural, and the form of active versus passive sentences. The examples below show markedness as it applies not only to form but also to form–meaning relations: affirmative versus negative sentences and statements versus yes–no questions.

In (1) are given examples for affirmative and negative sentences from English, Hungarian and Ute. In each language, the more complex meaning of the negative sentence is expressed with an added form.

(1) (a) English:

      (i) *The woman is killing the goat.*

      (ii) *The woman is **not** killing the goat.*

  (b) Hungarian:

      (i) *A   nő   meg-öli   a   kecskét.*
          the woman PERF-is.killing the goat
          'The woman is killing the goat.'

      (ii) *A   nő   **nem** öli   meg   a   kecskét.*
          the woman **not** is.killing PERF the goat
          'The woman is not killing the goat.'

(c)   Ute (Givón 1995: 42; IMM = immediate aspect):

(i)   *mamach   sivaatuchi paxa-y*
woman.SUBJ goat.OBJ kill-IMM
'The woman is killing the goat.'

(ii)   *mamach   **kacu-'u** sivaatuchi   paxa-**wa***
woman.SUBJ **NEG**-S3 goat.OBJ   kill-**NEG**
'The woman is not killing the goat.'

In (2) are given examples of statements and yes–no questions from Bengali, Finnish and Tagalog (Q stands for the question marker). In all three languages, the added meaning of interrogativity is expressed by a bit of added form: a question particle.

(2) (a) Bengali:

(i)   *Ram am   kheechilo.*
Ram mango ate.
'Ram ate a mango.'

(ii)   *Ram **ki** am   kheechilo?*
Ram **Q** mango ate
'Did Ram eat a mango?'

(b) Finnish:

(i)   *Söi Juham omenan.*
ate John   apple
'John ate an apple.'

(ii)   *Söi-**kö** Juham omenan?*
ate-**Q** John   apple
'Did John eat an apple?'

(c) Tagalog:

(i)   *Kinain ni   Juan ang   mansanas.*
ate   CASE John CASE apple
'John ate an apple.'

(ii)   *Kinain **ba** ni   Juan ang   mansanas.*
ate   **Q** CASE John ang   mansanas.
'Did John eat an apple?'

As was discussed in Chapter 4 (Sections 2.1 and 3.4.2), the relationship between unmarked and marked is characterized by more than just a difference in structural complexity. The unmarked member also tends to be dominant, more frequent within and/or across languages and more diversified.

The correlation between simpler structure and greater frequency is borne out in the two examples given above. While both affirmative and negative sentences occur in all languages and thus they do not differ in cross-linguistic frequency, frequency counts show that, at least in English, the structurally simple construction – affirmatives – is more frequent than the more complex construction: negatives (Givón 1995: 43). Text counts also show that statements are more frequent than non-declarative sentences, including questions (Givón 1995: 40–1). The distributional dominance of statement structures is shown by the fact that, with only the intonation pattern changed, they may function as questions, as in *Bill is coming with us?* Whether the remaining characteristic of the unmarked member – greater paradigmatic diversity – holds in these cases is not clear.

But markedness is not always observed in syntax. For example, in many languages, imperative sentences have a leaner syntactic (and morphological) structure than the corresponding declarative sentences. This is so in English: *Read the letter* versus *You are reading the letter.* But the imperative meaning is richer than the declarative meaning: it includes all of the latter plus the meaning element COMMAND. Thus, in this case, more meaning is expressed with less form – a violation of markedness.

Having seen examples of compliance and non-compliance with isomorphism and markedness in syntax, we will turn to the third and fourth dimensions of symbolic correspondence relations: compositionality and iconicity. In Section 3.1.3.1, these patterns will be discussed with respect to the selection of words and word forms and, in Section 3.1.3.2, with respect to linear order.

3.1.3 Compositionality and iconicity

3.1.3.1 The selection of words and word forms
Compositionality has to do with how the meaning of a given sentence is distributed over the parts of its form: it requires that the expression of meaning be both complete, with all meaning elements symbolized, and economical, with all bits of form corresponding to some meaning. The sequence of words in the syntactic structure of a sentence is **selectionally compositional** if each word in the sentence is linked to one and only one portion of the sentence meaning and each portion of the sentence meaning is linked to one and only one word. Syntactic structures are in turn **selectionally non-compositional** under the following scenarios (they parallel the general schemata in (5) of Section 2 above):

(1) (a) ONE-TO-ZERO RELATION BETWEEN MEANING
        AND FORM
        • Meaningless form:
          There is a syntactic constituent that does not correspond
          to any semantic constituent.
        • Formless meaning:
          There is a semantic constituent that is part of the meaning
          but not represented by a syntactic constituent.

   (b)   ONE-TO-MANY RELATION BETWEEN MEANING
         AND FORM
         • One form conveying more than one occurrence of a
           meaning:
           There is a syntactic constituent that corresponds to more
           than one occurrence of the corresponding semantic
           constituent.
         • One meaning expressed by more than one form:
           There is a semantic constituent that is expressed by more
           than one occurrence of the corresponding syntactic
           constituent.

All four types of selectional non-compositionality are common in the syntax
of natural languages. Just as one's ego is more than the sum of its parts, as
noted in the epigraph of this chapter, sentence forms can be more – or less
– than the sum of part meanings. Three of the four types of deviations from
syntactic compositionality were already illustrated by the Turkish sentence
first discussed in Chapter 1 and can be further shown by its equivalents in
other languages. Here are the data:

   (2)   ENGLISH
         Where are my two suitcases?

   (3)   TURKISH
         Iki bavul-ım   nerede?
         two suitcase-my where

   (4)   ITALIAN
         Dove sono i   mie due valige?
         where are the my two suitcases

   (5)   RUSSIAN
         Gde   mo-i   dva čemodan-a?
         where my-PL.NOM two baggage-SG.GEN

   (6)   HUNGARIAN
         Hol   a   két bǒrönd-öm?
         where the two suitcase-my

The meaning of the sentence can be informally represented as in (7):

   (7)   (QUESTION ((SUITCASE, TWO, DEFINITE, MY)
            (BE, PRESENT) (FOCUS, PLACE UNKNOWN)))

Disregarding linear order, a fully compositional syntactic structure for this
meaning would be the following:

(8) (QUESTION, PLACE UNKNOWN), (MY, DEFINITE, TWO, SUITCASE), (BE, PRESENT)

None of the sentences listed in (2)–(6) show exactly this structure. They deviate from it in the following ways:

(a) MEANINGLESS FORM
- genitive affix on the subject noun in Russian

(b) FORMLESS MEANING
- zero form for (BE, PRESENT) in Turkish, Russian and Hungarian
- zero form for DEFINITE in Turkish and Russian

(c) ONE MEANING EXPRESSED BY MORE THAN ONE FORM
- multiple expressions for PLURAL:
  - in English (plural numeral *two*, plural noun *suitcases*, plural verb *are*)
  - in Italian (plural numeral *due*, plural noun *valige*, plural verb *sono*, plural possessive pronoun *mie*, plural article *i*)
  - in Russian (plural numeral *dva*, plural possessive pronoun *moi*)

Here are other examples of these three non-compositional syntactic patterns:

(A) MEANINGLESS FORM
(9) (a) ***It** is clear that no cookies are left in the box.*
   (b) ***There** are no cookies left in the box.*
   (c) *My cats **do** not sleep all night.*

The words *it, there* and *do* in (9) are syntactically obligatory, if we leave them out, the resulting structures are ungrammatical. However, they are semantically empty, shown by (10): the same meaning can be expressed without these words in the same language or in a different one.

(10) (a) *That no cookies are left in the box is clear.* (no ***it***)
    (b) *No cookies are left in the box.* (no ***there***)
    (c) German: (no word corresponding to ***do***)
    Meine Katzen schlafen nicht die ganze Nacht.
    my   cats   sleep   not the whole night
    'My cats do not sleep all night.'

(B) FORMLESS MEANING
(11) (a) *Give me a day off.*
    (b) *Leave early to get there on time.*

In English imperative sentences, the 'you'-subject is generally absent.

> (C)   ONE MEANING EXPRESSED BY MORE THAN ONE FORM
> (12) Russian:
>> (a)   *horoš-ij*   *d'en*
>>   good-**MASC.SG.NOM** day.**MASC.SG.NOM**
>>   'good day'
>>
>> (b)   *horoš-aja*   *kn'ig-a*
>>   good-**FEM.SG.NOM** book-**FEM.SG.NOM**
>>   'good book'

The noun phrases in (12) exemplify agreement: number, gender and case is expressed both on the noun and on the adjective.

The fourth logically possible selectionally non-compositional pattern, not illustrated above, is if one form conveys more than one occurrence of the corresponding meaning element. Here are some examples:

> (D)   ONE FORM CONVEYING MORE THAN ONE OCCURRENCE
>   OF A MEANING
> (13) (a)   *Robert washed the dishes and ___ dried them.*
>   (b)   *Robert washed the plates and Bill, ___ the glasses.*
>   (c)   *Robert washed ___ and Bill rinsed the dishes.*
>   (d)   *Robert ___ and Bill washed the dishes.*

In (13a), *Robert* is mentioned once even though he is understood as the subject of both *washed* and *dried*. In (13b), the verb *washed* is mentioned once even though the meaning refers to two washings, one by Robert and one by Bill. In (13c), *the dishes* are mentioned once even though they are semantic arguments of two verbs *washed* and *rinsed*. And in (13d), the verb phrase *washed the dishes* is mentioned only once even though it is part of two semantic propositions, one involving Robert, the other involving Bill.

To summarize so far, sentences depart from selectional compositionality in all four ways defined in (5) of Section 2: a bit of meaning without form, a bit of form without meaning, a single bit of meaning expressed more than once in form, and a single bit of form expressing more than one occurrence of a bit of meaning.

While most of the above discussion about selectional non-compositionality pertained to the selection of words, some of the examples – such as those about Russian gender, number and case affixes – involved the selection of word forms, such as case form and verb inflection. Let us now take a closer look at the selection of word forms to see to what extent it conforms to selectional compositionality. As discussed in Chapter 3, there are two patterns of word form selection: agreement and government. We will begin with agreement.

A. Agreement

Agreement is redundant by its very nature. We defined agreement as involving one constituent (the target) having a marker which reiterates some properties of another constituent (the controller). For example, in the sentence *Felix is my best friend*, the verb is said to agree with the subject in that the verb *is* reiterates the singular-third-person feature of the subject *Felix*. Thus, agreement patterns are, by definition, non-compositional: they involve more than one expression of the same bit of meaning. In the suitcase examples in (2), (4) and (5) and in example (12), all cases of multiple expressions of the same meaning are instances of agreement: the numeral, the adjective, the noun, the possessive pronoun and/or the verb show agreement in English, Italian and Russian.

Apart from this fact, however, agreement may still be more or less selectionally compositional in other ways. Take, for example, the agreement marker. Controller properties reiterated by the agreement marker are often non-semantic. One example is gender: while there may be a semantic core to gender classes, they generally fall short of being semantically homogeneous. This is shown in German. In this language, most animate males (*der Junge* 'the boy', *der Lehrer* 'the male teacher') are expressed as 'masculine' nouns and most animate females as 'feminine' nouns (die *Frau* 'the woman', die *Mutter* 'the mother'). However, the masculine and feminine classes include many nouns that are inanimate and thus neither male nor female (*der Mond* 'the moon', *die Sonne* 'the sun'). Also, some male and female nouns are not in the masculine or feminine class; for example, *das Mädchen* 'the girl' is in the third, so-called neuter class. The article agrees with the gender of the noun that it goes with: *der* if the noun is 'masculine', *die* if it is 'feminine', and *das* if it is neuter. The agreement of the article with the noun is thus non-semantic since it follows a semantically largely arbitrary classification of nouns.

A further indication that agreement in gender does not trace meaning is that synonymous words may control different gender agreement across or even within languages. The Spanish word for 'apple', *manzana*, is feminine, which means the adjective agrees with it as it does with words for 'woman' and 'mother'. The corresponding word in German is *Apfel*, a masculine noun, that is, the article agrees with it as it does with 'man' and 'father'. And even though the Spanish words *costo* 'expense' and *costa* 'cost' are very close in meaning, the first controls masculine agreement on the adjective while the second takes feminine adjectives.

On the other hand, there is also cross-linguistic evidence for the semantic significance of the agreement features. There are four relevant scenarios:

(a) The agreement marker reflects semantic properties of the controller.
(b) The agreement marker provides semantic information about the controller that is not evident from the controller itself.

(c) The agreement marker identifies the right controller from among various candidates in the sentence.

(d) The agreement marker identifies a controller that is entirely missing in the sentence.

We will now see examples for each.

(a) The agreement marker reflects semantic properties of the controller
First, there are cases where semantic agreement overrides formal agreement. Thus, while – as noted above – in German, the noun *Mädchen* 'girl' controls neuter agreement with the article, the anaphoric pronoun referring back to the *Mädchen* in sentences such as 'The girl took the exam. She passed' tends to be the semantically appropriate feminine *sie*, rather than the neuter form *es*.

Another example of semantic agreement prevailing over formal agreement comes from Luganda (Corbett 1983a: 184; Talmy Givón, personal communication). In this language, every noun takes a prefix corresponding to the class that it belongs to. Although the classes are generally not semantically determined, the class labelled 1/2 in Bantu grammars includes only humans. Here is an example of two conjoined human nouns of class 1/2, with the verb showing the class 1/2 agreement marker:

(14) *omu*-kazi   ne   *omu*-sajja **ba**-*alabwa*
      1/2-woman and 1/2-man 1/2-were:seen
      'The woman and the man were seen.'

However, not all humans belong to this class; for example 'fat woman' belongs to class 5/6, and 'tall man' belongs to the class dubbed '11/10' in Bantu linguistics. Each of these classes calls for its own verbal prefix; but when two human nouns, one from each of these classes, are conjoined, the verb reverts to the prefix appropriate for human nouns: class 1/2:

(15) *ek*-kazi   ne   *olu*-sajja   **ba**-*alabwa*
      5/6-fat:woman and 11/10-tall:man 1/2-were:seen
      'The fat woman and the tall man man were seen.'

The same phenomenon of semantic agreement overriding the form of the controller is exemplified by English:

(16) (a) *The committee **has** met.*
      (b) *The committee **have** met.*
      (c) *The police **have** arrived.*

The nouns *committee* and *police* are singular by form. The verb shows singular agreement with *committee* in American English as one would expect based on the singular form of the noun; but in British English, the verb looks at the meaning of the noun and ends up in the plural. With the noun *police*, only semantic agreement is possible in both dialects: the verb must be plural.

(b) The agreement marker provides semantic information about the controller that is not evident from the controller itself

Second, the agreement marker may convey features of the controller that are not evident from the controller itself and thus may facilitate the interpretation of the sentence. A simple example is English words such as *teacher, nurse or engineer* in English, which can be understood as referring either to a man or to a woman. But when these words occur with a reflexive pronoun or an anaphoric pronoun, as in *The engineer hurt himself* or *The teacher entered and she started talking*, the agreeing pronoun reveals the intended gender of the noun. The agreement marker in these cases is semantically significant.

(c) The agreement marker identifies the right controller from among various candidates in the sentence

Third, the agreement marker may identify the right controller from among various candidates in the sentence and thus, again, aid semantic interpretation. Consider the Latin sentence cited in Chapter 2, Section 3.1.2. as an example of interlocking ordering.

(17) *Tiliae   cotermina quercu   collibus est Phrygiis*
linden.tree adjacent oak.tree in.hills is in.Phrygian
media   circumdata muro.
smallish encircled by.wall
'In the Phrygian hills, next to a linden tree there
was an oak tree encircled by a smallish wall.'

There are three discontinuous adjective–noun constructions: *quercus . . . circumdata* 'oak tree . . . encircled', *collibus . . . Phrygiis* 'hills . . . Phrygian', and *media . . . muro* 'smallish . . . wall'. Although in some instances, the meaning suggests which noun and adjective go together, it does not do the whole job; for example, as far as the meaning is concerned, 'Phrygian' could modify 'oak tree' rather than 'hills', and 'smallish' could go with 'hills' rather than 'wall'. The only way to know what the intended pairings of adjective and noun are is by the agreement markers on the adjectives as shown in (18):

(18) (a) *querc-us* . . .   *circumdat-a*
oak.tree-**FEM.SG.NOM** encircled-**FEM.SG.NOM**

(b) *coll-ibus* . . . *Phrygi-is*
hill-**PL.DAT** Phrygian-**PL.DAT**

(c) *medi-a* . . .   *mur-o*
smallish-**FEM.SG.ABL** wall-**FEM.SG.ABL**

For example, the fact that 'oak tree' is feminine singular nominative and 'encircled' has a feminine singular nominative ending shows that the two meanings must go together.

(d) The agreement marker identifies a controller that is entirely missing in the sentence

A fourth way in which agreement may be meaning-bearing is if the agreement marker is the sole identifier of a controller that is entirely missing in the sentence. In so-called pro-drop languages, personal pronouns act as agreement controllers but they can also be omitted. Examples from Latin and Serbo-Croatian were cited in Chapter 3 (Sections 3.3.1 and 4). In (19) are shown examples from Hungarian, where the possessed noun agrees with the possessor in number and person:

(19) (a) controller present:
      *az **én** könyv-**em***
      the **my** book-**S1**
      'my book'

      *a **te** könyv-**ed***
      the **you**$_s$ book-**S2**
      'your$_s$ book'

   (b) controller absent:
      *a könyv-**em***
      the book-**S1**
      'my book'

      *a könyv-**ed***
      the book-**S2**
      'your$_s$ book'

In sum, although, by definition, the agreement marker introduces redundancy and thus violates compositionality, in some cases it turns out to be meaning-bearing.

Let us now turn to the other pattern of word form selection: government.

B. Government

Are government constructions compositional? As noted in Chapter 3 (Section 3.3.3) government, like agreement, is a binary relation where the governor dictates the case marker of the governee. Typical examples are the verb selecting the case of its complements and the adposition selecting the case of the noun phrase it goes with.

Just like agreement, government can be non-semantic and thus in violation of compositionality. Consider the case governed by verbs for the meaning 'to be afraid':

(20) (a) English:
            *Bill is afraid **of** his boss.*
      (b) German equivalent:
            *Bill fürchtet sich   **vor**   seinem Boss.*
            Bill fears   himself **before** his   boss
      (c) Hungarian equivalent:
            *Bill fél   a   fönöké-**töl**.*
            Bill fears the his:boss-**from**

There are three different cases governed by the verb in these examples: in English, *be afraid* requires *of*; in German, the corresponding verb takes the preposition *vor*, which otherwise means 'before'; and in Hungarian, it takes the suffix *-töl*, equivalent of the preposition 'from'. Yet, all three sentences mean the same thing: the governed case has no semantic significance.

On the other hand, just as in the case of agreement, government can be semantically significant. There are at least three instances where case markers are informative:

(a) The case marker identifies the semantic role of the governee from among various candidate roles.
(b) The case marker conveys properties of the governee that are not evident from the governee itself.
(c) The case marker identifies a governor that is entirely missing in the sentence.

(a) The case marker identifies the semantic role of the governee from among various candidate roles

First, a noun phrase may alternatively serve as different semantic arguments and it is its case marker that says which role applies in a particular sentence. Consider (21):

(21) (a) *He put the dog **on** the chair.*
      (b) *He put the dog **under** the chair.*
      (c) *He put the dog **behind** the chair.*
      (d) *He put the dog **next** to the chair.*

The verb *put* can govern alternative cases each identifying a different semantic role of the governee. In these sentences, it is the prepositional case marker that is the sole indicator of the role of 'the chair' in the action. The same holds in the corresponding Hungarian sentences where the case marker is a postposition (in (22b) and (22c)) or an affix (in (22a) and (22d)).

(22) (a) *A   szék-**re**   tette   a   kutyát.*
            the chair-**onto** SG3:put the dog:ACC
      (b) *A   szék **alá**   tette   a   kutyát.*
            the chair **under** SG3:put the dog:ACC

(c)   *A   szék*   **mögé**   *tette*   *a*   *kutyát.*
the chair **behind** SG3:put the dog:ACC
(d)   *A   szék-hez*   *tette*   *a*   *kutyát.*
the chair-**next.to** SG3:put the dog:ACC

The choice of case marking can also differentiate between volitional agent and inert theme, as in Eastern Pomo (McLendon 1978: 3). The non-oblique case signals accidental involvement, the oblique case marks volitional agent. In (23) and (24), the verb is the same, it is only the case of the subject that differentiates between the two interpretations. Superscripts indicate tones.

(23) (a) *wí*^{1} *će·xélka*^{2}
I:NON-OBLIQUE slipping
'I am slipping (accidentally).'

(b) *há·*^{1} *će·xélka*^{2}
I:OBLIQUE slipping
'I am sliding (on purpose).'

(24) (a) *wí·*   *ba·téćki·*
I-NON-OBLIQUE got.bumped
'I got bumped (accidentally).'

(b) *há·*   *ba·téćki·*
I:OBLIQUE got.bumped
'I got bumped (on purpose).'

(b) The case marker conveys properties of the governee that are not evident from the governee itself
Second, case may provide information about the governee other than its semantic role. One kind of such information is the degree to which an entity is affected by the action. In the (b) sentences in (25), the locational participant – 'the wall' and 'the truck' – is understood as involved in its entirety while this is not so in the (a)-sentences. The sentence in (25b) implies that the entire wall was covered with paint while this is not implied in (25a); (25d) – but not (25c) – conveys that the entire truck was filled with hay. The difference comes from whether this constituent is expressed as a direct object or as a prepositional phrase.

(25) (a) *Jill sprayed paint **on the wall**.*
(b) *Jill sprayed **the wall** with paint.*

(c) *Jill loaded hay **on the truck**.*
(d) *Jill loaded **the truck** with hay.*

Other information about the governee that may be signalled by case marking is definiteness. In Finnish, the partitive case of the verb complement indicates indefiniteness while the genitive tends to signal definiteness.

(26) Finnish (Lehtinen 1963: 67)

    (a) *Halvan paisti-**a.***
        I:want steak-**PART**
        'I want **some** steak.'

    (b) *Halvan paisti-**n.***
        I:want steak-**GEN**
        'I want **a/the** steak.'

(27) (a) *Juomme   kahvi-**a.***
        we:drink coffee-**PART**
        'We drink coffee.'

    (b) *Juomme   kahvi-**n.***
        we:drink coffee-**GEN**
        'We drink (up) the coffee.'

(c) The case marker may identify a governor that is entirely missing in the sentence

As was seen in Section 4 of Chapter 3, just as agreement targets can occur without controllers, governees can occur without governors. In each case, the marking on the dependent constituent helps reconstruct the head. Take once again the example *About your grades*. The preposition *about* points at a governor such as *talk* or *speak* and thus helps to complete the meaning of the sentence 'Let's talk about your grades'. Other examples are *Your health!* and *To your health! Your health!* has no marking and it is most likely to be interpreted as a direct object of a sentence like *Watch your health!* addressed to a person when he is about to eat or drink something harmful. *To your health!* in turn is interpreted to mean 'I am drinking to your health'. This interpretation is prompted by the preposition *to*, the case marker governed by the verb *drink*.

To summarize Section 3.1.3.1: selectional compositionality does not uniformly hold for meaning–form relations in language: both the choice of words and the choice of word forms result in compositional structure in some cases and violate compositional structure in others.

3.1.3.2. Linear order: adjacency and precedence

The preceding section surveyed selectional compositionality in syntax. Let us now consider relational compositionality. Does the temporal order of syntactic constituents correspond to semantic relations? We will consider this question first for precedence and then for adjacency.

Clear instances of relational compositionality arising from **precedence** relations are given in (1):

(1) (a) *The elephant raised its trunk and sprayed water on the spectators.*
     (b) *Jack pinched his thumb and cried out.*
     (c) *Once the door is locked, you cannot get into the building.*
     (d) *If you have made a payment on this ticket, you cannot return it.*

In each case, two events are involved and they are mentioned in the order in which they do – or do not – occur: the order of mention signals the order of happening. In this case, syntactic precedence is iconic: a semantic relation is expressed by a syntactic relation that replicates the real-world relationship between the events. The shared property between the two relations in (1) is temporal sequence: the event happening earlier is conveyed by an expression mentioned earlier.

That iconic ordering is not logically necessary is shown by the fact that the order of mentioning the events could be reversed with the meaning intact, such as *The elephant sprayed water on the spectators after it raised its trunk.* This is a marked construction: a special marker – *after* – is employed to serve as a red flag indicating that the order of mention is not the same as the order of the events described.

The potential of iconic ordering in syntax is limited because many syntactic constituents do not refer to events and thus there is no real-world order that the syntactic order could parallel. For example, in the sentence *John mounted the horse,* the order of subject preceding object cannot be taken to be iconic in the above sense since *John* and *the horse* do not refer to events and are thus not capable of being temporally arranged. But the linear precedence of syntactic constituents can parallel meaning even if there is no actual involved: it may express some semantic – rather than real-world – relation. There are three relations that temporal precedence is commonly used to symbolize and that apply not only to events but also to entities.

First, old information that is already known and thus presupposed will often be mentioned before information based on these presuppositions. While temporal precedence does not apply to thoughts, the notion of logical precedence comes close to it. Second, entities that are ranked higher on some hierarchy of importance may be mentioned before those that are ranked lower. And, third, temporal order may simply distinguish subtypes of the same constituent type.

Examples for the old-before-new sequence come from expository discourse – such as a lecture or a paper – where definitions that will be needed later are presented first. It is also exemplified by sentences with so-called dislocational structure, such as *The art museum, it is always closed on Mondays.* Here, the art museum is the notion in which the sentence is anchored: it is assumed to be already active in the mind of the addressee and the rest of the sentence builds onto it by providing new information about it.

In some cases, the syntactic precedence of old versus new information holds even if the old and new constituents do not co-occur in the same sentence nor even in the same discourse. In Mandarin Chinese, subjects of intransitive sentences are understood as indefinite if post-verbal but definite if pre-verbal (Li and Thompson 1981: 20 (glossing simplified)):

(2) (a) *Lái   le   rén   le.*
come ASPECT person ASPECT
'**Some person(s)** has/have come.'

(b) *Rén   lái   le.*
person come ASPECT
'**The person(s)** has/have come.'

A second way, mentioned above, in which linear precedence may be meaningful is if it expresses ranking by importance. An example of the more-important-before-less-important sequencing principle is exemplified in the order of conjuncts. In the sentence *The editor-in-chief and the editorial board decided against accepting the article*, the fact that the editor-in-chief is mentioned before the editorial board conveys the importance of the former over the latter.

In the ordering of old-before-new and more-important-before-less impor-tant, it seems natural that the temporal precedence of the two terms be what it is: there is a natural priority to old versus new and to more important versus less important. In other instances of meaning-bearing linear order – the third type mentioned above – temporal precedence simply serves to dis-tinguish semantic constituents that co-occur in a sentence without any tem-poral, logical or evaluative priority attached to the precedent constituent over the subsequent one. In English, for example, temporal precedence serves to distinguish between subject and object, sometimes single-hand-edly, other times jointly with other markings.

(3) (a) *Bill is shaving Jack.*
    (b) *Bill is shaving him.*
    (c) *Bill is shaving me.*
    (d) *Bill is shaving Jack's beard.*

In all four sentences of (3), the subject of the sentence – *Bill* – is pre-verbal while the object is post-verbal. In (3a), this is the only way to tell who is the shaver and who is the shaved. In (3b) and (3c), additional formal devices join in: distinctive pronominal case form in both and third-person verb agreement in (3c). And in (3d), lexical meaning steps in: the two noun phrases allow for only one choice for the subject. Thus, the ordering of subject and object is meaning-bearing in (3a) while it is present but redundant in (3b)–(3d). Additional examples of meaning-bearing syntactic order were given in Chapter 2 (Section 3.2.3, examples (16)–(18)).

Often, however, syntactic order is non-semantic. This may be for two reasons: either the order is constrained but the constraints are not meaning-based or order is free. In Chapter 2, Section 3.2.3, we saw examples of non-meaning-related conditions on ordering in a language. The conditions may be lexical – for example in Igbo, the order of numeral and noun depends on the choice of numerals – or structural, such as in English where adjectives are normally prenominal but if they have complements, they must follow the noun.

The semantic vacuity of syntactic order is most evident in the variable ordering of the same constituents without any semantic difference: ordering is free. While this is sometimes the case in a single language – such as for post-verbal noun phrases in Tagalog also discussed in Chapter 2 (Section 3.2.3) – it is most clearly so across languages. The English phrase *red gloves* can be translated into languages where the adjective follows rather than precedes the noun without any change of meaning. Also, any English sentence of the SVO order pattern can be translated into languages with SOV or VSO patterns, again without any loss or gain of information.

While temporal precedence widely varies among languages, the other component of temporal relations, **adjacency**, tends not to do so: languages tend to use adjacency iconically for the expression of semantic closeness. In many instances, a change in adjacency relations between two constituents, with precedence kept invariant, will result in a change of meaning. This is illustrated in (4):

(4) (a) *This swimmer **from London** is faster than my friend.*
   *This swimmer is faster than my friend **from London**.*
   (b) *John **and Bill** will stay with Ann.*
   *John will stay with Ann **and Bill**.*

The semantic significance of adjacency was famously proclaimed by Otto Behaghel, a German linguist of the first part of the twentieth century, who wrote: 'Das oberste Gesetz is dieses, dass das geistig eng Zusammengehörige auch eng zusammengestellt wird' ('The foremost law is this: whatever belongs close together is also placed close together' (Behaghel 1932: 4)).

One might argue that adjacency expressing semantic coherence is necessary because otherwise how would one know what goes with what? However, just as temporal precedence, adjacency, too, is commonly employed redundantly: semantically cohesive constituents are placed adjacent even if the semantic coherence of the constituents is obvious from other kinds of markings.

For example, adjectives tend to stick with their nouns even if the sentence includes only one noun that the adjective could possibly go with or if there are additional means of identifying which adjective goes with which noun. For example, in the English sentence *The purple butterfly just emerged from its cocoon*, it is the adjacency of *purple* to *butterfly* that tells the hearer that *purple* is not to be construed with *cocoon*. But in the sentence *The purple butterfly has taken flight*, the adjacency of *purple* and *butterfly* is idle: there is no alternative noun which the adjective could sensibly modify. Similarly, adjectives stay with their nouns in languages like Russian or German even though adjectives agree with their nouns in gender, number and case. Thus, adjacency, just as precedence and as many other formal devices in language, has at times a meaning-bearing function but its use extends to structures where it is not meaning-bearing. As with many other social institutions, form may in some instances be motivated by function while in other cases it becomes a habitual convention void of meaning.

This closes our discussion of the correspondence relation between syntax and meaning. What about the relationship between syntax and sound form? The basic expectation is that phonetic structure simply spells out sentence meanings as represented in syntactic structure. In actuality, however, syntactic structure may 'peek ahead' at sound form: the make-up of a syntactic structure may be influenced by phonological material. This will be shown next.

3.2 SYNTACTIC STRUCTURE AND SOUND FORM

She's somewhere in the sunlight strong,	1
Her tears are in the falling rain,	2
She calls me in the wind's soft song,	3
And with the flowers she comes again.	4
Yon bird is but her messenger,	5
The moon is but her silver car.	6
Yea! sun and moon are sent by her	7
And every wistful waiting star.	8

These lovely words – entitled *Song,* by Richard Le Gallienne (1866–1947) – will be recognized as a poem by any speaker of English even if it is not broken up into lines in print. Part of the reason is its content: it is an expression of an emotion; it says things that are beyond everyday experience and the true meaning of which goes beyond the actual meanings of the words.

However, content by itself does not make a poem: the gist of what this piece says could be conveyed in prose as well. A necessary characteristic of many styles of poetry is that its syntax is patterned so as to serve a dual purpose: in addition to expressing an intended meaning, it also has to fulfil certain requirements in its sound form, such as rhythm and rhyme.

In this poem, each line consists of twelve syllables that are alternately stressed and unstressed; of the four lines that make up a verse, the first and the third rhyme, and so do the second and the fourth. This is shown in (1):

(1) rhythm (within a line): - ' / - ' / - ' / - '
     rhyme (within a strophe): A B A B

These regularities are achieved in part by the poet exploiting the options that syntax has to offer and in part by stretching the limits of these options. First, if the language offers a choice of alternative constructions, the one that conforms to the formal requirements is chosen. Thus, ordinary English usage would allow line 1 to start with *she is* rather than *she's*; of the two, *she's* is needed for rhythm. Also, in line 3, there are synonymous constructions available for the possessive construction: *the wind's soft song* and *the soft song of the wind*. Once again, rhythmic considerations and the need for a rhyming word seem to have determined the choice. Similarly, in line 7, there is the possibility of an active construction – *she sends sun and moon* – but both rhythm and rhyme call for the passive.

Second, if ordinary syntax does not permit a construction that form would call for, the limits of syntax may be stretched a bit for the sake of poetic form. Thus, the linear pattern of the preposed adverbial phrase in line 4 – *and with the flowers she comes again* – is unusual in prose, and the phrase in line 1 – *in the sunlight strong* – with the adjective postposed to its noun, would be downright ungrammatical.

Poetry offers extreme examples of how the selection and ordering of words can be influenced by phonetic form. Although poetic language is more sound-form-conscious than other forms of language, the difference is not abrupt. Even everyday language includes formulae where the selection and order of syntactic constituents are subordinate to sound form, such as proverbs (e.g. *A stitch in time saves nine*) or advertising slogans (*A sandwich is a sandwich, but a manwich is a meal*).

In addition to such sporadic examples, some languages have regular grammatical patterns that are in part determined by the phonetic composition of the words chosen. A morphological example from Tagalog was mentioned in a note to Chapter 2, Section 3.1.2. Tagalog has an affix *um* which derives verbs from nouns. The position of this affix depends on the first phonological segment of the word: if it is a vowel, *um* is prefixed, if it is a consonant, *um* follows this consonant (Schachter and Otanes 1972: 310).

(2) (a) *ulan* 'rain (N)'
um-*ulan* 'be raining'

(b) *kidlat* 'lightning (N)'
k-**um**-*idlat* 'be lightning'

This makes sense if we recognize that Tagalog has a strong preference for C(onsonant)V(owel)C(onsonant)V(owel) structure. If *um* were to be prefixed to consonant-initial stems, a VCCV structure (**umkidlat*) would result. The infixing of the *um* affix provides a compromise solution in the tug-of-war between phonology and grammar: the affix is positioned as close to the prefix slot as possible without violating CVCV structure.

While the Tagalog example is morphological, the choice and ordering of entire words, too, may be something that phonetic form has a say in. A phonetically based word order rule which crops up in several languages was noted by the German linguist Otto Behaghel mentioned earlier (in section 3.1.3.2): 'Das längere Wort, der längere Ausdruck tritt an die zweite Stelle' ('The longer word or the longer expression goes to the second place/relative to the shorter one' (Behaghel 1928: 367–8)). Some of his German examples and a couple of English ones are listed in (3):

(3) (a) *Land   und Leute*
country and people
'country and people'

(b) *wie   und warum*
how and why
'how and why'

(c) *why and wherefore*

(d) *hail and hearty*

An interesting example of the preference for short-before-long is the way seven-digit telephone numbers are broken up: both in the US and in Canada, the division is 3–4 (e.g. 332-0141) – a pattern recommended by the International Telecommunication Association.

A different kind of phonological influence on syntactic structure is that otherwise grammatical syntactic constructions may be barred because of phonological factors. Examples are certain conjoined structures in English and German. Consider first the English examples in (4) (Pullum and Zwicky 1986: 761).

(4) (a) *I certainly **will**, and you already **have**, **set** the record straight with respect to the budget.*

(b) **I certainly **will**, and you already **have**, **clarify/clarified** the situation with respect to the budget.*

Why is (4b) ungrammatical even though the very similar sentence in (4a) is fine? The auxiliaries *will* and *have* occur in both sentences; *will* requires the plain basic form of the verb while *have* takes the past participle form. As it happens, for the verb *set*, these two forms have the same phonological form: both *will set* and *have set* are grammatical. However, for the verb *clarify*, the two forms are distinct: *will clarify* but *have clarified*; thus neither form can satisfy the selectional requirements of both auxiliaries. The resulting conflict renders both versions of (4b) ungrammatical.

A similar example from German is (5) (Pullum and Zwicky 1986: 764–5):

(5) (a) *Sie findet und hilft   Frau-en.*
she finds and helps women-PL.ACC/DAT
'She finds and helps women.'

(b) **Sie findet und hilft   Männ-er/Männ-ern.*
she finds and helps men-PL.ACC/PL.DAT
'She finds and helps men.'

Both sentences include the conjunction of the verbs 'find' and 'help'. 'Find' governs the accusative case and 'help' governs the dative. For some nouns such as *Frau* 'woman', the two cases have the same phonological form in the plural: *Frauen*, and thus the same form can occur as the governee of both verbs. For other nouns, such as *Mann* 'man', the two cases have distinct phonological forms: *Männer* is the plural accusative and *Männern* is the plural dative. Thus, neither form can stand as the governee of both verbs and thus (5b) is ungrammatical.

All these examples show that, just as the selection and order of words can be meaningful – that is, determined by semantic requirements – the selection and order of words can also be 'soundful' – that is, influenced by phonetic constraints. But there is a large difference between the extent to which meaning and sound form influence syntactic form: semantically determined syntactic form is the rule rather than the exception while phonetically influenced syntactic form is the exception rather than the rule. The actually occurring examples of phonetically conditioned selection of words and word forms and their ordering stay well within the bounds of logical possibilities. For example, no language is known to line up words of a sentence in the order of increasing length, even if the semantic relations of the words would be recoverable by reference to their case or agreement.

4 Conclusions

In this chapter, we considered the closeness of fit between syntactic structure and the meaning it serves and between syntactic structure and the phonetic form that it is expressed in.

We have concluded that the effect of phonetic form on syntactic structure is meagre: syntax is mostly impervious to phonological requirements. On the other hand, syntax is very sensitive to meaning. In other words, when settling on a syntactic structure for a sentence, people are, understandably, mainly concerned with getting their messages across rather than with what their utterances will sound like.

Regarding the syntax-meaning interface, we considered four variables. Three have to do with quantitative resemblance between syntactic form and meaning: isomorphism (one-to-one relations between meaning and form across sentences), markedness (parallel proper-inclusion relations between meanings and forms across sentences) and compositionality (one-to-one relations between bits of meaning and bits of form within sentences). The fourth parameter, iconicity, has to do with quantitative and qualitative similarities between form and meaning.

We have found that natural language syntax receives no perfect score on any of these parameters: it is not perfectly isomorphic, it does not always obey markedness relations, it is not fully compositional and it is not fully iconic. Yet, human languages are, by and large, successful instruments of communication. This raises the question whether the parellelism between meaning and syntactic form as measured on these four scales is desirable in symbol systems at all.

Two of the close correspondences – **markedness and iconicity** – are not at all necessary, although both help. Thus, it is not necessary for 'more meaning' to be conveyed by 'more form' as markedness would require, witnessed by the fact that nouns whose singular is formally marked but their plural is formally unmarked are easily imaginable and in fact occurrent in languages. Similarly, there is no reason why negative sentences could not be formally simpler than affirmative ones. And, given the plethora of morphosyntactic devices which can signal relations among syntactic constituents, there is no need for adjacency and precedence to be iconic.

What about the other two patterns: **isomorphism and compositionality**? In a symbol system that is closed – that is, one which is not designed for the communication of new messages – there is no need for meaning form correspondence to be constrained in either of these ways: each form–message correspondence may be individually memorized by the users of the system. This is the case in the system of traffic lights. But in an open-ended symbol system, as natural languages are, sentence meanings must be predictable from the meanings of the parts at least to an extent. Two kinds of meaning–form parallelism need to be present: some degree of compositionality and perhaps not too much ambiguity.

In order to see this, consider the English sentence *John spilled the beans*, which is both ambiguous – between the concrete and the idiomatic meaning – and non-compositional with respect to the idiomatic meaning. If all sentences of English were either this ambiguous and this non-compositional, it is hard to see how an infinite number of novel ideas could be expressed and understood.

Nonetheless, full compositionality and complete lack of ambiguity are not necessary even in open-ended symbol systems because the context in which symbols are used helps to interpret partially compositional forms and to unravel ambiguity. For example, the sentence *No, in Chicago* is not fully compositional of the meaning 'No, she was born in Chicago' but it becomes so if it is preceded by the question *Was Joan born in Milwaukee?* Similarly, the statement *I want this* is not compositional of the meaning 'I want this apple' but it becomes so if it is accompanied by a gesture pointing at an apple. In the same way, alternative interpretations of ambiguous symbols can be dealt with because of the disambiguating effect of context. For example, raising a hand in a classroom means the person has something to say but the same gesture if performed by a crossing guard is understood to mean 'stop'.

Whereas therefore some degree of isomorphism and compositionality seems to be necessary in open-ended symbol systems, it is not certain that compositionality beyond this minimum is even desirable. This is because the use of symbols involves both an encoder and a decoder and the interests of the two can point in opposite directions. From the point of view of the decoder – the receiver of the message – it would seem that the more closely form parallels meaning, the easier the task. Take our earlier example of road signs warning of deer crossing. A sign that shows the outline of a deer is more compositional than one the shows the outline of the head of a deer and the decoder is likely to prefer the first. However, from the point of view of the encoder, the deer head is better since it is simpler to draw than the whole animal. Thus, a less compositional, more sketchy form may be more difficult from the point of view of comprehension but easier in terms of production.

Notes

Section 1   Preliminaries
The proper representation of meaning is a much-debated issue in the literature (cf. for example Allan 2001). In this book, these discussions will be bypassed and meanings will be represented in simple terms similar to those employed by Sanders (e.g. 1972) and Wierzbicka (e.g. 1988).

Section 2   Symbolic correspondence: some possibilities

- Gerald Sanders, whose theory of Equational Grammar (1972) first proposed symbolic correspondence as the cornerstone of grammatical descriptions, used the term symbolic equivalence for the relation between signans and signatum. Since in the more recent literature, the term symbolic correspondence has been adopted (e.g. Langacker 1999), this practice is followed in this book. William Croft's term is symbolic relation (Croft 2001).
- The term isomorphism is taken from Haiman 1985.
- For iconicity in symbolic systems in general, see Peirce 1932.

Section 3.1.2   Markedness
On markedness, see for example Greenberg 1966; Croft 1990: esp. 64–94; Givón 1995: esp. 25–69; Battistella 1996.

Section 3.1.3.1   The selection of words and word forms

- For detailed discussions of iconicity in natural language and in syntax in particular, see for example Haiman 1985a, 1985b; Newmeyer 1998: 114–18, 155–61; Croft 1990: 164–92.
- For an argument concerning the semantic nature of the relationship between controller and target, see Keenan 1974: 303.
- For the distribution of semantic versus formal agreement, see Corbett 1983b, Corbett forthcoming.
- Recent cross-linguistic discussions of unusual uses of case marking are presented in Aikhenvald *et al.* 2001.

Section 3.2   Syntax and sound form

- *Song* by Richard Le Gallienne is taken from page 39 of *A Centenary Memoir-Anthology*, New York: The Apollo Head Press, copyright 1966 by the Poetry Society of America; reprinted with the permission of the Poetry Society of America. The word *yon* in line 5 is an archaic form for 'that' or 'the'.

- Paul Kiparsky (1973) convincingly argued that the formal devices employed in poetry were closely akin to those figuring in the normal phonological or more broadly grammatical systems of languages. For example, the number of syllables in a word often figures both in poetic form and in some rules of grammar; while, in turn, the number of sound segments in a word is never appealed to by constraints on poetic form nor by prosodic rules of everyday language.

- The ordering of Tagalog clitics, partially discussed in Chapter 2, Section 3.2.1, also shows short-before-long order; see Schachter and Otanes 1972: 411–15.

Section 4   Conclusions

For arguments regarding how unmarked constructions are more favourable to the listener than to the speaker, see Gundel *et al.* 1988.

Exercises

1. On digital alarm clocks that are on the twelve-hour cycle, a little red light differentiates am and pm. In some clocks, the red light comes on for am, on others it comes on for pm. Is either of the two systems more in line with markedness than the other? Is either of them iconic?

2. What does a shopping list look like if it is selectionally compositional but relationally non-compositional? What does the list look like if it is also relationally compositional?

3. Consider the formation of the comparative and superlative degree of English adjectives such as those below. What conditions determine whether the comparative and the superlative are formed with an affix or with a degree word? Is phonetic form a factor?

(a) *soft, softer, softest*
(b) *light, lighter, lightest*
(c) *pretty, prettier, prettiest*
(d) *lazy, lazier, laziest*
(e) *beautiful, more beautiful, most beautiful* (*beautifuller, *beautifullest)
(f) *rambunctious, more rambunctious, most rambunctious* (*rambunctiouser, *rambunctiousest)
(g) *intelligent, more intelligent, most intelligent* (*intelligenter, *intelligentest)
(h) *unbearable, more unbearable, most unbearable* (*unbearable-er, *unbearable-st)

4. Why is (a) grammatical but both versions of (b) are not?

    (a) *Then before me sat one of the ugliest creatures I ever have or ever will come upon in the whole of my life.*

    (b) **Then before me sat one of the ugliest creatures I ever have or ever will encountered/encounter in the whole of my life.*

Find two other examples of sentence pairs that differ in the same way.

5. Consider the following sentences from Warlbiri. How is it signalled which noun is modified by the adjective 'small'? What role, if any, do case marking, adjacency and precedence play? (Data and transcription from Riemsdijk 1981)

    (a) ***wita-ngku***   *ka*   ***maliki-rli*** *kurdu*   *yarlki-rni*   *kartirdi-rli*
         small-ERG AUX **dog-ERG** child:ABS bite-NONPAST teeth-ERG

         'The **small dog** bites the child with its teeth.'
         (BUT NOT: 'The dog bites the **small child** with its teeth.')
         OR:
         'The dog bites the child with its **small teeth**.'
         OR:
         'The **small dog** bites the **small child** with its
         teeth.'
         OR:
         'The **small dog** bites the child with its **small
         teeth**.')

    (b) *maliki-rli* *ka*   *kurdu*   *yarlki-rni*   ***kartirdi-rli*** ***wita-ngku***
         dog-ERG AUX child:ABS bite-NONPAST **teeth-ERG** **small-ERG**

         'The dog bites the child with its **small teeth**.'
         (BUT NOT: 'The **small dog** bites the child with its teeth.'
         OR:
         'The dog bites the **small child** with its teeth.'
         OR:
         'The **small dog** bites the child with its **small
         teeth**.'
         OR
         'The dog bites the **small child** with its **small
         teeth**.')

    (c) *maliki-rli* *ka*   ***wita-ngku*** *kurdu*   *yarli-rni*   ***kartirdi-rli***
         dog-ERG AUX **small-ERG** child:ABS bite-NONPAST **teeth-ERG**

         'The **small dog** bites the child with its teeth.'
         OR:
         'The dog bites the child with its **small teeth**.'
         (BUT NOT: 'The dog bites the **small child** with its teeth.'

OR
'The **small dog** bites the child with its **small
teeth**.')

6. Here are again the Persian sentences presented at the end of Chapter 4,
this time with English glosses. Compile a lexicon – morpheme forms and their
meanings – and construct a syntactic description in three parts: inventory of
categories, selection and order. Compare this new description with the one
you constructed before. If the rules are different, how so?

GRAMMATICAL SENTENCES: UNGRAMMATICAL SENTENCES:

1. *man amadam*   *amadam man*
   'I came.'   *man amad*
                         amadam
                         man

2. *mahmud amad*   *amad mahmud*
   'Mahmud came.'   *mahmud amadam*
                         mahmud
                         amad

3. *u amad*   *amad u*
   'He came.'   *u amadam*
                         mahmud u amad
                         man u amad

4. *man mahmud ra didam* *man ra mahmud didam*
   'I saw Mahmud.'   *mahmud ra man didam*
                          didam man mahmud ra
                          man mahmud ra amadam
                          man mahmud didam
                          man didam

5. *mahmud man ra did*   *man ra mahmud did*
   'Mahmud saw me.'   *did mahmud man ra*
                          mahmud man ra didam
                          mahmud man did

6. *man u ra didam*   *man ra u didam*
   'I saw him.'   *didam man u ra*
                          man u ra did

7. *u man ra did*   *did u man ra*
   'He saw me.'   *u man did*
                          u
                          did
                          man ra

8. *u ræft*   **ræft*
 'He went.'   **u ræftam*
          *ræft did
          *did ræft
          *u mahmud ra ræft

9. *man ræftam*   **ræftam man*
 'I went.'   **ræftam*
          *man u ra ræftam

10. *u man ra šænid*   **šænid u man ra*
 'He heard me.'   **u šænid*

11. *man u ra šænidam* **šænidam man u ra*
 'I heard him.'   **man šænidam*
          *šænidam

12. *mahmud man ra šænid* **šænid mahmud man ra*
 'Mahmud heard me.' **mahmud man šænid*

Chapter Six

Variation and Change

> Things around here are not what they used to be. People who have just moved in, they do not know this: they think everything was always like it is now. But I have been here long enough and have seen enough things to know otherwise.
>
> (Comment by an elderly apartment house manager)

1 Preliminaries

In June 1699, a solitary 52-year-old woman boarded a ship at a European harbour bound for Surinam. A native of Germany, Maria Sibylla Merian had spent most of her life studying the life forms of insects in Germany and The Netherlands and now she was about to undertake entomological studies in this distant South American country. Fighting the hot and humid climate which, after two years, forced her to cut her stay short, she managed to carry out a comprehensive survey of the local insects and subsequently captured their life cycle on 60 copper engravings accompanied by copious comments (Merian 1994 (reprinted)).

In the preface of the book, Maria Sibylla describes how, as a young woman, her imagination was first captured by silkworms that she spotted around her native city of Frankfurt am Main. Withdrawing from all social relations with people, she devoted herself single-mindedly to the study of how various caterpillars, worms and larvae differed in colour and shape and how they transformed themselves into adult insects. This preoccupation stayed with her for the rest of her 70 years. Hers was a life dedicated to the study of variation and change among insects.

The great wealth of the world of insects and 'the marvel of (insect) metamorphosis' (Farb 1984: 55) have fascinated untold generations from Aristotle all the way to our time. There are approximately 750,000 different species of insects. This is a striking fact in and of itself: if they are all insects, they must all be the same in some ways; but then how can they differ in so many ways? Are there any limits to their variability – that is, are there insects that are 'logically possible' but do not occur? And how do insect forms change ontogenetically – that is, in the course of the life span of an individual – and phylogenetically, in the course of thousands and millions of years?

The very same questions about variation and change arise with respect to all things such as stars, trees, social orders, religions, literary genres, musical instruments, book bindings, shoes, spoons, human fingerprints – and human languages. Currently, there are over 6,000 languages in the world. If they are all to be considered languages, they must have some characteristics in common; but if we see them as different, they must have some distinguishing properties. How do languages resemble and differ from each other? How do languages change over the centuries and millennia and how does language change within the brief lifespan of a human being?

Let us take a closer look at the concepts of variation and change, starting with the former. Given that there is **variation** within a particular domain, three basic questions arise. The first is about constraints on the range of variants within the type of object under study: what occurs and what does not? The second question is about the distribution of the variants: under what conditions do the particular variants occur? And, third, why are the variants and their attendant conditions the way they are?

If we apply these questions to insects, we find that variation among them is vast but limited. An invariant property of all insects that exist today is that they have a breathing apparatus that 'consists of a network of extremely small air tubes that branch through the interior tissues and open to the outer atmosphere through a row of small holes, called spiracles, on each side of the body' (Farb 1984: 142). Other characteristics of this breathing apparatus may vary; for instance, dragonflies have gills attached to their air tubes that are capable of straining oxygen out of water. The various subtypes of breathing organs are not distributed at random: variation is conditioned by the insects' habitat. Not surprisingly, gills attached to the breathing tubes are found only in insects that live near water.

Variation in language is similarly limited and some of it is similarly conditioned. An example of a limited range of variants across languages is vowels: languages widely differ in what vowels they have. But there is a limit to variability: no language is known that does not have an [a] – that is, a low central or back vowel. Another example of constraints on the distribution of the variants is how voiced and voiceless bilabial stops occur across languages. Neither is present in all languages; but all languages that have /p/ also have /b/.

Let us now turn to the concept of **change**. Change is a temporally directed variation, with the variants keyed to subsequent points along the time axis. Just as variation, change is ubiquitous both in nature and in culture. An example of linguistic change has to do with English front-rounded vowels. In the span of a few hundred years of the history of Old English, the front high-rounded vowel /ü/ of Old English lost its rounding and turned into /i/. Could /ü/ have turned into something else? Could [i] have evolved from something other than [ü]? What were the conditions that triggered the change? And why? Another example is the free word order of Old English that, over the centuries, stabilized into SVO. Could it have stabilized into, say, SOV or VSO? What conditions triggered the change?

Questions about change parallel those about variation. We need to identify the range of changes (i.e., given a structure, what could it have come from and what can it become?), find the distribution of changes (i.e., the conditions under which they can take place) and find the reasons for the limitations on the range of changes and their attendant conditions.

It is revealing to realize that variation and change are not 'carved into' reality; rather, they are relations conjured up and imposed upon the world by the human mind. Our variational and evolutionary views of reality are the result of the human predisposition to categorize things. If we did not have the concept of subtypes within types, we would either see everything in the world as equally different, or everything as exactly the same; but nothing would be regarded as both the same and different since that would be a contradiction. As discussed in Chapter 4 (Section 2), taxonomy provides the means for a more refined view: while some things may indeed be completely different and other things completely the same, many things can be both different in some respects and the same in other respects, whether at a given point in time or in the course of history. It is only because we can see things as the same in some ways even though they are different in other ways that we can talk about variation and change.

The humanly imposed nature of the notions 'same' and 'different' is shown by the fact that people differ in their judgement on what things are the same and what things are different. Are Jekyll and Hyde the same person or two different persons housed in the same body? Is an adult the same as the child that she used to be? Is the person whose mental capacities are ravaged by Alzheimer's disease still the same person as he was before the onset of the ailment? Various views of abortion poignantly highlight the alternative concepts that people form about variation and change. If you kill a foetus, do you kill a human being? The key issue is whether the foetus is to be seen as a human being or as something other than that; in other words, whether, when a foetus becomes a child, it undergoes a category change turning from non-human to human, or only a change of subcategories – fetal human to full-scale human. Arguments have been offered both ways illustrating the highly relativistic decisions that we make about what things are the same and what things are different.

In sum, the descriptive and explanatory questions about variation and change are the following:

Re variation:

(1) **Range of variants**
What variants of a type occur?
(2) **Distribution of variants**
Under what conditions must or may a given variant occur?
(3) **Explanations**
Why are the variants and their distribution the way they are?

Re change:

(1) **Range of changes**
What changes occur? That is, what changes into what?
(2) **Distribution of changes**
Under what conditions must or may a given change occur?
(3) **Explanations**
Why are the changes and their distribution the way they are?

In this chapter, we will mostly focus on the two descriptive questions ((1) and (2)) regarding syntactic variation and change; the question about explanations will be taken up in Chapter 7. As in the preceding chapters, we will first consider the relevant logical possibilities (Section 2). Sections 3 and 4 will then present case studies of syntactic variation and change.

2 Variation and change: some possibilities

The purpose of this section is to examine the metalanguage of variation and change – that is, the various types of statements that are instrumental in describing such phenomena in language in general and outside it. We will start with variation.

The most obvious domain of linguistic variation is within a single language. The first example comes from phonology. Consider the English words *sane, seal, slip, spell, string* and *sprain*. The following observation can be offered:

(1) In English, **some** words start with an /s/.

This statement says that /s/-initial words are possible in English but it does not say which words start with an /s/. A statement that would do that is the following:

(2) In English, **all** words must start with an /s/.

This statement has predictive power; however, it is clearly untrue: there are many English words – *pane, aim* and so on – that do not start with /s/.

Is there a way to formulate a prediction about the occurrence of word-initial /s/ that does hold true? One is offered in (3):

(3) In English, **all** words **whose** first three segments are consonants must start with an /s/.

This statement is correct: there are words like *string* and *spring* but no words like **ftring* or **lpring*. The statement in (3) does not specify the entire distribution of word-initial /s/ in English but it predicts some of its occurrences.

In (1)–(3) are exemplified three statement types that can be made about variation within a set of objects: (1) is an existential statement – it says that there are some English words that start with an /s/; (2) and (3) are universal statements – they say that every member of a particular universe of words starts with an /s/. However, (2) and (3) differ in the size of the universe they pertain to: (2) is an unrestricted universal in that it pertains to the entire universe of English words, while (3) is a restricted universal in that it pertains to a smaller universe, one that is properly included in the former: all those English words that start with a triple consonant cluster.

A second example to illustrate variational statements about the structures of a single language comes from syntax. Consider the sentence *What has the clown done?* In this sentence, the auxiliary *has* comes before the subject *the clown*. Based on this example, the following observation can be made:

(4) In English, in **some** sentences, the auxiliary verb precedes the subject.

This statement describes a possible order pattern of English. It is of the permissive kind: it says that this order may occur in the language but it does not specify the conditions under which it must occur. Given a sentence, this statement does not predict whether the auxiliary of that sentence will or will not precede the subject. In order to formulate a predictive statement, it would have to be of universal scope, such as in (2).

(5) In English, in **all** sentences, the auxiliary verb must precede the subject.

This statement would be useful – but it is false. In other sentences, such as *The clown has poked a hole in the balloon*, the auxiliary verb follows the subject rather than preceding it.

Given that the auxiliary does not always precede the subject, is it nonetheless possible to formulate a statement of universal scope predicting the conditions under which it does so? Once again, the answer lies in finding a sub-universe within the larger one for which the prediction does hold. The resulting statement is given in (6).

(6) In English, in **all** sentences **that** are wh-questions where the wh-word is not the subject, the auxiliary verb must precede the subject.

(4), just like (1), is an existential statement; (5), just like (2), is an unrestricted universal; (6), just like (3), is a restricted universal.

These examples illustrate statements about variation **within a language**. But suppose we broaden the domain and wish to capture variation **across languages**. To state facts about cross-linguistic variation, the same statement types are available as those regarding language-internal variation. For an illustration, let us take the nasal consonants /m/ and /n/. The existential statements 'Some languages have /m/' and 'Some languages have /n/' are true but not predictive. The unrestricted universals 'All languages have /m/' and 'All languages have /n/' are predictive but untrue. But the restricted universal 'All languages that have an /m/ also have an /n/' is both predictive and true: there are no known languages with an /m/ but no /n/.

Exactly where does the empirical force of universal statements come from? The force of these statements arises from the fact that, out of a set of logical possibilities, they say that some actually occur but others do not. Let us first consider zoological examples.

(7) (a) **All animals** must have reproductive systems.
(b) **All animals that have feathers** must be bipedal.

The unrestricted universal in (7a) has to do with two logically possible animal types: those that do and those that do not have reproductive systems, and it says that, of the two, only the former exists. In (8) + stands for having a characteristic; − stands for not having it; * indicates a type claimed not to occur:

(8)
	having reproductive systems
animal type I	+
*animal type II	−

The restricted universal in (7b) makes a claim regarding the occurrence versus non-occurrence of four logically possible animal types that the two properties, having feathers and having two legs, define and it claims that only three of the four actually occur.

(9)
	having feathers	being bipedal	
animal type I	+	+	(e.g. birds)
animal type II	−	−	(e.g. dogs)
animal type III	−	+	(e.g. apes)
*animal type IV	+	−	(unattested)

(10) and (11) similarly illustrate the predictive force of an unrestricted and a restricted universal, this time for language:

(10) All languages must have oral consonants.

	having oral consonants
language type I	+
*language type II	−

(11) All languages that have an /m/ must also have an /n/.

	having /m/	having /n/	
language type I	+	+	(e.g. English)
language type II	−	−	(e.g. Quileute)
language type III	−	+	(e.g. Tlingit)
*language type IV	+	−	(unattested)

To summarize so far, we have seen examples of three statement types about variation within and across languages. Their logical schemata are given in (12): S/L stands for 'sentences of a language; or languages', A and B are language properties.

(12) (a) EXISTENTIAL STATEMENTS:
     In some S/L, there is A.
   (b) UNIVERSAL STATEMENTS:
      (i) UNRESTRICTED UNIVERSALS:
        In all S/L, there is A.
      (ii) RESTRICTED UNIVERSALS:
        In all S/L, if there is B, there is also A.

Existential statements pertain to the first question raised about variation at the end of Section 1: what variants occur? **Universal statements** address the distribution of variants – the second question.

Exploring variation among the sentences of a single language by identifying structural patterns and establishing their distribution is the task of single-language grammars. This task was the main topic of Chapters 2–5. This chapter focuses on variation across languages. The research area that aims at formulating existential and universal statements about cross-linguistic variation is called **language typology**.

We have so far seen two subtypes of universal statements: unrestricted and restricted universals. The latter are also called typological implications or typological universals; of their two terms, B is dubbed the **implicans** ('implier') and A is the **implicatum** ('implied'). For example in (11), /m/ is the implicans and /n/ is the implicatum.

In addition to the basic division between unrestricted and restricted universal statements, universals differ from each other in other ways as well. First, they can differ in their modality. Compare the two statements in (13).

(13) (a) If a language has prepositions and the demonstrative must follow the noun, so **must** the adjective (Hawkins 1983: 71; emphasis added).

(b) 'When the descriptive adjective must precede the noun, the demonstrative and the numeral, **with overwhelming more than chance frequency**, do likewise' (Greenberg 1963: #18; emphasis added).

Whereas (13a) predicts the occurrence of something with certainty, (13b) predicts something as probable but not certain. Universal statements can thus vary in the degree of certainty with which they make their claim: some – as (13a) – are absolute and others – as (13b) – are probabilistic (also called statistical). The statement that all languages have vowels is an unrestricted universal of the absolute kind while the assertion that most languages have nasals is an unrestricted universal of the probabilistic kind. While existential statements say what may occur, probabilistic universals say what is likely to occur and absolute universals state what must occur. Using the terminology introduced in Chapter 1, Section 2.1.2, existential statements are enabling, or permissive, statistical universals are probabilistic, and absolute universals are nomological explanations.

For restricted universals, there are two other subdivisions. One has to do with the relationship between implicans and implicatum, the other with their complexity.

Consider the typological implications in (14):

(14) (a) In all languages, if the inflected verb must precede the subject in yes–no questions, so must it in wh-questions as well (Greenberg 1963: 111, #11a).

(b) In all languages, if in wh-questions the inflected verb must precede the subject, the wh-word is normally initial (Greenberg 1963: 111, #11b).

(c) In all languages, if yes–no questions are differentiated from declaratives by an intonation pattern, the position of this pattern is reckoned from the end of the sentence rather than from the beginning (Greenberg 1963: 110, #8).

The three generalizations differ in how their implicans and implicatum relate to each other. In (14a), the claim is about the construction repertoire of languages: verb-before-subject order in yes–no questions predicts the presence of the same pattern in wh-questions. Implicans and implicatum are properties of different sentence types: wh-questions and yes–no questions.

In (14b), this is not so: implicans and implicatum are both properties of a single sentence type: wh-questions. Since (14a) proposes an implication across constructions, it is a paradigmatic implication; while (14b), linking one part of a construction to another part of the same construction, forms a syntagmatic implication.

The statement in (14c) also applies within a sentence but implicans and implicatum are not two distinct parts but co-occurring properties of one part. It takes one feature of a constituent of a construction – namely, an intonation pattern signalling questions – and specifies something else about that constituent: its linear position. We will call this type reflexive implication (since, like reflexive pronouns, implicans and implicatum converge on the same entity).

The three kinds of implicational universals – paradigmatic, syntagmatic and reflexive – apply outside linguistics as well. A paradigmatic generalization in zoology is one that restricts the co-occurrence of different life forms within an ecological system; for example, if an ecological system includes bees, it must also include flowering plants. A zoological instance of syntagmatic implications is a statement restricting the co-occurrence of body parts in an animal body, such as the statement cited above (7b): if an animal has feathers, it must have two legs. A reflexive implication in zoology is one that restricts the co-occurrence of properties of individual body parts, such as that, for primates, limbs must be articulated.

The diagrams in (15) show the three subtypes of restricted universals for cross-linguistic variation. The rectangles are constructions of a language; a and b are implicans and implicatum; dots stand for other properties of constructions; arrows indicate the direction of implication.

(15) (a) reflexive implication:
If a, then b (where a and b are features of the **same constituent**)

(b) syntagmatic implication:
If a, then b (where a and b are features of **different constituents co-occurring in the same construction**)

(c) paradigmatic implication:
If a, then b (where a and b are features of **different
constructions of the same language**)

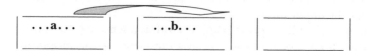

...a...	...b...	

A further difference among restricted universals has to do with the complexity of the terms. The implicational statements reviewed so far have a
simple logical structure: one implicans and one implicatum. Consider now
the statements previously given in (13) to illustrate different modalities;
they are repeated here under a different focus.

(13) repeated:
    (a) If a language has prepositions **and** the demonstrative must
        follow the noun, so must the adjective (Hawkins 1983: 71;
        emphasis added).

    (b) 'When the descriptive adjective must precede the noun, the
        demonstrative **and** the numeral, with overwhelming more
        than chance frequency, do likewise' (Greenberg 1963: #18;
        emphasis added).

In these statements, one of the two terms is complex. In (13a), it is the implicans that contains two conditions: preposed adpositions and postposed
demonstratives. In (13b), it is the implicatum that is complex: preposed
demonstratives and preposed numerals. Their respective logical structures
are shown in (16):

(16) (a) In all languages, if B1 and B2, then also A.
     (b) For all languages, if B, then also A1 and A2.

These schemata are familiar from Section 3.2.3 of Chapter 3, where we saw
that terms in selection rules may have simple or complex terms. This is no coin-
cidence: both selection rules of a single language and generalizations across
languages belong to the broad class of distributional generalizations: they state
the 'location', or conditions of occurrence, of a grammatical pattern.
    The two generalizations (16a) and (16b) differ in their efficiency. In (16a)
a single prediction is made based on more than one piece of information,
while in (16b) more than one prediction is made based on a single piece of
information. In other words, (16a) assumes much and predicts little, while
(16b) assumes little and predicts much. Since, guided by the requirements of
generality and simplicity in scientific statements, we want to be able to infer
much information from little evidence, (16b) is more valuable than (16a).
    It follows that ideal typologies involve a minimal implicans and/or a
maximal implicatum. What do such typologies look like?

A typological universal with a maximal implicatum is one where the implicatum includes all structural properties of a language except for the one serving as the implicans, as in the following highly hypothetical example:

(17) In all languages,
- if the direct object stands before the verb,
- then the language has
  - demonstrative before the noun
  - agglutinating morphology
  - fricatives
  - vowel harmony
  - at least six synonyms for 'ask'
  - and so on

Linguists have long been searching for the 'magic implicans' that would allow for the prediction of many, if not all, other structural characteristics; but such so-called holistic typologies, or even one that is near-holistic, are yet to be discovered (cf. Plank 1986).

A typological universal with a minimal implicans is one that does not contain an implicans at all, that is, an unrestricted universal: 'In all languages, A' with no 'B' as a condition for the occurrence of 'A'. In other words, an unrestricted universal is nothing other than a typological implication of the most general sort.

This consideration establishes the logical relatedness of unrestricted universals and typological implications. Both statement types are universal with respect to some universe of languages; whether they are 'restricted' or 'unrestricted' just depends on the universe that we fix our eyes on. If we focus on the universe of all human languages, then those statements that predict something for all members of this universe are unrestricted and those that predict something for a sub-domain of this universe are restricted. If our selected universe is smaller, consisting of all those human languages that meet a particular condition, a statement that is a restricted universal for the domain of all human languages becomes an unrestricted universal for this smaller domain. And if we 'switch universes' again, this time by broadening the domain to the universe of all communication systems, what is an unrestricted universal for the universe of all human languages becomes a restricted one: it holds only for those communication systems that are human languages.

Here is the summary of the various statement types instrumental in describing cross-linguistic variation:

(1) STATEMENTS ABOUT CROSS-LINGUISTIC VARIATION DIFFER by logical type: they can be
- existential or
- universal.

(2) UNIVERSAL STATEMENTS DIFFER
   (a) by their degree of certainty: they can be
      • **absolute or**
      • **probabilistic;**
   (b) by the universe they pertain to: they can be
      • **unrestricted or**
      • **restricted**.

(3) RESTRICTED UNIVERSAL STATEMENTS DIFFER
   (a) by the relationship between their terms: they can be
      • **reflexive** (implicans and implicatum are properties of a single constituent); or
      • **syntagmatic** (implicans and implicatum are properties of different constituents co-occurring in a construction); or
      • **paradigmatic** (implicans and implicatum are properties of different constructions co-occurring in the same language);
   (b) by the complexity of their terms: they may have
      • **single** implicantia and/or implicata; or
      • **multiple** implicantia and/or implicata.

Similar statement types serve to describe change. Existential statements will tell us what changes are possible, that is, what can change to what; universal statements will describe the conditions under which the changes occur. Universal statements about change have the same subtypes as those about variation. The basic typology of statements about change in (18) parallels those about variation as given in (12) above.

(18) (a) EXISTENTIAL STATEMENTS:
      In some languages, A changes to B.
      In some languages, B has arisen from A.
   (b) UNIVERSAL STATEMENTS:
     (i) UNRESTRICTED UNIVERSALS:
        In all languages, if A changes to anything, it must change to B.
        In all languages, if A has arisen from something, it must have arisen from B.
     (ii) RESTRICTED UNIVERSALS:
        In all languages, if there is C, then, if A changes to anything, it must change to B.
        In all languages, if there is C, then, if A has arisen from something, it must have arisen from B.

We are now ready to turn to case studies of syntactic variation across languages (Section 3) and of historical and individual change (Section 4).

3 Syntactic variation

3.1 VERB AGREEMENT

As noted in Chapter 3 (Section 3.3.2), in some languages, verbs agree with some of their arguments. German (as English) has subject–verb agreement in person:

(1) German
  (a) ***Du   sandt-est   den Jungen zur   Salma.***
      You_S sent-**SBJ.S2** the boy   to.the Salma
      'You sent the boy to Salma.'

  (b) ***Er sandt-e   den Jungen zur   Salma.***
      he sent-**SBJ.S3** the boy   to.the Salma
      'He sent the boy to Salma.'

The Hungarian example in (2) shows both subject–verb agreement in person and verb agreement with the direct object in definiteness.

(2) Hungarian
  (a) ***Te   egy fiú-t   Salmához küldt-él.***
      you_S a   **letter-ACC** to:Salma sent-**S2.SBJ.INDEFOBJ**
      'You_S sent a boy to Salma.'

  (b) ***Te   a fiú-t   Salmához küldt-ed.***
      you_S the boy-**ACC** to:Salma sent-**S2.SBJ.DEFOBJ**
      'You_S sent the boy to Salma.'

  (c) ***Ő egy fiú-t   Salmához küldött-0.***
      he a   boy-ACC to:Salma sent-**S3.SBJ.INDEFOBJ**
      'He sent a boy to Salma.'

  (d) ***Ő a fiú-t   Salmához küldt-e.***
      he the boy-ACC to:Salma sent-**S3.SBJ.DEFOBJ**
      'He sent the boy to Salma.'

Like German and Hungarian, Lebanese Arabic has subject–verb agreement (in gender). Like Hungarian, it also has verb agreement with the direct object and, unlike Hungarian, it also has verb agreement with the indirect object.

(3) Lebanese Arabic (Koutsoudas 1969: 119–25; transcription simplified; note that *Samiir* is the name of a man and *Salma* is the name of a woman)

– verb agrees with subject:

(a) ***Samiir*** *baat-0*   *l*   *walad la Salma.*
   Samiir sent-**MSC.SBJ** the boy   to Salma
   'Samiir sent the boy to Salma.'

(b) ***Salma*** *baat-it*   *l*   *walad la Samiir.*
   Salma sent-**FEM.SBJ** the boy   to Samiir
   'Salma sent the boy to Samiir.'

– verb agrees with subject and direct object:

(c) ***Samiir*** *baat-0-u*   *la*   *l*   ***walad*** *la Salma.*
   Samiir sent-**MSC.SBJ-MSC.DO** ACC the **boy**   to Salma
   'Samiir sent the boy to Salma.'

(d) ***Salma*** *baat-it-ha*   *la*   *l*   ***bint*** *la Samiir.*
   Salma sent-**FEM.SBJ-FEM.DO** ACC the **girl** to Samiir
   'Salma sent the girl to Samiir.'

– verb agrees with subject and indirect object:

(e) ***Salma*** *baat-it-lu*   *l*   *walad la* ***Samiir.***
   Salma sent-**FEM.SBJ-MSC.IO** the boy   to **Samiir**
   'Salma sent the boy to Samiir.'

(f) ***Samiir*** *baat-0-la*   *l*   *walad la* ***Salma.***
   Samiir sent-**MSC.SBJ-FEM.IO** the boy   to **Salma**
   'Samiir sent the boy to Salma.'

The examples in (1)–(3) show that verb agreement with the subject, with the direct object and with the indirect object are all possible patterns in languages. This is stated in (4):

(4) (a) In some languages, the verb agrees with the subject.
    (b) In some languages, the verb agrees with the direct object.
    (c) In some languages, the verb agrees with the indirect object.

But such existential statements do not render the occurrence of the various subtypes of agreement predictable: we need to identify the conditions under which each pattern holds in a language. As a first stab at the problem, we may formulate the following unrestricted universals:

(5) (a) In all languages, the verb agrees with the subject.
    (b) In all languages, the verb agrees with the direct object.
    (c) In all languages, the verb agrees with the indirect object.

While these statements are just the logical type that we are looking for, they are patently untrue: not all languages have all three agreement types. The actual distribution of the three types of verb agreement over the eight logical possibilities is shown in (6):

(6)	VERB-SUBJ. AGREEMENT	VERB-DIR. OBJ AGREEMENT	VERB-INDIR. OBJ. AGREEMENT	EXAMPLE LANGUAGE
type I	+	+	+	Leb. Arabic
type II	+	+	−	Hungarian
type III	+	−	−	German, English
type IV	−	−	−	Korean
*type V	−	+	+	none
*type VI	−	−	+	none
*type VII	+	−	+	none
*type VIII	−	+	−	none

Let us now explore how the conceptual tool of restricted universals could help us state a universal distribution for these non-universally distributed patterns of agreement. In (7) are offered two absolute paradigmatic implications:

(7) (a) In all languages where the verb agrees with the direct object, it also agrees with the subject.
  (b) In all languages where the verb agrees with the indirect object, it also agrees with the direct object.

The true statements in (7) and the false ones in (5) are all universals but they pertain to different universes: those in (5) have to do with all human languages while those in (7) have to do with subsets of all human languages – those that have a particular characteristic. The statement in (7a) predicts the presence of subject–verb agreement for those languages that have verb agreement with the direct object, such as Hungarian. The statement in (7b) predicts verb agreement with the direct object for those languages that have verb agreement with indirect objects, such as Lebanese Arabic.

Note, however, that these generalizations do not predict all agreement patterns. Neither generalization predicts subject–verb agreement for languages such as German (or English) since the implicans – verb agreement with direct objects – is not present. Neither statement predicts verb agreement with direct objects for languages such as Hungarian, either, where, again, the necessary predictor (verb agreement with indirect objects) does not occur. Finally, neither (7a) nor (7b) predict verb agreement with indirect objects for languages like Lebanese Arabic since neither generalization provides an implicans for this pattern.

The second case study of constraints on cross-linguistic variation in syntax comes from constituent order.

3.2 CONSTITUENT ORDER

The three major sentence constituents – subject, direct object and verb – have six logically possible orders. As was discussed in Chapter 2 (Section 3.1.1), all six orders occur across languages. Examples are Thai (SVO), Hindi (SOV), Tagalog (VSO), Malagasy (VSO) and two Brazilian languages for object-initial order: Hixkaryana (OVS) and Urubú (OSV). The existential statements in (1) capture these observations:

(1) (a) In some languages, the dominant order is SVO.
    (b) In some languages, the dominant order is SOV.
    (c) In some languages, the dominant order is VSO.
    (d) In some languages, the dominant order is VOS.
    (e) In some languages, the dominant order is OVS.
    (f) In some languages, the dominant order is OSV.

Language-typological research of the past 40 years has found that the order of major sentence constituents in a language is not independent of how other constituents are ordered. One correlation holds between the ordering of verb and object order and the ordering of noun and adposition. Based on a genetically and areally balanced sample of 625 languages, Dryer found the following statistical implications to hold (1992: 83–6):

(2) (a) Most languages that have OV order have postpositions.
    (b) Most languages that have postpositions have OV order.
    (c) Most languages that have VO order have prepositions.
    (d) Most languages that have prepositions have VO order.

Note that phrases such as 'have OV order' or 'have prepositions' refer to majority patterns in a language. For example, English is a prepositional language even though, as noted before, it does have some postpositions, such as *ago*.

In (3) and (4), evidence is presented from languages that bear out the pattern.

(3) Postpositions in OV languages:
    (a) Turkish
          OV: *Barbarlar-ı*   **yendiler**.
               barbarians-ACC **they:defeated**
               'They defeated the barbarians.'

          NAdp: *vapur ile*
               boat **with**
               'with boat'

(b) Hindi

    OV: *Mai bhai-ko*   **dekhta hu**.
       I brother-ACC **see**   **am**
       'I see the brother.'

    NAdp: *bhaike*   **sath**
       brother **with**
       'with brother'

(4) Prepositions in VO languages:

    (a) Tagalog

       VO: **Dumadalaw** *key*   *Rosa si*   *Maria.*
       visit   CASE Rosa CASE Maria
       'Maria is visiting Rosa.'

       AdpN: **para** *sa binlana*
          for the window
          'for the window'

    (b) Irish

       VO: **Chonaic** *Seán an madadh.*
       saw   John the dog
       'John saw the dog.'

       AdpN: **chun** *na fuinneoge*
          for   the window
          'for the window'

The four restricted universals in (2) are stated as probabilistic implications since, were they stated as absolutes, they would not hold true: there would be counterexamples. Thus, Persian is OV but prepositional; and Finnish is VO but mostly postpositional. The statements are paradigmatic since implicans and implicatum do not necessarily occur together in a sentence; and they are simple since both implicans and implicatum refer to a single property.

A second implicational relationship linking the order of verb and direct object to the ordering of other constituents has to do with possessor and possessee: genitives and their nouns. In (5) are given examples of GenN order for the two OV languages mentioned in (3); in (6) are given examples of NGen order in the two VO languages of (4).

(5) GenN and OV

    (a) Turkish

       GenN: *Mehmed-in*   **parası**
          Mehmed-GEN **his:money**
          'Mehmed's money'

   (b) Hindi (simplified transcription)
       GenN: *lar-ko*   ***ma***
             boy-GEN **mother**
             'the boy's mother'

(6) NGen and VO
   (a) Tagalog
       NGen: ***ang***   ***ama***   *ni Juan*
             CASE father of John
             'John's father'
   (b) Irish
       NGen: ***an tathair*** *Sheain*
             the father of:John
             'John's father'

Dryer has shown that there is an overwhelming preference for GenN order among OV languages (1992: 91). In each of the six geographic areas that Dryer divided the world into, most genetic language groups show the clustering of OV and GenN. The preference for NGen order among VO languages is somewhat weaker but still evident. Examples of languages that go against the two tendencies are Persian, which has NGen even though it is an OV language, and Swedish, which has GenN even though it is VO. English straddles the line between compliance and non-compliance: it is a VO language but it has both NGen and GenN order (e.g. *the fame of the school, the school's fame*). These observations are captured in the following simple, paradigmatic, probabilistic implications:

(7) (a) Most languages that have OV order have GenN order.
     (b) Most languages that have GenN order have OV order.
     (c) Most languages that have VO order have NGen order.
     (d) Most languages that have NGen order have VO order.

As we saw in Section 2, there is an obvious way of seeking to convert probabilistic universals into absolute ones: by finding a sub-universe for which the prediction holds without exceptions. If the probabilistic statement is an unrestricted universal, we try to convert it into a restricted universal by finding an implicans that defines the sub-universe within which the prediction is exceptionless. For example, as seen earlier, rather than being content with a statement according to which most languages have /n/, we formulate a statement according to which all languages have /n/ that have /m/. If in turn a probabilistic universal is already of the restricted sort, we need to find an additional implicans to further restrict its universe so that the prediction becomes exceptionless. In other words, we buy absolute predictability at the price of narrowing the universe for which the prediction is to hold.

John Hawkins has proposed such an additional implicans (1983: 64) for (7a). He noticed that the languages in his sample that were exceptions to the 'if OV then GenN' pattern, such as Persian, had the adjective after the noun, whereas the languages that bore out the trend had pre-nominal adjectives. This observation points to the following generalization that held exceptionless for Hawkins' sample.

(8) All languages that have both OV order and AdjN order have
    GenN order.

Both (7a) and (8) are implicational generalizations with OV as implicans and GenN as implicatum. They differ in that (7a) is probabilistic while (8) is an absolutized version of (7a), made possible by the added implicatum: AdjN order.

So far we have seen two case studies of syntactic variation across languages: one about verb agreement, the other about constituent order. The generalizations in both made crucial mention of the major sentence constituents subject, object and verb. Our last case study has to do with the varying semantics and varying syntactic classification of these terms across languages.

3.3 ACCUSATIVE AND ERGATIVE SYSTEMS

Consider the English sentences in (1):

(1) (a) *The hunter is chasing the wolves.*
    (b) *He is chasing them.*

How do we know who is chasing whom? English provides multiple cues for differentiating subject and direct object. First, there is word order: the subject is pre-verbal and the direct object is post-verbal. Second, there is verb agreement: if, as in these sentences, the two noun phrases differ in number, number marking on the verb picks out the agent. Third, there is case marking: if, as in (1b), one or both of the two noun phrases is a pronoun, case form signals whether the pronoun is the agent or the patient.

Consider now the intransitive sentences in (2).

(2) (a) *The wolves are running.*
    (b) *They are running.*

In these sentences, it is easy to tell who is running: there is no choice because there is only one noun phrase present. Since there is no other noun phrase competing for subjecthood, one would not expect any marking on the subject: it does not need to be differentiated from anything else. And, if the subject of an intransitive sentence is nonetheless marked in some way, all bets are off regarding the nature of the marking: it could be marked the same way as the subject of the transitive sentence, or as the direct object of the transitive sentence, or in some third way.

These three logically possible marking patterns of intransitive subjects are shown and exemplified in (3) (cf. Comrie 1978: 332): A(gent) stands for transitive subject (even though not all transitive subjects have the semantic participant role of agency), P(atient) stands for direct object (even though not all direct objects are semantic patients), and S(ubject) stands for intransitive subject.

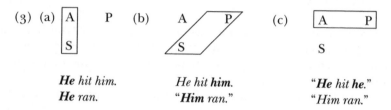

(3) (a)	(b)	(c)
He hit him.	*He hit him.*	"*He hit he.*"
He ran.	"*Him ran.*"	"*Him ran.*"

What we actually find is that in English, only pattern (3a) is grammatical: intransitive subjects are case-marked the same way as transitive subjects.

While all three patterns in (3) occur in languages, they do not occur with equal frequency. One common pattern is the English type – (3a); the other common pattern is (3b). The pattern in (3a) is called **accusative pattern**; (3b) is labelled **ergative pattern**. Both labels are taken from the name of the case of the noun phrase which is 'the odd one out', i.e. that is not the same as either of the other two. In an accusative case marking system, this special case is that of the P, called the **accusative case**; the shared case of A and S is called the **nominative case**. In an ergative pattern, the special case is that of the A: it is called the **ergative case**, and the shared case of P and S is called the **absolutive case** (or sometimes, confusingly, the nominative).

Here are examples of accusative and ergative case markings juxtaposed for comparison. Latin has suffixed case markers, Tongan has prepositions.

(4) ACCUSATIVE CASE MARKING: Latin
  Fili-us   can-em   occidit.
  son-**NOM** dog-ACC killed
  'The son killed the dog.'

  Fili-us   cucurrit.
  son-**NOM** ran
  'The son ran.'

(5) ERGATIVE CASE MARKING: Tongan
  Na'e tamate'i 'a   Kolaiate 'e   Tevita.
  PAST kill   **ABS** Goliath ERG David
  'David killed Goliath.'

> *Na'e alu 'a   Kolaiate ki Fisi.*
> PAST go **ABS** Goliath to Fiji
> 'Goliath went to Fiji.'

The following probabilistic universal holds:

(6) In most languages that have case markers, the markers are used to differentiate S either from A or from P but not from both.

The statement in (6) is about accusative and ergative patterns as they apply to case marking. But these patterns may hold for other structural properties, such as verb agreement or word order. If in a language, the verb agrees with both transitive and intransitive subjects, the pattern is accusative because it shows a likeness between transitive and intransitive subjects as opposed to objects. If, on the other hand, the verb agrees with intransitive subjects and objects, the pattern is ergative because the class of controllers includes intransitive subjects and objects but not transitive subjects. Similarly, AVP and SV order is accusative-style since pre-verbal position is shared by A and S; but PVA and SV is ergative since pre-verbal position is shared by P and S. English follows the accusative pattern not only in its pronominal case marking but also in terms of verb agreement and constituent order: the verb agrees with both intransitive and transitive subjects; and both kinds of subjects precede the verb.

Even though linguists talk about 'accusative languages' and 'ergative languages', these labels – just as others, such as 'SOV language' or 'SVO language' – capture only the majority patterns that the language in question exhibits. In actuality, there is perhaps no language that is fully accusative or fully ergative. In what follows, we will consider a few mixed systems.

First, in some languages one kind of marking device – such as case – follows one alignment pattern and another kind of marking – say, word order – follows the other. An example is French. In this language, the split is between case marking on the one hand and verb agreement on the other. The case marking of pronouns follows the accusative principle: *il* 'he' is the form for both A and S and *le* 'him' is the P form. This is shown in (7):

(7) (a) ***Il le*** *voit.*
     he him sees.
     'He sees him.'

   (b) **Il** court.
     he runs
     'He is running.'

However, verb agreement with pronoun objects is ergative: the past participle of the perfective verb agrees in number and gender with intransitive subjects and with pronominal objects. This is illustrated in (8). Although in

(8b) the two object pronouns occur in phonologically reduced form and thus seem the same, in their full form they are different: *le* for the masculine gender in (i), and *la* for the feminine gender in (ii). (The masculine and feminine agreement markers are differentiated only in spelling, not in pronunciation.)

(8) (a) verb agreement with intransitive subjects

      (i) **Le**   *chapeau est arriv-é.*
          the.MSC.SG hat   has arrived-**MSC.SG**
          'The hat has arrived.'

      (ii) **La**   *chemise est arriv-ée.*
          the.FEM.SG shirt   has arrived-**FEM.SG**
          'The shirt has arrived.'

   (b) verb agreement with pronoun objects

      (i) *Le*   *chapeau ... je l'-ai*   *achet-é.*
          the.MSC.SG hat   I **it:MSC**-have bought-**MSC.SG**
          'The hat ... I have bought it.'

      (ii) *La*   *chemise ... je l'-ai*   *achet-ée.*
          the.FEM.SG shirt   I **it:FEM**-have bought-**FEM.SG**
          'The shirt ... I have bought it.'

The French example shows that different marking systems of a language – here case marking and agreement – can go separate ways in whether they show accusative or ergative alignment. But the very same marking system – such as case marking – may also be split between the two kinds of alignment. Two examples are Georgian and Lithuanian, each representing a different conditioning factor for accusative and ergative case markings.

In Georgian, case marking is accusative style in the present but ergative style in the past (Comrie 1978: 351–2). This is shown in (9):

(9) (a) present-tense sentences:
      transitive: *Student-i*   *çeril-s*   *çers*
               student-**NOM** letter-**ACC** writes
               'The student writes the letter.'
      intransitive: *Student-i*   *midis.*
               student-**NOM** goes
               'The student goes.'

   (b) past-tense sentences:
      transitive: *Student-a*   *çeril-i*   *daçera.*
                student-**ERG** letter-**ABS** wrote.
               'The student wrote the letter.'

          intransitive: *Student-i   mivida.*
                    student-**ABS** went
                    'The student went.'

Notice the distribution of the case suffix *i.* In all these sentences, it appears on intransitive subjects and it also marks a noun phrase of a transitive sentence. However, while in the present-tense sentences, this other noun phrase is the transitive subject, in past-tense sentences, the additional *i-* marked noun phrase is the object. The language thus has both accusative and ergative case marking depending on the tense of the verb. Cross-linguistic surveys indicate that the reverse pattern – ergative case marking in present-tense sentences and accusative case marking in past-tense sentences – never occurs (see Dixon 1994: 97–101).

In Lithuanian, it is the affirmative versus negative mode of the sentence that dictates the choice between accusative and ergative case marking (Senn 1966: 392, 394). The language marks noun phrases by accusative alignment in affirmative sentences but in many negative sentences, case markers are ergatively distributed.

(10) (a)   affirmative sentences:
               transitive: *àš dár turiù tév-**a***
                         I still have father-**ACC**
                         'I still have a father.'
               intransitive: *tévá-**s**   yrà namiẽ*
                         father-**NOM** is   at:home
                         'Father is at home.'

        (b)   negative sentences:
               transitive: *àš nebeturiù tév-**o***
                         I not:have father-**GEN**
                         'I don't have a father.'
               intransitive: *tév-**o**   nerà namiẽ*
                         father-**GEN** not:is home
                         'Father is not home.'

An additional language whose syntax is split between accusative style and ergative style is none other than English. As noted above, if we compare intransitive sentences with active transitive ones in English, we find that not only pronominal case marking but also verb agreement and constituent order conform to the accusative pattern. Now consider the following:

(11) (a)   (i)   *Bees are swarming **in the garden**.*
              (ii) ***The garden** is swarming with bees.*

        (b)   (i)   *Water abounds **in the area**.*
              (ii) ***The area** abounds in water.*

The sentences in (11) illustrate that prepositional phrases – *the garden* and *in area* – can be alternatively expressed as intransitive subjects. As shown in (12), prepositional phrases show a similar alternation with direct objects.

(12) (a) (i) *John planted flowers **in the garden**.*
  (ii) *John planted **the garden** with flowers.*

  (b) (i) *John loaded hay **on the truck**.*
  (ii) *John loaded **the truck** with hay.*

Thus, (11) and (12) show a common characteristic of intransitive subjects and direct objects: they both constitute alternative expressions for certain prepositional phrases. Furthermore, the semantic difference between the alternatives is the same: when the locative expression is a direct object or an intransitive subject, its referent is understood as completely affected by the action while this is not so in the prepositional version. For example, in ((11)(aii)), the whole garden is understood to be full of bees, while this is not suggested by (ai). Similarly, ((12) (aii)) – but not (ai) – suggests that the entire garden has been planted with flowers. Thus, (11) and (12) show the existence of an ergative pattern in English.

While the alternations in (11) and (12) are available only to some verbs, a second bit of ergative syntax is more central to English grammar: the very existence of the passive construction. Below is a comparison between intransitive sentences and both active transitive sentences (13a) and passive ones (13b):

(13) (a) active sentence: **He** hit her.
  intransitive sentences: **He** runs.

  (b) passive sentence: **She** was hit by him.
  intransitive sentences: **She** runs.

English is an accusative language only as long as we compare intransitive sentences with active transitive ones. If in turn we compare intransitive sentences with passive ones, the patterning is ergative. The reason why English is nonetheless considered an accusative language is that active sentences are the unmarked option: passives involve a complex, periphrastic verb form as opposed to the mostly simple active verbs, and passives are also less frequent than their active counterparts.

To summarize this section, the following generalizations about the marking of grammatical relations emerge:

(14) (a) (repeated from (6))
      In most languages that have case markers, the markers are used to differentiate S either from A or from P but not from both.

(b) Most (if not all) languages have grammatical patterns of both the accusative and the ergative kind.

(c) In all those languages where the choice between accusative and ergative case marking depends on verb tense, the ergative case marking appears in the past tense and the accusative case marking in the present tense.

(d) In some languages, whether case marking follows the accusative or the ergative pattern depends on whether the verb is affirmative or negative.

The statement in (14d) is existential; all the others are universals. The generalization in (14a) is restricted, reflexive and probabilistic; (14b) is unrestricted and probabilistic; and (14c) is a restricted, syntagmatic and absolute universal.

4 Syntactic change

If you walk around in an unfamiliar city looking at the buildings, you first see everything in its present-day reality. However, once you know something about the history of the city's architecture, your view becomes more differentiated: you recognize some houses as relics from the nineteenth century, other buildings as representing current styles, while a few of them may be harbingers of new architectural trends making their first cautious appearance. As the epigraph of this chapter says, one's view of things is different if knowledge of earlier times is available.

This is the same with languages. At first blush, all the various grammatical constructions of English seem equally 'present'. But the characteristics of today's English can be telescoped along the time axis: while some form a relatively stable core of the present-day language, others are relics, and again others are innovative constructions gradually easing their way into the grammatical system. For example, the case distinctions observable in pronouns – *he* versus *him* versus *his*, and so on – are an old tradition that has been around for many centuries and so has multiple negation (such as in *He did not see nothing*), non-standard in today's English but fully acceptable in Old English. On the other hand, reflexive pronouns such as *myself* and *yourself* are relatively young: as recently as 500 years ago, personal pronouns (*me, you*) were employed in this function. The use of the auxiliary *do* in negative sentences is even more recent: it did not get firmly established before the twentieth century. And the use of *who* in non-subject function – as in *Who did you talk to?* – is still in the process of pushing out the earlier form *whom*.

Change in language is observable on two levels: in the language of a community as a whole extending over centuries and millennia, and in the language of individuals over the span of a single human life. The former is called **historical change**; we will refer to the latter as **individual change**. Language arises, changes and dies on both levels. On the individual level, language changes throughout our lives but change is most apparent at its onset as we learn our first language or when we learn a second or third language and, at the other end, when we can lose a language by lack of use or by aging or by becoming aphasic because of brain injury or disease. The birth and the death of a language as we experience them in our lives have parallels in historical change, as new languages constantly evolve – such as pidgins and creoles – and languages die out in great numbers for reasons of diminishing speaker populations.

In what follows, we will take up one case of historical change (Section 4.1) and one area in individual change (Section 4.2) and formulate some generalizations about them.

4.1 THE HISTORICAL EVOLUTION OF DEFINITE ARTICLES

As we consider the histories of different languages, two facts jump out. First, the various stages are not specific to one language: the same stages recur across languages. An earlier form of English may be the present-day form of another language or it may be one lurking in the future of another language. For example, Modern French, as seen in Chapter 4 (Section 3.3.2), puts personal pronoun objects before the verb; Old English showed the same tendency. Another example is the use of the copulative verb in sentences such as *My brother is a lawyer*. While English does use the copula *is*, Russian present-tense sentences simply juxtapose the two noun phrases: 'My brother lawyer'. But the copula in English seems to be on its way out: it is already reduced in sentences like *My brother's a lawyer*, and it is frequently absent in African-American English ushering in what may be in store for the Standard English of the next century.

Second, it is not only that the same stages crop up in different languages, but contiguous sets of them do, too. That is, there are certain pairs of adjacent stages that recur in the histories of different languages and they recur in the same order. For example, both English and French evidenced a stage where nouns were inflected and a stage where nouns had no inflection; and the first stage preceded the other. Historical change is generally unidirectional. These two points will be evidenced in the following discussion about the evolution of articles.

Definite and indefinite articles are very frequent words in English: there is hardly any sentence that does not include at least one *the* or *a(n)*. Yet, these grammatical elements are not universal across languages. Matthew Dryer (1989) reports that a mere one-third of the world's languages have articles of either kind. Some have only a definite article (e.g. Irish), others have only an indefinite article (e.g. Turkish), and some, such as English or Spanish, have both. The less-than-universal distribution of articles across languages suggests that articles can arise and fade out in the course of linguistic history. In what follows, we will focus on definite articles and probe into the onset of their life cycle: their origin.

Consider the determiners in the following English phrases:

(1) (a) **the** *man*
        the *station*
        the *beauty*

    (b) **that** *man*
        that *station*
        that *beauty*

If we compare the definite article *the* and the demonstrative *that*, two observations leap to the eye. First, the two are similar both in phonological form and in meaning. Phonologically, they both start with a voiced interdental fricative and contain a non-back vowel. Semantically, they both serve to single out a particular instance of a type. The second observation is that the article *the* has a more meagre form and a more meagre meaning than the demonstrative *that*. The form of the demonstrative is larger than the form of the definite article: *that* has three phonological segments while *the* has only two. Similarly, the meaning of the demonstrative properly includes the meaning of definite article: *that* identifies an individual by the spatial feature of remoteness from the speaker (as opposed to *this*, which refers to something near the speaker), while *the* lacks spatial reference.

Why is there both a formal and a semantic resemblance between the English definite article and the distal demonstrative? The answer is found in the history of the language. Old English (about AD 500–1100) did not have a definite article but it did have two demonstratives, each with masculine, feminine and neuter form: *thes, theos, this* 'this', and *se, seo, thæt* 'that'. The distal demonstrative gradually generalized its meaning: beginning with the twelfth century, some of its uses did not refer to things identifiable as distant from the speaker but to things identifiable otherwise, such as having been mentioned in the discourse or being known by everybody as unique, for instance the sun or the heaven. Twelfth-century examples of the distal demonstrative already reduced in form and reduced in meaning to that of an definite article are **the** *king Stephne* 'the king Stephen' and *henged up by* **the** *fet* 'hung up by the feet' (Traugott 1972: 135).

Romance languages show a similar development. In (2) are listed the forms of the definite article in French and Spanish and the Latin demonstrative pronoun that they both evolved from. As in the history of English, the Latin demonstrative lost part of its form and generalized its meaning.

(2) (a) French: **le** *garçon*   'the boy'
              la *maison*   'the house'

    (b) Spanish: **el** *libro*   'the book'
              la *puerta*   'the door'

(c) Latin: *liber **ille***   'that book'
             *domus **illa***   'that house'

Swahili is a third case in point. In Swahili, both 'that' and 'the' have the same phonological form *yule* but when used as a demonstrative, *yule* is stressed and follows the noun; when used as an article, it is stressless and precedes the noun (Givón 1984: 419). This is shown in (3):

(3) Swahili: (a)   *mtóto **yúle*** 'that child'
                     child **that**

         (b)   ***yule** mtóto* 'the child'
                     the child

Another non-Indo-European example of the same historical process is Hungarian. The form *az* can be used in the sense of 'that' and in the sense of 'the', with the former being the historically earlier use. The word *az* precedes the noun in both demonstrative and article use but, while the definite article immediately precedes the noun (or its modifiers), the demonstrative non-immediately precedes the noun (or its modifiers). This is because the definite article is an obligatory part of the demonstrative construction and it must intervene between the two (cf. Chapter 4, Section 3.1).

(4) Hungarian: (a)   ***az** alma* 'the apple'
                       the apple

           (b)   ***az**   az alma* 'that apple'
                       that the apple

Besides Germanic, Romance, Bantu and Finno-Ugric, the evolution of a demonstrative into a definite article has also taken place in Greek and in various Caucasian languages and it is ongoing in Indonesian. The opposite path of definite articles evolving into demonstratives has not been observed in any language.

The process of demonstratives evolving into definite articles by losing some of their form and some of their meaning is comparable to agreement markers developing out of pronouns (discussed in Chapter 3 (Section 4)) and to the evolution of the French discontinuous negative marker (discussed in Chapter 2 (Section 4)). All these changes are instances of grammaticalization – a process to be taken up again in Chapter 7, Section 4.2.

Can we then conclude that definite articles are the only source for definite articles and that demonstratives in turn never change into anything other than definite articles? Neither statement is exceptionless: definite articles may arise from other sources, such as numeral classifiers and verbs, and demonstratives can turn into other grammatical elements such as conjunctions (cf. English *that* in *They told us that the tornado was approaching*) and third person pronouns (cf. French *il* 'he', *elle* 'she' from Latin *ille, illa* 'that'). But those instances where the definite article comes from a demonstrative share a characteristic: the source is always a distal demonstrative – 'that', rather than 'this'.

All in all, the following statistical and absolute universals can be stated:

(5) (a) In most languages that have definite articles, the historical source is a demonstrative.

(b) In all languages, if a demonstrative evolves into a definite article, the source must be a distal demonstrative rather than a proximate one.

(c) In no language may demonstratives evolve from definite articles.

Note that generalizations about historical change such as those in (5) do not predict **when** a change will take place or even **whether** it ever will. What these generalizations do is state what are possible, probable or necessary terms of a change **if** and **when** it does occur.

The next section will take up change on a micro-level as it happens in the course of a human life.

4.2 THE FIRST-LANGUAGE ACQUISITION OF WH-QUESTIONS

A newborn child does not comprehend and produce speech; yet, in a matter of just a few years, he has mastered the language that he was born into. The question is: what happens between the null-language stage and the full-language stage? The same question arises in connection with second languages: how does a person find his way from zero knowledge of a foreign language to a stage of more or less complete command of it?

One thing is certain: nobody acquires a language, whether first or second, without exposure to that language. Thus, the most obvious factor in the learning process is the ambient language that the learner attempts to acquire.

But this cannot be the whole story. If language were acquired merely by the mechanical imitation of input from the ambient language, the following would have to be true:

- the learner says **everything** that he has heard;
- the learner says **only** what he has heard.

There is ample evidence in both first and second language acquisition that this is not what happens. Let us start by considering first-language acquisition. On the one hand, children's imitations are not fully true to the model that they emulate: they omit, add and change aspects of the model. On the other hand, children also construct novel utterances with no exact models. These two observations show that, miraculous though the very ability of direct imitation is, the child brings additional capabilities to the task of language acquisition. The challenge for linguists and psychologists is to describe both the child's imitative efforts and the ways in which his novel utterances depart from what he has heard. What is it that the newborn baby's mind brings to the task of acquiring a language? Are specific language-related abilities involved or is the language-learning ability just an application of general human intelligence? What, if any, role do social conditions play in the process? And are there any similarities in the acquisitional stages and their sequencing across children learning the same language and those learning different languages?

The questions about second-language acquisition are similar. Foreign-language learners, too, imitate what they hear but their production both falls short of the models and goes beyond them. What are the conceptual resources that they draw upon? A fundamental difference between first and second language acquisition is that, in the latter case, knowledge of the first language is clearly a significant factor: some of the native-language habits are transferred to the foreign language. The question is what role transfer plays and what other physical and psychological abilities come into play.

The following discussion of these major issues will be restricted to first language acquisition and within it, to some facts about how English-learning children acquire wh-questions.

Children do not acquire all subtypes of wh-questions at the same time. Here are three observations:

(1) (a) *What*-questions tend to be acquired before *who*-questions.
     (b) *Where*-questions tend to be acquired before *when-*, *how-*, and *why*-questions.
     (c) Those *what*-questions that have *what* as subject tend to be acquired before those that have *what* as direct object.

To start with (1a); why do children tend to ask questions like *What this?* before producing questions like *Who this?* Lois Bloom and others have suggested an explanation in terms of children's communicative need. Children are more likely to know the people they see than the things around them. If so, they may have a bigger need to ask about what something is than who somebody is.

Let us now turn to the second observation in (1). Side by side with the child's needs, there is another factor that would seem likely to play a role in the acquisition process: the abilities available to the child for fulfilling his needs. In areas other than language development, children learn simple things before more complex ones. For example, children can maintain body postures favoured by gravity earlier than those that require straining against gravity: babies lie before sitting and sit before standing up. Similarly, babies can cope with food that is easier on the digestive system sooner than they can cope with food that is harder to digest. If the simple-before-complex principle were to hold for language as well, it would have to be the case that children learn simpler grammatical structures before they learn more complex ones.

Appeal to the simple-before-complex principle may provide an explanation of the second observation in (1). Patricia Clancy suggests that *where*-questions are generally acquired before *when*-, *how*- and *why*-questions because spatial relations – which is what *where*-questions are about – are more easily perceived by the child than time and manner.

The third observation stated in (1) has to do with the acquisitional sequence of subject and object wh-questions. The simple-before-complex principle may again offer a clue. To test the general hypothesis that simpler constructions are acquired before complex ones, one must have a way of independently determining how grammatical structures stack up on the complexity scale. One aspect of grammatical complexity that has been suggested by William O'Grady is the degree of match between semantic and syntactic closeness (O'Grady 1997: 136). As discussed in Chapter 5 (Section 3.1.3.2), languages show a strong tendency to place semantically related constituents next to each other. Nonetheless, not all syntactic constructions obey this desideratum. Since constructions where semantic cohesion and temporal adjacency go hand in hand would appear to be simpler than those where there is no such match, we would expect constructions of the former type to be acquired before those of the latter type.

This prediction holds true for several acquisitional orders, among them the one noted in (1c) above. Consider the following questions (from O'Grady 1997: 133, 137, 138):

(2) (a) *What is bothering Sue?*
    (b) *What will Sue say ___?*
    (c) *What will Sue talk about ___?*
    (d) *What will Sue read a book about ___?*
    (e) *What do you think Sue will read ___?*

In (2a), *what* is in its semantically justified position – as subject, it directly precedes the verb. In the rest of the sentences, however, *what* is displaced from its semantically expected position (indicated by the blank). Furthermore, the distance between the two positions varies:

- in (2b), *what* is the object of the verb;
- in (2c), *what* is the object of a preposition which is the complement of the verb;
- in (2d), *what* is the object of a preposition which is an adjunct of the verb;
- in (2e), *what* is the object of a clause which is the object of the main verb.

As noted in (1c), most experimental evidence about children's ability to imitate, comprehend or produce such questions bears out the predicted acquisitional sequence. Children seem to have the least trouble with subject wh-questions, where semantic and syntactic position coincide (as in (2a)), and the most trouble with wh-questions where the wh-word semantically belongs to an embedded sentence (as in (2e). The remaining question types (in (2b) through (2d)) are also acquired in the predicted order. These observations may thus provide additional support for the simple-before-complex principle: that children acquire simpler, relationally compositional constructions before more complex ones.

There is an additional factor that may come into play in all three observations made in (1): the frequency with which constructions occur in the language environment of the child. Perhaps the child hears *what*-questions more often than *who*-questions, *where*-questions more often than *what*-questions, and subject wh-questions more often than object wh questions. Obtaining reliable data on frequency of occurrence in ambient speech is very problematic and thus it is difficult to gauge the significance of frequency. However, even if the acquisitional sequence of various constructions turns out to correlate with the frequency with which they are used in the ambient language, this finding does not negate the simple-before-complex principle. It is presumably simpler for children to learn a construction that they are frequently exposed to than to learn something that they hear infrequently.

We may sum up this section with the following possibly universal hypotheses about the role that means and ends play in language acquisition:

(3) (a) In all languages, children acquire constructions that they need before they acquire constructions that they do not need.

(b) In all languages, children acquire simpler (and/or more frequently heard) constructions before they acquire more complex ones.

5 Conclusions

While Chapters 2–5 focused on syntactic patterns mainly in single-language contexts, in this chapter, we considered syntax across languages and across language stages. We saw that three main statement types – existential statements and restricted and unrestricted universals – are the basic tools in generalizing over sentences of different languages, just as they are in generalizing over sentences of a single language.

In Charles Dickens' novel *A Christmas Carol*, the Ghost of Christmas Past guides Scrooge back into his childhood. When Scrooge sees a young boy left alone in the empty school building after all the other children returned to their families for the holidays and he realizes that the boy is his former self, compassion blossoms in his crusty old heart not only for the young Scrooge but also for the little boy that had stopped by his office the night before and broke into a Christmas carol only to be ruthlessly chased away. By recognizing himself in his own past self, Scrooge comes to recognize himself in another human being. Barriers between present and past and between self and other melt away.

This is the kind of experience that is impressed upon us as we study variation and change in language. Russian with its rich inflectional system and multiple agreement and government structures may appear to be completely different from English; and so may Vietnamese with its lack of inflection. But the Russian structures of today are not so different from what Old English had a thousand years ago; and the Vietnamese type of grammar may be the one that English is headed towards.

Notes

Section 2   Variation and change: some possibilities

- For overall discussions of language typology, see for example Comrie 1989; Croft 1990; Lyovin 1997; Ramat 1987; Song 2001; Whaley 1997. For a vast collection of universal and typological statements proposed in the literature, consult the Konstanz Universals Archive at http://ling.uni-konstanz. de/pages/proj/Sprachbau.htm Cross-linguistic patterns may go back to various reasons including common genetic origin and areal influence. For comprehensive discussions, see Nichols 1992; Nettle 1999.
- For the distinction between syntagmatic and paradigmatic implications, see Bakker 1994: 24–5. Note that the type of implication we labelled reflexive is dubbed 'provision' in the Konstanz Universals Archive mentioned above.
- For a discussion of complex implicantia and complex implicata, see also Chapter 3 (Section 2) and Hammond *et al.* 1988: 4–8.

Section 3.1   Verb agreement
For examples of verb agreement with other arguments, see Lehmann 1982; Corbett forthcoming.

Section 3.2   Constituent order
For typological generalizations about constituent order, see Dryer 1992; Hawkins 1994.

Section 3.3   Accusative and ergative systems
For discussions of mixed accusative and ergative languages, see for example Comrie 1978; Moravcsik 1978b; Dixon 1994; Plank 1979, 1995.

Section 4.1   The historical evolution of definite articles

- On the forms, functions, cross-linguistic distribution and historical evolution of definite articles, see Krámský 1972; Dryer

1989; Harris and Campbell 1995: 341–2; Diessel 1999: 128–9; Heine and Kuteva 2002: 109–11; Rijkhoff 2002: 185–94.

- In spelling Old English interdental fricatives, we deviate from the use of the special symbol called the 'thorn' and use *th* instead.
- On definite articles arising from numeral classifiers and verbs, see Rijkhoff 2002: 186. On demonstratives turning into something other than a definite article, see Diessel 1999: 118–50; Heine and Kuteva 2002: 106–16.

Section 4.2   The first-language acquisition of wh-questions
The discussion about wh-questions follows Chapter 7 of O'Grady 1997.

Exercises

1. Work out the schematic structure of the following cross-linguistic generalizations taken from Joseph Greenberg's classic paper on language universals (1963) and identify their kinds according to the typology of cross-linguistic generalizations summarized at the end of Section 2.

(a)   'All languages with dominant VSO order have SVO as an alternative or the only alternative basic order' (#6).

(b)   'Question particles of affixes, specified in position by reference to a particular word in the sentence, almost always follow that word. Such particles do not occur in languages with dominant VSO order' (#10).

(c)   'If the verb has categories of person-number or if it has categories of gender, it always has tense-mode categories' (#30).

(d)   'If either the subject or object noun agrees with the verb in gender, then the adjective always agrees with the noun in gender' (#31).

(e)   'Whenever the verb agrees with a nominal subject or nominal object in gender, it also agrees in number' (#32).

(f)   'A language never has more gender categories in nonsingular numbers than in the singular' (#37).

2. Zebras have striped bodies and striped tails; leopards have spotted bodies and spotted tails; civets have spotted bodies and striped tails; but there are no animals known to have striped bodies and spotted tails. Construct a table with the logical possibilities of the distribution of striped and spotted bodies and tails and state an implicational universal.

3. Construct a typology of cuisines – the cooking styles of various countries. Are there any unrestricted and typological universals regarding inventories of individual food ingredients in a cooking style, ingredients that can be selected to make a food, and foods that make up cuisines?

4. The English indefinite article *a(n)* has historically evolved from the numeral *one*. Find other languages where the indefinite article is similar in form to the numeral 'one' and where presumably the same process has taken place.

5. Here is a set of data from Luiseño (adapted from Langacker 1972: 69). It contains both transitive and intransitive sentences.

(a)   Is case marking accusative or ergative?

(b)   Is verb agreement accusative or ergative?

(c)   Most verb have two alternative stem forms. Is their distribution accusative or ergative?

1. *nóo pókwaq*	'I am running.'
2. *nóo kwótaq*	'I am getting up.'
3. *čáam ŋóoraan*	'We are running.'
4. *čáam waráavaan*	'We are getting up.'
5. *húnwut pókwaq*	'The bear is running.'
6. *ʔehéŋmay wíilaq*	'The bird is flying.'
7. *húnwutum ŋóoraan*	'The bears are running.'
8. *ʔehéŋmayum wáapaan*	'The birds are flying.'
9. *nóo húnwuti tóowq*	'I see the bear.'
10. *nóo húnwuti móqnaq*	'I am killing the bear.'
11. *nóo húnwuti wótiq*	'I am hitting the bear.'
12. *nóo qeʔéeq húnwutumi*	'I am killing the bears.'
13. *čáam tóowwun ʔehéŋmayi*	'We see the bird.'
14. *čáam móqnawun húnwuti*	'We are killing the bear.'
15. *čáam wótiwun húnwuti*	'We are hitting the bear.'
16. *čáam wuváʔnawun ʔehéŋmayumi*	'We are hitting the birds.'
17. *húnwut néy tóowq*	'The bear sees us.'
18. *húnwut wuváʔnaq čáami*	'The bear is hitting us.'
19. *húnwutum čáami tóowwun*	'The bears see us.'
20. *húnwutum ʔehéŋmayumi qeʔéewun*	'The bears are killing the birds.'

Chapter Seven

Explaining Syntax

We do not only wish to know **how** Nature is (and **how** her processes develop) but also wish, if possible, to arrive at the perhaps utopian and pretentious-seeming goal to know **why** Nature is as it is and not otherwise. In this domain lie the highest satisfactions of the scientist.

(Albert Einstein, cited in Pais 1994: 131–2; emphasis original)

1 Preliminaries

The central topic of the preceding chapters was the description of syntactic patterns. However, our ultimate goal is not just to describe syntax but to understand why the patterns are the way they are. Let us see whether our discussions provided any answers to this further question.

Recall what we mean by explanation. As seen in Chapter 1 (Section 2.1), asking for an explanation means searching for a way to close the gap between observation and expectation. We ask a why-question when we observe something that is unexpected: we see it as likely but not necessary, or as possible but not likely, or as not even possible. Permissive explanations bring the impossible into the realm of possibilities, probabilistic explanations make things likely although not necessary; and nomological explanations render observed facts necessary.

As we now review the preceding chapters for explanatory content, the first thing to note is that the syntactic patterns discussed were formulated at **different levels of generality**. Some of them concerned very specific facts about a language, such as that in English, the verb *be content* governs *with*. Others were patterns that held for entire syntactic categories of a language; for example, that in English, the present-tense verb agrees with the subject in person and number, or that in Turkish, the order of major sentence constituents is SOV. And some patterns applied across languages: that all known languages have constraints on the linear order of syntactic constituents, or that grammaticalization is a recurrent type of change in language history.

All these generalizations have some explanatory force. Consider the following example:

(1) *Jerome is content with his job.*

The fact that this particular sentence includes the preposition *with* follows from the fact that *be content* must take a *with*-complement. That the sentence has the word *is* in it follows from the fact that present-tense English verbs must agree with their subjects. And the generalization that all languages have some constraints on the order of words renders it likely – although not necessary – that in this particular English sentence, word order is not free.

Although all generalizations have some explanatory force, they differ in their scope – that is, in the range of facts that are derivable from them. A particular fact about a particular word in a given sentence may thus be explained on different levels: it may be given a low-level explanation by a generalization that applies to all occurrences of that word in the language; a higher-level explanation by a statement that applies to the entire category in that language that the lexical item belongs to; and an explanation on an even higher level if it is derivable from a generalization that holds across languages. Generalizations that apply to categories of a language are more powerful than those that apply to individual lexical items; and generalizations that apply across languages are more powerful than those that hold only for a single language.

A second thing to note about the syntactic statements in the preceding chapters is that they also differed in whether they were **permissive, probabilistic** or **nomological**. The generalization stated in Chapter 2 (Section 3.2.3), according to which syntactic constituents may be ordered into numerical positions (such as first or second) is a permissive generalization. That definite articles mostly evolve from demonstratives is a probabilistic one (Chapter 6, Section 4.1). And the claim that if in a language the verb agrees with the direct object, it also agrees with the subject is exceptionless for the languages that have been examined in this respect and it is therefore a nomological generalization (Chapter 6, Section 3.1).

In addition to explanatory scope and explanatory force, there is a third way in which the generalizations that have been discussed differ. Recall how we explained the fact that the verb in Lebanese Arabic agrees with the subject. This fact was shown to be derivable from the restricted paradigmatic universal mentioned above: that if the verb agrees with the direct object in a language, so does the subject. Here we explained a structural fact with a structural generalization. This is an example of **structural explanations**.

The argument regarding why there is verb agreement to begin with as given in Chapter 3 (Section 4) was different. The explanation took us out of synchronic structure and explained verb agreement as the result of a historical process: grammaticalization. This is an example of a **historical explanation**.

Now recall how we accounted for how children acquire the various kinds of wh-questions in English. The acquisitional sequence seemed to fall out of two assumptions: children first learn what they need most and what they can acquire most easily. This explanation relies on something outside both synchronic language structure and language history: it appeals to the goals and means of the language user. It is a **functional explanation**.

The three kinds of explanations may be illustrated from outside linguistics as well. First, suppose we want to explain why sparrows have wings. One way to do this is by noting that all birds have wings. In this example, a property of the body of one kind of bird is explained by that property holding for all bird bodies. This is thus a structural explanation.

Second, the existence of wings on sparrows might be explained by noting that millions of years ago, sparrows did not have wings but had an additional pair of legs which, as result of some principles of anatomical evolution, turned into wings. Or we can explain the existence of sparrow wings by reference to the embryonic development that sparrow foetuses undergo. Either way, the explanatory principles have to do with change from an earlier stage, whether historical or developmental. We will use the cover term 'evolutionary' for both historical and developmental explanations.

Third, if we take it as given that sparrows must be able to move over long distances through the air, the existence of wings is explained by the fact that the only way for an animal to propel itself by air over great distances is through the use of wings. Here, the existence of a structural feature is rendered inevitable by reference to the function of this structural element. This is an example of a functional explanation.

Here is an analogous syntactic example illustrating all three kinds of explanatory approaches pertaining to the same fact. To explain why the word *a(n)* precedes the noun in English, we can refer to the fact that *a(n)* is an article, that articles are determiners and that all English determiners – that is, not only the articles *a(n)* and *the* but also the demonstratives *this, these, that* and *those* – precede their nouns. In this case, a fact about the ordering of a word is explained by its membership in a word category in which all members are ordered the same way. The explanation is structural in that the explanans appeals to a structural category: determiner.

Alternatively, the same fact of *a(n)* preceding the noun can be explained by noting that the historical source of *a(n)* is the numeral *one*, which preceded the noun in Old English just as it does today. If we can assume that words that undergo a category change – in this case, from numeral to article – do not alter their linear position, we have provided a evolutionary explanation for our explanandum.

A third approach to explaining the pre-nominal position of the indefinite article in English is by noting that Art & N order tends to correlate cross-linguistically with V & O order (Dryer 1989; 1992: 103–4). This is predicted by a hypothesis by Matthew Dryer.

Dryer proposes that languages tend to place all branching – i.e. multiword – constituents either before all non-branching (single-word) ones or after all branching ones. In the verb–object construction, verbs do not branch but objects do. In the article–nominal construction, articles are like verbs: they are one-word and thus non-branching constituents, but the nominal they precede, like the verb's object, may include more than just the noun – adjectives, relative clauses and other modifiers. English is a non-branching-before-branching language: since verbs precede their nominals, the order of articles before nouns is predicted by the hypothesis.

This so far is a structural explanation for why *a(n)* precedes the nominal in English. But, as Dryer suggests (1992: 128–32), the fact that languages tend to exhibit uniform ordering for branching and non-branching constituents may in turn be explained functionally: 'structures with a consistent direction of branching are easier to process than structures that involve a mixture of left- and right-branching' (1992: 133). This explanation is functional because it makes reference to the language user's goals – to produce and comprehend sentences with ease – and his limited resources in achieving these goals.

The next three sections will expand on the three types of explanations: structural, evolutionary and functional, and will provide two more detailed syntactic examples for each. The explanatory arguments will be made explicit through highlighting the three components of explanations seen in Chapter 1 (Section 2.1): the explanandum (a statement of what needs to be explained), the explanans (at least one general principle) and the bridge statement that states the connection between the explanandum and the explanans.

2 Structural explanations

2.1 WH-QUESTIONS IN ENGLISH

In English wh-questions, question words such as *who, what, where, when* and *how* are generally sentence-initial.

(1) (a) ***What*** *did Jim tell the reporter?*
    (b) ***Who*** *did Jim tell the news to?*
    (c) ***Where*** *did you buy this hat?*
    (d) ***When*** *are the cherries going to be ripe?*
    (e) ***How*** *should I cook the rice?*

If you compare the structure of these sentences with the corresponding declarative sentences (*Jim told the news to the reporter, I bought this hat at Macy's,* and so on), you will find that the interrogative structures both include an extra element and lack one. First, the questions in (1) include a question word at the beginning of the sentence that the statements do not. Second, the verbs seem to be missing their complement in the position in which that complement occurs in a statement – that is, following the verb. For example, *tell* generally takes both a direct and indirect object; cf. *Jim told **the news to the reporter;*** but in (1a), *tell* is not followed by a direct object; and in (1b), it is not followed by an indirect object.

Upon further analysis, however, it turns out that the two observations dovetail: what seem to be extra elements in the questions are understood as the missing complements of the verbs. In (1a) for example, the word *what* is understood as the direct object of *tell*. In addition to meaning, there is a syntactic parallelism between the question word and the verb complement: they observe the same selectional constraints relative to the verb. For example, the inanimate form *what* in (1a) questions matches the fact that *tell* takes an inanimate direct object. Similarly, the animacy of the question word *who* in (1b) corresponds to the fact that *tell* takes an animate recipient. In other words, the question words fit the argument frame of the verb even though they do not follow the verb as the corresponding complements do in declarative sentences.

Government and Binding Theory proposes an account of these facts. This framework – a version of Noam Chomsky's Transformational Generative Grammar – assumes that a sentence has not just one but several structural representations with differing partonomic and taxonomic structures and that the representations of a sentence are connected by rules that convert one into another. Regarding wh-questions in English, the theory makes two assumptions. One is that, in the underlying representation, question words occur in their post-verbal complement positions. For example, the underlying structure of (1a) is *(Did) Jim tell the reporter what*. The second assumption is that there is a movement rule that extraposes question words to a sentence-initial slot that is outside the clause proper: *[What [(did) Jim tell the reporter]$_S$]$_S$?* (The formation of these questions also involves the inversion of the subject and an auxiliary verb but we will not discuss this here.)

However, not all wh-questions that would be derived by this analysis turn out to be grammatical: there are limitations on which underlying positions the question words can be moved from. In (2) and (3), blanks show the underlying positions:

(2) (a)   *What do you claim ___ ?*
     (b)   *What do you claim ___ caused the problem?*
     (c)   * *What do you make the claim that ___ caused the problem?*

(3) (a)   *Who did Jill see ___ ?*
     (b)   *Who do you think Jill saw ___ ?*
     (c)   * *Who do you know the park where Jill saw ___ ?*

A plausible reason for the ungrammaticality of the (c)-sentences is that the sentence-initial wh-word has strayed too far from its underlying, semantically appropriate position. But what does 'too far' mean? Notice that it does not simply have to do with the number of intervening words: if we add words to the grammatical sentences in (2b) and (3b) and thus increase the distance between the underlying and surface position of the wh-word, the sentence is still grammatical:

(4) (a) *What would you, the greatest expert on this matter, claim ___ caused the problem?*

(b) *Who do you think and perhaps even know for sure Jill saw ___?*

If not the number of intervening words, then what makes the distance between the underlying and surface positions of wh-words 'too big'? Here is the answer provided by Government and Binding Theory. The structures in (5) sketch the underlying forms of the sentences in (2); a similar analysis holds for (3).

(5) (a) *[You claim **what**]$_S$?*

(b) *[You claim [**what** caused the problem]$_S$]$_S$?*

(c) **[You make [the claim that [**what** caused the problem]$_S$]$_{NP}$]$_S$?*

If we move *what* in (5a) and (5b) to the front, we get grammatical sentences but the same movement of *what* in (5c) leads to ungrammaticality. Note now that in (5a), *what* moves out of its clause to the beginning of the sentence outside the clause: *[**What** [you claim ___]$_S$]$_S$.* In the process, *what* crosses only one major syntactic juncture: the left boundary of the sentence. In (5b), *what* is understood as the subject of an embedded clause. Wh-movement applies twice: first, it moves *what* outside its own clause resulting in *[You claim **what** [caused the problem]$_S$]$_S$?*, and then it moves *what* to the front of the entire sentence. Each time, *what* crosses only one clause boundary.

In (5c), however, the wh-word's trip to the left is more complex. As in (5a) and (5b), it is first moved out of its clause resulting in the structure *[You make [the claim that **what** [caused the problem]$_S$]$_{NP}$]$_S$?* But now, before it gets to cross the left boundary of the entire sentence, it has to cross the left boundary of the noun phrase that its clause is embedded in, resulting in *[**what** [the claim that caused the problem]$_{NP}$]$_S$.* Noting this extra hurdle for the question word to pass in (5c), we can take a first stab at explaining why (2c) is ungrammatical:

(6) A question word cannot move in a single step across both a clause boundary and a noun phrase boundary.

This principle, known as the Complex NP Constraint, originally formulated by John R. Ross in 1967, has considerable explanatory force: the ungrammaticality of various sentences other than (2c) and (3c), all involving the movement of a question word out of a noun phrase and a clause, follows from it. For example, it also explains the ungrammaticality of the following:

(7) (a)   *What* *did you catch a rabbit and?*
    (b)   *Who* *did John talk to Mary and?*

The underlying structures of these sentences can be sketched as follows:

(8) (a)   *[You caught [a rabbit and* **what***]ₙₚ]ₛ*
    (b)   *[John talked to [Mary and* **who***]ₙₚ]ₛ*

In these sentences, the underlying position of the wh-word is an immediate constituent of a noun phrase: *[a rabbit and* **what***]ₙₚ* and *[Mary and* **who***]ₙₚ*. As in (5c), when the question word moves left, it crosses both the left boundary of a noun phrase and the left boundary of the sentence that it will end up preceding. By doing so, it violates (6). The ungrammaticality of (7a) and (7b) is thus explained by the Complex NP Constraint, just as the ungrammaticality of (2c) and (3c) is.

But the constraint is even more general. Consider the following passive sentences.

(9) (a)   **John** *was invited to Mary's house.*
    (b)   **John** *seems to have been invited to Mary's house.*
    (c)   **John** *seems that it is likely to be invited to Mary's house.*

Here are sketches of the underlying structures as posited in Government and Binding Theory.

(10) (a)   *[Was invited* **John** *to Mary's house.]ₛ*
     (b)   *[Seems [to have been invited* **John** *to Mary's house.]ₛ]ₛ*
     (c)   *[Seems that [it is likely [to be invited* **John** *to Mary's house.]ₛ]ₛ]ₛ*

The movement of the direct object *John* differs from wh-movement in two ways. First, what moves here is not a question pronoun but a full noun phrase (*John*). Second, the constituent boundaries that are crossed are not the same as in the examples that we have seen so far. The movement of *John* from (10a) to (9a) involves no crossing of any noun phrase or clause boundary (unlike the wh-words, the subject is assumed to be inside the clause). The movement of *John* from (10b) to (9b) involves the crossing of a single boundary of a clause: *[to have been invited John to Mary's house]ₛ*. But the movement of *John* out of its underlying structure in (10c) involves the crossing of two clause boundaries: the left boundary of the clause *[to be invited . . .]ₛ* and the left boundary of the clause *[it is likely to . . .]ₛ*.

Thus, if we expand the statement of the Complex NP Constraint in (6) so that it applies not only to question words but also to constituents in general and so that it bars not only the crossing of a clause and a noun phrase boundary but also the crossing of two clause boundaries, the ungrammaticality of (9c) is accounted for. In the resulting expanded version stated in (11), 'major constituent boundary' is a cover term for clause and noun phrase boundary.

> (11) A constituent cannot move in a single step across more than one major constituent boundary.

This principle is called **Subjacency**. The name comes from the fact that the principle requires that the moved element be directly 'lying under' (or 'be subjacent to') its landing site rather than being in a more distant relationship to it.

Here is the summary of the explanatory argument presented above:

EXPLANANDUM
Sentences such as *What do you make the claim that ___ caused the problem?* ((2c) above) are ungrammatical.

EXPLANATORY PRINCIPLE ((11) above)
Subjacency: a constituent cannot move in a single step across more than one major constituent boundary.

BRIDGE STATEMENTS
- Question words are constituents; noun phrase and clause are major constituents.
- The formation of wh-questions involves the movement of question words from their underlying positions to the left outside the entire clause.
- In sentences such as (2c), the underlying position of the wh-word and its surface position are separated by two major constituent boundaries.

This explanation is structural: a fact is explained by a generalization about structure; and it is nomological since the explanatory principle is stated in absolute, non-probabilistic terms.

For the past 50 years, structural explanations have been the focus of syntactic research. In addition to Government and Binding, there are many other approaches each opting for different ways of providing structural explanations for syntactic facts. (For a survey of the large number of contemporary theoretical frameworks, see for example Brown and Miller 1996.)

2.2 RELATIVE CLAUSES IN BASQUE

Relative clauses modify noun phrases by describing their referents. For example, in *Jill liked the cat that ran away*, the relative clause *that ran away* describes the head noun *the cat*: the cat referred to by the head noun is the same as the one that ran away. Relative clauses thus must include reference to the head noun.

In *Jill liked the cat that ran away*, reference to the head noun is made by the subject of the relative clause: the cat is the one that ran away. This is not always the case: reference to the head noun can be made by the object of the relative clause, as in *Jill liked the cat that Joe had given to her*. Here, the cat is understood as the direct object of the relative clause.

In addition to subjects and direct objects, relative clauses may be formed on any other constituent of the relative clause; that is, any constituent of the relative clause is 'relativizable'. This is illustrated in (1):

(1) (a) SUBJECT IS RELATIVIZED
     *the man **who** has given the book to the woman*

   (b) DIRECT OBJECT IS RELATIVIZED
     *the book **which** the man has given to the woman*

   (c) INDIRECT OBJECT IS RELATIVIZED
     *the woman **to whom** the man has given the book*

   (d) ADVERBIAL PHRASE IS RELATIVIZED
     *the book **with which** the man replaced the notebook*

   (e) GENITIVE IS RELATIVIZED
     *the book **whose** cover was designed by the man*

   (f) STANDARD OF COMPARISON IS RELATIVIZED
     *the book **which** the newspaper article is better than*

While in English, all six constituent types are relativizable, this is not so in all languages. Basque has relative clauses formed on subject, direct object and indirect object but not on adverbial phrases, genitives and standards of comparison. This is shown in (2). Note that Basque relative clauses precede the head and that they do not involve a relative pronoun but have an invariant relative clause marker on the verb, functioning somewhat like English *-ing*. For example, (2a) means 'the man who has given the book to the woman', but its more literal translation is 'the to-the-woman the-book having-given man'. In the examples below, the head and the relative marker are in bold.

(2) (a) SUBJECT IS RELATIVIZED
     *emakume-a-ri   liburu-a eman dio-**n**   **gizon-a***
     woman-the-IO book-the give has-**REL man-the**
     'the man who has given the book to the woman'

(b) DIRECT OBJECT IS RELATIVIZED
    *gizon-a-k   emakume-a-ri   eman dio-n   **liburu-a***
    man-the-SBJ woman-the-IO give has-**REL book-the**
    'the book which the man has given to the woman'

(c) INDIRECT OBJECT IS RELATIVIZED
    *gizon-a-k   liburu-a   eman dio-n   **emakume-a***
    man-the-SBJ book-the give has-**REL woman-the**
    'the woman to whom the man has given the book'

These examples correspond to the English examples in (1a–c). There are no Basque equivalents of (1d–f).

Why does Basque not have the full range of relative clauses that English does? The explanandum can be stated as in (3).

(3) In Basque, subjects, direct objects and indirect objects can be relativized but adverbial phrases, genitives and standards of comparison cannot.

A partial explanation is offered by an observation made by Edward Keenan and Bernard Comrie (1977). They have found that there are many languages that, like Basque, do not allow the relativization of all constituent types; and, furthermore, that the range of relativizable constituents was determined by general constraints. One of the constraints is stated in (4). Keenan and Comrie use the term 'oblique object' for what we called adverbial phrase above.

(4) In all languages, if a constituent type is relativizable, all other constituent types to its left on the Accessibility Hierarchy are also relativizable.

Accessibility Hierarchy:

SUBJECT	DIRECT OBJECT	INDIRECT OBJECT	OBLIQUE OBJECT	GENITIVE	STANDARD OF COMPARISON

The Accessibility Hierarchy is a chain involving a set of absolute typological implications of the paradigmatic sort (cf. Chapter 6 (Section 2)). It says that if in a language, standards of comparison are relativizable, so are genitives; if genitives are relativizable, so are oblique objects; and so on. In its logical structure, it is similar to the scale used to predict controllers of verb agreement (Chapter 6 (Section 3.1)).

The scale in (4) allows for some language types while excluding others. The following six language types are ruled in:

TYPE 1   languages where only **subjects** are relativizable
TYPE 2   languages where only **subjects and direct objects** are relativizable
TYPE 3   languages where only **subjects, direct objects and indirect objects** are relativizable
TYPE 4   languages where only **subjects, direct objects, indirect objects and oblique objects** are relativizable
TYPE 5   languages where only **subjects, direct objects, indirect objects, oblique objects and genitives** are relativizable
TYPE 6   languages where **subjects, direct objects, indirect objects, oblique objects, genitives and standards of comparison** are relativizable

English is of Type 6; Basque is of Type 3. The number of excluded language types is very large; for example, languages where subjects and genitives but no other sentence parts are relativizable; or languages where only direct objects and obliques are.

How does the Keenan–Comrie generalization in (4) explain the fact that in Basque, only Subject, Direct Object and Indirect Object are relativizable? First, it predicts the relativizability of direct objects from the relativizability of indirect objects. Second, it explains why subjects are relativizable since this in turn follows from the relativizability of direct objects.

Note, however, that the Accessibility Hierarchy does not explain every-thing about Basque relative clauses. First, note that we have no explanation for why indirect objects are relativizable in Basque. The relativizability of this constituent type would be predicted only if some lower-ranking constituent type – adverbial phrases or genitives or standards of comparison – would also be relativizable in the language; but this is not the case. Second, the expla-nation does not tell us why Basque stops at indirect objects in the hierarchy while English, for example, does not. In other words, a link between the rel-ativization constraint and other grammatical properties of Basque is missing.

In sum, here is the explanatory argument:

EXPLANANDUM ((3) above)
In Basque, subjects, direct objects and indirect objects can be relativized but adverbial phrases, genitives and standards of comparison cannot.

EXPLANATORY PRINCIPLE ((4) above)
In all languages, if a constituent type is relativizable, all other constituent types to its left on the Accessibility Hierarchy are also relativizable.

Accessibility Hierarchy:

SUBJECT	DIRECT OBJECT	INDIRECT OBJECT	OBLIQUE OBJECT	GENITIVE	STANDARD OF COMP- ARISON

BRIDGE STATEMENTS
In Basque, indirect objects are relativizable.

The explanatory principle is a restricted universal of the paradigmatic sort and it is stated as an absolute, nomological principle.

3 Evolutionary explanations

In contemplating synchronic structural principles for explaining word order universals, Joan Bybee remarks (1988: 352): 'My own intuitions about explanations are not satisfied by such principles, however, unless they provide answers to the "how" question – how do such generalizations arise in language? What are the mechanisms that bring the state of affairs about?' In other words, Bybee is asking not just for reasons but for **causes** of synchronic phenomena.

As discussed in Section 1, evolutionary explanations may be historical or developmental. Within each, there are three further options. For an analogous example, consider an old painting of a woman with green hair. How did the green paint get there? One explanation would be that the artist painted the hair green to begin with. In other words, things may be the way they are because they have always been that way. Another possible explanation is that somebody smeared green paint on the original colour. The explanation in this case is by reference to intervention, or forced change. Third, the original yellow paint may have spontaneously turned green in the course of time.

In what follows, two examples of evolutionary explanation will be presented, one historical and one developmental. For each explanandum, we will explore the three avenues of evolutionary explanation: appeal to no change or to forced change or to spontaneous change.

3.1 DIRECT OBJECTS IN FRENCH

In English, all direct objects – whether nominal or pronominal – follow the verb, as in (1):

(1) (a) *Bill has swallowed **a fly**.*
    (b) *Bill has swallowed **it**.*

French is different in this respect: the noun object follows the verb just like in English but the pronominal object precedes it (cf. Chapter 4, Section 3.3.2). In (2) are given the French equivalents of (1).

(2) (a) *Bill a   avalé   **une mouche.***
         Bill has swallowed **a   fly**

    (b) *Bill l'-a   avalée.*
         Bill **it**-has swallowed

What explains the differential behaviour of noun objects and pronoun objects in French? Here is our explanandum.

(3) In French, noun objects follow the verb and pronominal objects precede it.

Note first that the pattern is not unique to French: noun and pronoun objects differ the same way in some other Romance languages as well. In (4) and (5) there are examples from Spanish and Brazilian Portuguese:

(4) SPANISH
    (a) *Yo compré **los libros.***   'I bought the books.'
         I   bought **the books**

    (b) *Yo **los**   compré.*   'I bought them.'
         I   **them** bought.

(5) BRAZILIAN PORTUGUESE
    (a) *Vi   a   **Juan.***   'I see John.'
         I:see **PREP John**

    (b) ***Lo**   vi.*   'I see him.'
         him I:see

A similar pattern can be documented in languages outside the Romance family. In Swahili, nominal objects follow the verb but pronominal objects are prefixed to it.

(6) SWAHILI
    (a) *Ni-li-ona   **kitabu.***   'I saw the book.'
         S1-PAST-see **book**

    (b) *Ni-li-**ki**-ona.*   'I saw it.'
         S1-PAST-***it***-see

Old English, too, tended to place pronominal objects before the verb while nominal objects generally followed the verb as they do in today's English.

(7) OLD ENGLISH (Traugott 1972: 89)
  *he **him*** * hamweard ferde to his agnum rice*
  he **him(self)** homeward took to his own   kingdom
  'He went (betook himself) to his own kingdom.'

Such observations have led Joseph Greenberg to the following generalization: 'If in a language, the pronominal object follows the verb, so does
the nominal object' (1963: 25). In other words, there may be languages
where both noun and pronoun objects follow the verb (as in Modern
English) and languages where both precede the verb (as in Turkish).
However, if one follows the verb and the other precedes it, it is always the
pronoun that precedes, not the noun.

Here we have structural principles of increasing scope. The rule which
states that pronominal objects in French are pre-verbal and nominal objects
are post-verbal has explanatory value itself but it is restricted to French. If
we state a joint rule for a subset of Romance languages (French, Spanish and
Brazilian Portuguese), we gain added explanatory mileage since the new
rule predicts the relevant ordering in three languages. And Greenberg's
typological implication is even more general since it predicts pre-verbal
pronominal objects for an entire universe of languages: for all of those that
have prenominal noun objects.

Could Greenberg's rule be derived from an even higher-level generalization? On the one hand, we might look for a further generalization of the
structural sort, stated on more comprehensive categories of which nouns,
pronouns and verbs are subtypes. Another possibility would be to look for a
functional explanation by searching for some difference between the functions of nouns and pronouns that would account for their differential linear
positions. Neither of these options has been explored in the literature; but
a third has been. A look into the past history of French and the other languages that exhibit this pattern offers a clue.

As discussed in the beginning of this section, historical explanations may
be of three kinds depending on whether they claim no change, forced
change or spontaneous change. In this case, a **no-change theory** would say
that French has the order it does because 'this is what it always had'. But this
argument does not hold. French, along with the other Romance languages,
is historically derived from Latin where both nominal and pronominal
objects were generally pre-verbal. Thus, a change has taken place.

A second option is a hypothesis of **forced change** – some external factor
that would have brought about the change, such as the influence of another
language. But no such external influence can be detected to explain this
particular word order change in Romance.

We are left with the third option: explaining the French ordering pattern
by reference to a general principle of **spontaneous language change**. As
noted above, there is evidence that French and the other Romance languages – all daughters of Latin – started out with a uniformly pre-verbal order
for all objects. This order has also been reconstructed for Proto-Germanic –

the parent language of English – as well as for Proto-Bantu from which Swahili is derived. We can posit the following three stages of the historical process (O_N stands for noun object, O_{Pr} stands for pronominal object; changes are in bold):

ORDER PATTERNS: NOUN OBJECT	PRONOUN OBJECT	LANGUAGES: ROMANCE	GERMANIC	BANTU
Stage I SO_NV	$SO_{Pr}V$	Latin	Proto-Germanic	Proto-Bantu
Stage II **SVO_N**	$SO_{Pr}V$	French Italian Spanish Brazilian Portuguese	Old English	Swahili
Stage III SVO_N	**SVO_{Pr}**	–	Modern English	–

What this says is that a change from pre-verbal to post-verbal order of objects occurred in all three language families and that in each case, nominal objects were in the vanguard with pronominal objects lagging behind. English, however, has completed the change by extending it to pronominal objects as well. Thus, the French pattern – along with that of Italian, Spanish, Brazilian Portuguese, Old English and Swahili – can be explained by the hypothesis that in word order change, pronouns are more conservative than nouns.

But is there independent support for the claim that in historical change, pronouns lag behind nouns? There is. For an example, consider the loss of gender and case of English nominals. In Old English, both nouns and pronouns had case, gender and number inflection. In today's English, nouns still show number but they have no case inflection except for the genitive clitic *'s*, and they have lost their gender inflection entirely. Personal pronouns, however, still retain not only number but also some gender and case distinctions, such as *he* versus *she*, and *he* versus *him*. The same thing happened in French regarding case: nouns have lost case distinctions but personal pronouns have retained them.

These facts independently motivate the principle according to which pronouns are slower to change than nouns, whether involving word order or inflection. This principle thus serves to explain the differential order patterns of pronominal and nominal objects in French and other languages on a fairly high level.

Notice, however, that the explanation proposed does not explain everything. We have not explained why French – along with the other Romance, Germanic and Bantu languages – changed their object–verb order at all, rather than keeping SOV both for nouns and pronouns – a pattern that is familiar from Turkish, Japanese and many other languages. Nor have we explained why, once French and English began to change to post-verbal object order, the process was arrested in French at the point where nouns have undergone it but pronouns have not, while in English the change has been completed. In other words, our explanation renders the change permissible but not necessary or even probable.

This is typical of historical explanations. They can restrict the range of changes that will take place – provided they do happen at all and whenever they do. Given a source structure, they can limit the kinds of structures that it will change into; and given a later target structure, they predict the range of source structures that it could have come from. But principles of historical change cannot predict that a change will take place and if so, when it will begin and whether and when it will be completed. Just as we cannot be sure when a demonstrative of a language will evolve into a definite article or whether it ever will (cf. Chapter 6 (Section 4.1), we cannot be sure when the SOV order in a language will begin to change to SVO – or whether it ever will.

In sum, here is the explanatory argument:

> **EXPLANANDUM** ((3) above)
> In French, noun objects follow the verb and pronominal objects precede it.
>
> **EXPLANATORY PRINCIPLE**
> Historical change affects nouns before affecting pronouns.
>
> **BRIDGE STATEMENTS**
> - At an earlier stage, French placed both nominal and pronominal objects in front of the verb.
> - A change of placing objects after the verb then began.
> - French has not completed the change for all objects.

Next, we will turn to an explanation that also posits change, not on a macro-level, but within the life span of an individual human being.

3.2 DIRECT AND INDIRECT OBJECTS IN ENGLISH

In English, some sentences with three-place predicates have two alternative expressions:

(1) (a) *Sue gave a silver tray* **to her church**.
    (b) *Sue gave* **her church** *a silver tray*.

    (a) *Bill told the news* **to his friend**.
    (b) *Bill told* **his friend** *the news*.

(a)   *Felix showed his thesis **to his adviser**.*
(b)   *Felix showed **his adviser** his thesis.*

(a)   *Paula baked a pudding **for her dolls**.*
(b)   *Paula baked **her dolls** a pudding.*

The alternative patterns differ in two ways. Let us label the verb complements by their semantic participant roles. The noun phrase expressing the
directly affected referent will be called Theme, and the noun phrase for
whom the act is carried out is the Recipient. One difference between the (a)
and (b) sentences is word order: in each (a)-sentence, the two occur in the
order Theme & Recipient while in (b), the order is reversed. The other difference is selectional: the Recipient has a preposition (to or for) in each (a)-
sentence but not in (b). Here are the two schemata:

(2)   (a)   VERB & THEME & **PREPOSITION & RECIPIENT**
     (b)   VERB & **RECIPIENT** & THEME

We will refer to pattern (2a) as the **prepositional construction** and to (2b),
as the **double-object construction**.

   Not all three-argument verbs allow for both patterns: there are none that
occur only with double objects but some only occur in the prepositional
construction:

(3)   (a)   *Sue donated a silver tray **to her church**.*
     (b)   **Sue donated **her church** a silver tray.*

(a)   *Bill reported the news **to his friend**.*
(b)   **Bill reported **his friend** the news.*

(a)   *Felix demonstrated his claim **to his adviser**.*
(b)   **Felix demonstrated **his adviser** his claim.*

(a)   *Paula invented a pudding **for her dolls**.*
(b)   **Paula invented **her dolls** a pudding.*

We will refer to such verbs as prepositional verbs; verbs such as *show* and *give*
that occur in both constructions will be called double-object verbs.

   Why can some verbs occur in the double-object construction while others
cannot? We might look for a structural explanation: contrasting semantic or
phonological properties of the two classes of verbs might explain why
members of the two classes behave differently.

   This avenue has indeed been explored in the literature. Although it has
proven to be difficult to find watertight criteria separating double-object
verbs from prepositional ones, there seem to be two factors at work. First,
double-object verbs tend to be of Anglo-Saxon, rather than Latin, origin.

This condition accounts for why Anglo-Saxon *give, tell, show* and *bake* take a double object but not their semantically related Latinate counterparts *donate, report, demonstrate* or *invent*. Second, double-object verbs generally imply a transfer of an object that the Recipient will become the possessor of while non-double-object verbs are non-committal in this regard. Thus, you can *bake somebody a cake* but not **cut somebody a cake*, and you can say *I rent you a boat* but not **I wash you a boat*.

Whatever the crucial structural property that separates double-object verbs from the others, we are still left with the question of the link between that property and the double-object construction. For example, if the operative property of double-object verbs is that the referent of their Recipient becomes the possessor of the referent of the direct object, why should this property make such verbs opt for the double-object construction?

In search of an answer to this question, one might look for functional factors. The adjacency of the Recipient to the verb may iconically signal the Recipient's greater affectedness by the action in the sense that he actually comes to possess the object that is being transferred. Another option is to take a historical perspective and explore how the two classes of verbs have come to be associated with the alternative patterns in the course of the history of English.

But even if we could find successful structural and historical explanations for the facts, a further question would still remain: just how do individual speakers of English learn which verbs take which construction? This is the issue that will now be addressed. Here is the explanandum:

(4) English speakers know which verbs can take double objects.

In ontogeny, just as in phylogeny, there are three kinds of possible answer to consider. First, one might suppose that the requisite pattern 'was there to begin with'. In the present case, this would mean (5):

(5) THE INNATENESS HYPOTHESIS
Information about which English verbs can take double
objects is innate in children learning English.

However, (5) cannot be true: the grammars of particular languages are not genetically transmitted from parent to offspring. Suppose a child is born to Thai-speaking parents and is adopted by English-speaking parents. Even though Thai does not have verbs that take the double-object construction, the child will learn which are the double-object verbs in English just as any child born to English-speaking parents does. Thus, English-speaking children cannot have received from their parents' genes that, say, *give* is a double-object verb but *donate* is not.

Another version of the innateness hypothesis might be that all grammatical patterns of all languages are innate in children.

(6) THE REVISED INNATENESS HYPOTHESIS
Information about which verbs can take double objects
in any language is innate in all children regardless of
what language they are learning.

Under this hypothesis, the child's acquisition of his language would not
amount to learning new grammatical patterns but rather to suppressing
those patterns that are innately available to him but which do not happen
to be present in his ambient language.

But this version of the innateness hypothesis is not supported by the facts,
either. If it were correct, we would expect all children to use these innate
patterns immediately as they begin to speak. For example, children acquiring English should immediately use the double-object construction with
just those verbs that take it but not with others. This prediction is not borne
out: at the early stages, children make mistakes. Here are some examples
(Bowerman 1988: 79; see also Pinker 1996: 312–13) showing prepositional
verbs *say, whisper, choose, button* and *open* used erroneously in double-object
constructions by a child who is acquiring American English.

(7) (a) *I said her 'no'.*
     (b) *Don't say me that or you'll make me cry.*
     (c) *Shall I whisper you something?*
     (d) *Choose me the ones that I can have.*
     (e) *Button me the rest.* (Request to have remaining snaps on the
          child's pyjamas fastened.)
     (f) *Mommy, open Hadwen the door.*

If knowledge about double-object verbs were readily available for the child
upon birth, no errors of this kind could occur.

Provided the requisite knowledge about double-object verbs is not 'there
to begin with' in babies' minds, we might turn to the second type of evolutionary explanation and hypothesize that this knowledge gets there by external intervention. In language history, this line of explanation posits the
influence of another language: one language takes a prestigious language
as a model and imitates it. In individual development, the intervention idea
corresponds to caretakers teaching children grammatical patterns. The
hypothesis is stated in (8):

(8) THE INTERVENTION HYPOTHESIS
Information about which English verbs can take double objects is
taught to children.

However, this guess also fails in the light of evidence. Adults rarely coach
children on points of grammar and when they do, children generally resist:
they are likely to continue to use mistaken forms in spite of their parents'
patient efforts to teach them otherwise.

This leaves the third possible avenue of evolutionary explanation for how English children come to know double-object constructions, stated in (9):

(9) THE DEVELOPMENTAL HYPOTHESIS
Information about which verbs can take double objects in English is acquired by children through spontaneous development.

What does 'spontaneous development' mean? 'Development' cannot start from nothing nor can it take place in a vacuum: something must be there to begin with which subsequently evolves under external influence. The developmental hypothesis thus assumes the presence of two components: something that child brings with him and something that comes from outside. The claim is that children grow into their language by gradually extracting the grammar from the ambient language data with the help of their innate cognitive capabilities. The hypothesis thus adopts elements from both the Innateness Hypotheses and the Intervention Hypothesis considered above: it relies on the interaction between 'nature' – innate capacity – and 'nurture' – the effect of the environment.

What exactly should be assumed to be innate and what exactly comes from the environment? The second question is easier to answer: what comes from the environment is the ambient language. The importance of the linguistic environment is clearly shown by the fact that children invariably learn the language that they are surrounded by and that children who are deprived of language do not learn it.

The other question – what are the innate properties that foster language acquisition? – is more difficult to answer. That something having to do with our ability to learn language must be innate is evidenced by the simple fact that human babies learn language but, say, kittens or chimps do not, even if raised in the same environment. Is it the overall ability to learn language that is innate or is it that some actual components of human language grammar are innately available to all children by virtue of their humanness?

Let us assume the second option: that some concrete grammatical properties are universally innate. What might they be? We have already seen that they cannot be specific grammatical patterns that vary across languages. According to Noam Chomsky, it is the language-universal, rather than language-particular, aspects of grammar that are genetically given. This knowledge forms a uniform blueprint for human languages. It includes knowing that sentences have partonomic, taxonomic and symbolic structure, as well as more detailed language properties, such as Subjacency (see Section 2.1 of this chapter). Whether these innate language universals are specific to linguistic competence or whether they are more general so that they apply to other aspects of human cognition as well – such as vision, hearing and spatial orientation – is a debated issue among psychologists.

Let us now try to sketch the process of a child acquiring the double-object construction in English. What is given is some innate knowledge –

something that child is born with – and the linguistic input that he is born into. How might the process begin?

In addition to innate linguistic knowledge, there are two very general psychological tendencies pervading general human – and even some animal – behaviour that can be plausibly assumed to be innate: paying attention to the environment and imitating others' behaviour. These inborn inclinations will make babies pay attention to speech and try to produce what they hear.

But imitating what the child has heard is a long way from his learning a language. There are two additional steps that the child must take. First, children do not just produce what they hear: they extrapolate from the input by producing sentences that they have not heard before. In other words, they generalize from the data. But, while some of the child's novel utterances will be grammatical in the ambient language, others will not. Thus, the second step is the child rescinding his creative use of language by abandoning ungrammatical structures so that his sentences come to fall within the range of grammaticality We will call these two issues expansion and retreat.

Let us first consider the issue of **expansion**. What makes the child come up with novel grammatical structures? The answer must be that the child wants to say new things and that for the purposes of doing so he unconsciously formulates general hypotheses about grammatical structures that might be suitable for expressing these new things. Thus, the child may produce *I say her 'no'* or *May I whisper you something?* because he has heard *I told her 'no'* and *May I tell you something?* and he assumes that not only *tell* but all three-argument verbs can occur in the double-object construction.

Extrapolation of this kind is widely documentable both in child language acquisition and in human learning in general. Morphological examples are ungrammatical forms *foots* or *comed* in child English, produced by the overextension of the regular plural rule and the past tense rule of English.

But this leaves the second, more thorny question, that of **retreat**. Why does the child at some point in his development stop saying ungrammatical double-object constructions like *I say her 'no'* and *May I whisper you something?* What makes the child abandon a more general hypothesis for a narrower one?

One obvious answer would be that the child gradually abandons the use of certain double-object constructions because he does not actually hear them used. But this is too simple an idea. After all, children, both in their linguistic and in their non-linguistic behaviour, continue to be highly creative throughout their lives, constantly going beyond the models that they have been exposed to. Nor could any version of the 'intervention hypothesis' be successfully invoked to explain why children abandon ungrammatical patterns: as noted above, much research has demonstrated that children generally do not receive this kind of 'negative evidence'. It is thus very unlikely that the child would be corrected for every verb that he incorrectly uses in the double-object construction (Pinker 1996: 320).

The crucial piece of the puzzle may be the **Uniqueness Principle** first proposed by Kenneth Wexler. According to Wexler, the child innately assumes that 'when he or she is faced with a set of alternative structures fulfilling the same structure, only one of the structures is correct unless there is direct evidence that more than one is necessary' (Pinker 1996: 113). In other words, the child assumes an isomorphic, one-to-one relationship between meaning and form and thus resists synonymy. The principle explains why children, once they are exposed to the correct forms *feet* and *came*, expunge the forms *foots* and *comed* from their usage. Given that they have heard the correct forms, the principle tells them that *foots* and *comed* – words of his own making that they never actually heard – cannot also be correct.

How would the Uniqueness Principle apply to the child learning the proper use of the double-object construction? Since this construction is very common for the verbs that allow it, the child may hear *Give Pete the bear* before he hears *Give the bear to Pete*. The child then generalizes the double-object construction to other verbs including some of those that do not actually allow it, such as *open* or *whisper*. When he subsequently hears *give, show* and other double-object verbs also used in the prepositional construction, he is baffled: his innate Uniqueness Principle militates against the use of verbs in alternative constructions. He does have evidence, however, that this phenomenon exists – he has heard *give, show* and so on used in both constructions.

He is now faced with a conflict between evidence and principle. The Uniqueness Principle militates against synonymy; yet, he has evidence that synonymy exists. He solves the conflict through attempting to minimize it by finding the limits of this objectionable phenomenon – that is, by looking for conditions under which it occurs. Once he has hit upon the constraints – such as that in the double-object construction the Recipient becomes the possessor of the Theme – he abandons his earlier general rule about all verbs being able to occur in the double-object construction. In this way, the extent of the violation of the Uniqueness Principle is reduced to only a subset of verbs.

In sum: we started out with the problem of how children learn the double-object construction in English. The explanation we ended up with assumes the presence of relevant language input and a child with certain innate principles that come into play in responding to the linguistic environment. Here is the skeleton of the argument:

EXPLANANDUM
English speakers know which verbs can take double objects ((4) above).

EXPLANATORY PRINCIPLES
(a) All children have innate knowledge about sentences having partonomic, taxonomic and symbolic structure.
(b) All children have innate tendencies
  • to pay attention to the ambient language;
  • to imitate utterances of the ambient language;
  • to want to say new things;
  • to generalize observed patterns;

- to resist synonymy (the Uniqueness Principle);
- to resolve a conflict between a principle and actual facts by minimizing the extent of the conflict.

BRIDGE STATEMENTS
- Children are not born with the knowledge of which verbs can take double-objects.
- Verbs occurring both in the double-object and in the prepositional construction create a conflict with the Uniqueness Principle.

To the extent that the explanans includes tendencies, the explanation is probabilistic rather than nomological.

In the preceding two sections, examples of structural and evolutionary explanations were discussed. We will now turn to the third kind: functional explanations.

4 Functional explanations

According to Niko Tinbergen, a researcher of animal behaviour, there are four questions that can be asked about the behaviour of animals. One is about the mechanism underlying the behaviour: what are the physiological and cognitive structures involved and why are they the way they are? A second question is about phylogeny: what is the ancestral history of the behaviour; and why? A third question is about ontogeny: what factors influence individual development that gives rise to the behaviour and why? And the fourth one is about function (Tinbergen 1963).

Daniel Nettle, who cites Tinbergen's questions known as the 'four why-s', notes that they boil down to three 'how'-s and a single 'why' (Nettle 1998: 458–60). The why-question asks about function. Once function is identified, the rest of the questions are mere how-questions: how function motivates historical and individual change and, by way of these changes, how it motivates the resulting structures.

This applies to language as well. Thus, having considered structural, historical and developmental explanations for syntactic structures in the preceding sections, we will now turn to exploring the ultimate explanatory force for syntax: function.

Function in language involves two factors: the goals that people are after when using language and the means that they have at their disposal to attain those goals.

It is easy to see that considering goals without the available means is not going to lead to functional explanations of artifacts. Humans, beavers and birds all build shelters for protection; yet, bird nests, beaver dens and people's homes look very different. This may in part arise from differences in secondary goals; but the difference in capabilities must be the dominant factor.

Simon Kirby cites an example of Stephen Gould's that further shows how the means available to an organism will bear on its ways of achieving its goals (Kirby 1998: 159–60). While locomotion is an important goal for animals of all kinds, no animal body is known to have evolved wheels for moving around. The explanation given by Gould is that wheels must spin freely and thus they cannot be fused to the object that they move. But animals need to have all parts of their bodies physically connected so that nutrients can flow everywhere. This physical limitation constrains the range of the locomotional devices animal bodies can develop.

Given that language is an instrument, functional explanations would seem easy to construct: we just select a grammatical phenomenon and then show that it is dictated by language function – that is, by the goals of the speaker–hearer coupled with his cognitive and physical powers and constraints. But there are several reasons why this is not so, two of which are as follows.

First, one cannot expect all grammatical phenomena to be equally determined by language function. In thinking about functional explanations of instrumental objects in general, Gerald Sanders takes knives as an example (Sanders 1977a). He notes that while all structural properties of a knife have to be compatible with its function, not all of them are necessary for it: structure is not fully determined by function. For example, a carved geometric pattern on the knife's shaft is compatible with but immaterial to its cutting function. Second, the knife may have properties that are justified by, or conducive to, its function but still not necessary, such as a convenient length and shape of the knife's handle. And, third, there are certain features – such as having a handle at all that is not made of cotton – that are determined by the knife's function.

In other words, functional explanations may not be nomological; in some cases they are only probabilistic or permissive. All properties of actual instruments can be given a permissive functional explanation by showing that the properties in question are compatible with the instrument's function. Some of the properties may be subject to probabilistic explanations if we can show that they favour the optimal use of the instruments. And some instrument properties are indispensable for function and thus may be accounted for nomologically.

The second factor that complicates functional explanations is that language serves more than one function and the various functions may be in conflict. One such potential conflict is that language must serve the goals of both the speaker (encoder) and the hearer (decoder). The speaker is concerned with ease of expression; the hearer is interested in ease of comprehension. But comprehensibility often requires redundancy while ease of expression calls for economy – the opposite of redundancy.

In addition to the basic conflict between encoder's and decoder's interests, there are also other conflicting functions. While the speaker's and hearer's communicative preferences may shape the development of novel structures, their propagation is often influenced by social factors that may be at cross-purposes to these desiderata. People may prefer structures that are used by prestigious speakers even if they are less communicatively effective.

The functional explanations discussed in the preceding chapters illustrate some of these points. The need to appeal to both goals and means is shown by the discussion of the acquisitional sequence of wh-questions in child language (Chapter 6, Section 4.2). The explanation appealed to children's goals – to say what they need most – and their means: to use the simplest or best-known constructions.

The influence of both speaker's and hearer's needs is apparent in the explanation of why accusative and ergative case marking patterns are more common across languages than the other logically available ones (Chapter 6, Section 3.3). The explanation is that these two patterns both aid the addressee's comprehension of sentences by differentiating Agent and Patient, and do this in a way that is most economical for the speaker. In this case, the interests of speaker and addressee converge but the explanation is only probabilistic since the other patterns also occur in a few languages.

A third explanation of a functional sort discussed in the preceding chapters pertained to the very existence of syntax in natural language (Chapter 1, Section 4). As we saw, the existence of syntactic selection and order rules comes from the fact that many sentences include more than one word and that the selection and order of these words is not free. That sentences consist of more than one word is not explained: languages with big multimorpheme words could equally well serve to express new meanings. Similarly, the existence of syntactic ordering rules is not necessary: the order of meaningful units could be free without hampering the expression of meanings. But the fact that the selection of meaningful units in sentences is constrained is necessarily linked to the goal of the speaker to express meanings in a decodable way.

We will now turn to two more detailed examples of functional explanations. Section 4.1. presents a functional explanation for a structural pattern; Section 4.2. is an example of how function can explain historical change.

4.1 CO-ORDINATE ELLIPSIS IN ENGLISH AND JAPANESE

Consider the following:

(1) (a) *The gardener raked the flower beds and he swept up the leaves.*
    (b) *The gardener raked the flower beds and ___ swept up the leaves.*
    (c) **___ raked the flower beds and the gardener swept up the leaves.*

As (1b) shows, it is possible in English to leave out an overt reference to something if it is mentioned in another clause of a co-ordinate structure. Furthermore, (1c) shows that omission of a subject is possible only in the second clause. The same holds for the ellipsis (omission) of identical verbs:

(2) (a)   *The gardener raked the flower beds and his son raked the lawn.*

(b)   *The gardened raked the flower beds and his son, ___ the lawn.*

(c)   **The gardener ___ the flower beds and his son raked the lawn.*

The omissibility of the second mention of a constituent makes intuitive sense from the point of view of the addressee: he needs to have heard an overt mention before he is able to reconstruct the missing referent.

But notice that if it is the object that is mentioned only once, as in (3), it is omitted in the first clause, rather than the second.

(3) (a)   *The gardener raked the flower beds and his son watered them.*

(b)   *The gardener raked ___ and his son watered the flower beds.*

(c)   **The gardener raked the flower beds and his son watered ___.*

The generalization is that the overt mention of subjects and verbs must be in the first clause but the overt mention of objects must be in the second clause. The grammatical and ungrammatical options are listed in (4) (blank indicates the elided constituent).

(4) subject ellipsis: SVO _VO   * _VO SVO
    verb ellipsis: SVO S_O   *S_O SVO_
    object ellipsis: SV_ SVO   *SVO SV_

Gerald Sanders has proposed an account of these facts (Sanders 1970b: esp. 486–93). He first noted that in English, the order of truncated and untruncated conjuncts fell out from the general ordering rules of subjects, objects and verbs in English. The relevant rules are as follows:

(5) (a)   If (S, O), then S & O
          In prose: Any phrase containing the subject must precede any
                    phrase that contains the object.

(b)   If (V, O), then V & O
      In prose: Any phrase containing the verb must precede any
                phrase that contains the object.

These rules yield both the correct SVO pattern of untruncated clauses and the three elliptic patterns listed in (4). For subject ellipsis, the permitted pattern is SVO _VO; the ungrammatical pattern is * _VO SVO. The permitted order of constituents after ellipsis is in conformity with the basic constituent order in untruncated clauses because, in both instances, the subject comes before the verb and the verb before the object. The ungrammatical pattern – _VO SVO – would violate the generalization, since in this case the subject would not precede all verb-containing phrases.

The same is true for verb and object ellipsis. The ellipsis of the second verb maintains the '(all)verb(s)-before-(all) object(s)' pattern while the ellipsis of the first verb would violate it since one object would come before the verb. Similarly, ellipsis of the first object upholds the rule '(all)-verb(s)-before-(all)object(s)', while the ellipsis of the second object would violate it because one verb would come after the object.

Sanders' second observation was that uniform ordering of constituents in untruncated and elliptical sentences held not only in English but also in Japanese (1977b: 248–9). Japanese and English differ both in the basic constituent order of untruncated sentences and in the ellipsis patterns of truncated ones. In particular, Japanese has SOV order in full clauses as opposed to English having SVO; and, while both languages restrict subject ellipsis to the second clause, Japanese has object ellipsis in the second clause and verb ellipsis in the first clause – the exact opposite of the English pattern. Sanders' insight is that the two differences converge on the generalization that the order of constituents in truncated and untruncated sentences has to be uniform in both languages. Here are the relevant orders of Japanese:

   (6) (a) BASIC CONSTITUENT ORDER
             SOV

      (b) ELLIPSIS PATTERNS

subject ellipsis:	SOV _OV	*_OV SOV
object ellipsis:	SOV S_V	*S_V SOV
verb ellipsis:	SO_ SOV	*SOV SO_

The rules for Japanese are given in (7). The first rule ordering subjects and objects is the same as for English (see (5a)). The two languages differ only in the rule ordering verb and object ((5b) versus (7b)).

   (7) (a) If (S, O), then S & O
          In prose: Any phrase containing the subject must precede any
                  phrase that contains the object.

      (b) If (V, O), then V & O
          In prose: Any phrase containing the verb must follow any phrase
                  that contains the object.

These considerations so far illustrate two levels of structural explanations. A rule showing that SVO order holds across full and elliptical sentences in English is explanatory all by itself. Showing that the principle of uniform ordering across truncated and untruncated constructions applies to Japanese as well broadens the explanation further by adding validity to it across two languages.

Even though English and Japanese thus turn out to be alike in that each orders constituents uniformly in truncated and untruncated sentences, they differ in what constituent can be elided in which conjunct. Both languages allow subject ellipsis in the second conjunct but they differ in verb and object ellipsis. English allows verb ellipsis only in the second conjunct, while Japanese allows it only in the first conjunct; and English allows object ellipsis only in the first conjunct, while Japanese allows it only in the second conjunct. These differences are highlighted in (8).

(8) ENGLISH: JAPANESE:
    (a) ellipsis in second conjunct:
        subject: SVO _VO   subject: SOV _OV
        verb: SVO S_O   **object**: SOV S_V
    (b) ellipsis in first conjunct:
        object: SV_ SVO   **verb**: SO_ SOV

In subsequent work (1977b) Sanders proposed a higher-level explanation. He suggested that the differences could be eliminated by assuming a different taxonomy of ellipsis sites: if rather than tagging them in terms of grammatical function, they are identified in terms of serially numbered positions. This is shown in (9), where A, B etc. are first, second etc. constituent across two conjoined clauses regardless of their grammatical function. As (9) shows, a generalization emerges that holds for both languages: first and second constituent are elided in the second conjunct; third constituent is elided in the first conjunct.

(9) BOTH ENGLISH AND JAPANESE:
    Serial positions: ABC DEF
    (a) ellipsis in second conjunct:
        D: ABC _EF (D = subject in both English and Japanese)
        E: ABC D_F (E = verb in English, object in Japanese)
    (b) ellipsis in first conjunct:
        C: AB_ DEF (C = object in English, verb in Japanese)

Whereas (9) shows English and Japanese as belonging to the same type in regard to permissible ellipsis sites, Sanders found that not all languages worked like these two: languages do differ in what positions they allow ellipsis. However, there is one ellipsis position in all languages in Sanders' sample: D, the first constituent of the second conjunct. In other words, the ABC _EF schema was found to be grammatical throughout Sanders' sample regardless of which category occupied the D-position.

The question that now arises is why this ellipsis site should be universally privileged? We will take this to be our explanandum, stated in (10):

(10) In all languages, the first major constituent in a second conjunct can be omitted and still be understood.

The explanation proposed by Sanders is functional: it makes reference to how people process serial structures. First, he points out that, while truncated constructions are favoured by the speaker since they are shorter and thus take less effort to pronounce, they are difficult for the hearer since he needs to recover the bit of meaning that is not expressed. If we can assume that the listener's interest takes precedence over the speaker's, we expect that the cross-linguistically most popular ellipsis site will be one that poses the least problem for the decoder.

There is a psychological principle about serial processing that zeroes in on the D position in three-constituent elliptical structures as the easiest to decode. As has been shown by many experiments, not all positions in a linear string are equally easy to remember. When given a string of words or numbers, people recall the very first one best; the second and the last are next in ease of recall. Notice now that in order to infer the constituent elided in D position, what one needs to remember is A. But A is the very first member of the string, occupying the position that is known to be best remembered. If we assume that what is easiest to process is what is most widely distributed across languages, the cross-linguistic popularity of D as an ellipsis site is explained.

This additional assumption – that ease and frequency are correlated – is independently motivated in human behaviour. There are more people who can simply skate than those who can figure-skate; more people who can play scales on the piano than those who can perform complex pieces; and more people can climb a hill than those who can make their way to the top of Mount Everest.

Thus, the cross-linguistic preference for D-ellipsis is functionally explained by way of two principles of human psychology:

(11) (a) In serial processing, the first member of the series is remembered best.
  (b) What is the easiest is the most frequent.

Here is the summary of the explanatory argument:

EXPLANANDUM ((10) above)
In all languages, the first major constituent in a second conjunct can be omitted and still be understood.

EXPLANATORY PRINCIPLES
GOAL-RELATED:
• The listener must be able to reconstruct the meaning of a missing constituent.
MEANS-RELATED ((11) above):
• In serial processing, the first member of the series is remembered best.
• What is the easiest is the most frequent.

BRIDGE STATEMENT
The elided first constituent of a second conjunct refers to the first constituent of the first conjunct.

Explanations of structural patterns that refer to function are suggestive but not complete unless they also point at the process by which function comes to affect structure. Our final example of functional explanations posits such a process.

4.2 CONSTITUENT ORDER IN MANDARIN CHINESE

Archaic Mandarin (eleventh to fourth centuries BC) was similar to Modern English in that it had SVO order. Modern Mandarin in turn is like Japanese: it has generally SOV order. How did this change happen? Why would object and verb switch positions? Charles Li and Sandra Thompson (1974) show that the change did not happen through the actual re-ordering of the verb and the object. Instead, it happened when the verb, while sitting tight in its original position preceding the object, underwent a category change.

Since Archaic Mandarin order was SVO, conjoined clauses looked like this: SVO SVO, just as English *Jack grabbed the books and Jill carried the bag.* Now, let's picture a Mandarin sentence where the two clauses refer to the same subject and object with only the verb different; such as the equivalent of *Jack grabbed the books and Jack burned the books.* Li and Thompson hypothesize that in such instances, both the identical subject and the identical object were omissible in the second clause resulting in SVO _V_ ('Jack grabbed the book and ___ burned ___').

In some such sentences, the two verbs were closely linked so as to refer to a single act, similar to the verbs in the English sentences ***Try and pull*** *the nail*, or ***Go (and) get*** *the pliers.* Such verb sequences, which occur in many languages, are called serial verb constructions. While the second verb is semantically more significant and can vary, the first verb is generally 'lighter' in meaning and is restricted to a small set, such as 'go', 'try' or 'stand'.

Prior to the ninth century AD, the Mandarin verb that often occurred as the first in serial verb constructions was *bǎ* meaning 'take hold of'. Reduced forms of sentences of the structure 'Jack *bǎ* the book and Jack burned the book.' were 'Jack *bǎ* the book ___ burned ___'.

Because of the close semantic relationship between the two verbs and the small semantic contribution that *bǎ* made to their joint meaning, the two clauses came to be interpreted as a single clause and the first verb came to be regarded as just a marker of the object of the second verb. Thus, a sentence like 'Jack grabbed the book and ___ burnt ___' came to be analysed as 'Jack object-marker the book burnt'. The re-analysis of *bǎ* as an object marker and the fading of the boundary between the two clauses yielded a simple clause with SOV order.

That the *bǎ*-verb has indeed undergone the change from verb to preposition is shown by the fact that in today's Mandarin, it precedes objects even when the original 'take hold of' meaning does not apply, such as when the main verb is a non-physical act such as 'criticize' or 'scrutinize'.

The process is summarized in (1). Identical subscripts indicate identical reference:

(1) STAGE 1:

(a) Unreduced co-ordinate structure:
[[SUBJECT$_1$ & $b\check{a}_V$ & OBJECT$_2$] & [SUBJECT$_1$ & VERB & OBJECT$_2$]]

(b) Elliptical co-ordinate structure:
[[SUBJECT & $b\check{a}_V$ & OBJECT] & [___ VERB ___]]

STAGE 2:
The verb $b\check{a}$ reinterpreted as a preposition of the direct object; the two clauses reinterpeted as a single clause:
[SUBJECT & $b\check{a}_{CM}$ & OBJECT & VERB]

Thus, a change from SVO to SOV took place without verbs actually being inverted with objects.

But why did this change happen in Mandarin? This is the further explanandum that we still need to address.

(2) In the course of the history of Mandarin Chinese, a verb became a preposition and two conjoined clauses merged into a single clause.

There are really two questions hidden here. First, why did this change occur in Mandarin? Second, why does such a change occur in human languages at all?

By way of answering the first question, Li and Thompson point out that the order of some other constituents was Dependent before Head way back in history. Relative clauses had preceded their head noun phrases, and question particles – analysable as heads – had followed sentences since the time of Archaic Chinese. Thus, the verb–object object – Head before Dependent – was an anomaly and its change to object–verb order may be regarded as an attempt for verbs and objects to catch up with the other head–final patterns already in existence.

But what is the answer to the second question: why do changes like the ones in Mandarin happen in human languages at all? How is it that a verb can evolve into an adposition and that clause boundaries can be eliminated? Such developments are not unprecedented in languages. For example in Ewe (a West African language, Kwa group), the verb 'give' evolved into a dative case marker (Haspelmath 1998: 328–9). Similar changes are widespread across languages involving categories other than verbs and prepositions. The common feature of this broader class of changes is that a lexical category – noun, verb, demonstrative and so on – turns into a non-lexical, grammatical category such as an adposition, an auxiliary or an article. We have seen several examples of this process earlier in this book: French *pas* 'step' turning into part of a negative marker (Chapter 2, Section 4), personal pronouns turning into agreement markers (Chapter 3, Section 4), demonstratives turning into definite articles (Chapter 6, Section 4.1) and the numeral 'one' turning into an indefinite article (Section 1 of this chapter).

The other aspect of the Mandarin case – the reduction of a bi-clausal structure to a single clause – is also independently illustrable. An example of clause fusion is the evolution of modal verbs in English, such as *can* or *must* which, in Old English, were full-fledged main verbs, with the other verb describing the action in a separate clause.

The historical change illustrated in all these cases, called grammaticalization, is characterized by two processes:

- the rich meaning of the constituent is 'bleached' – some of it is lost
- the form of the constituent is reduced – it may be shortened and it loses its phonological independence by becoming a clitic or affix.

Thus, the change of *bǎ* from verb to preposition and the elimination of the clause boundary between the two clauses are typical components of grammaticalization.

This so far is a historical explanation: we have explained the word order change in Mandarin by reference to the general historical process of grammaticalization. But why does grammaticalization happen? Contemplating the process of main verbs like 'want' or 'intend' changing into markers of the future tense in various languages, Joan Bybee writes (1988): '[These changes] are themselves in need of explanation. Why do certain lexical items undergo these related semantic changes and develop grammatical characteristics? To answer this question, we are drawn back to the synchronic plane to investigate the way language is used' (p. 370); 'we must ask what cognitive processes are behind the historical changes' (p. 354).

As has been suggested by several linguists, the key factor is frequency: the frequent use of words results in semantic and formal reduction. Frequently occurring elements undergo habituation – a phenomenon that is rampant in human (and animal) behaviour outside language as well (other telling terms for it are conventionalization, automatization and ritualization). When the meaning is predictable, the speaker can afford to simplify the phonetic body of the utterance.

More generally, what is involved is that a symbol with a complex meaning and a complex form is 'worn out' over the centuries: both form and meaning are eroded so that the symbol ends up having a simpler form conveying a thinner meaning (Haspelmath 1998: 320–2; Langacker 1977: 98–130). Striking examples are found in the history of writing. Egyptian hieroglyphs were used to depict objects and they stood for entire concepts. Later the pictures became simplified in form and gradually came to represent only the first letter of the objects' names. An example from body language is the greeting gesture of early twentieth-century European men touching their hats. This stems from an older custom: when meeting somebody, men actually took off their hats in an expression of humility and respect. The gesture was then conventionalized: it was reduced to a simply touch of the hat with its meaning also shrinking to a simple greeting.

What these examples show is that historical reasons are not the last word in explaining structural phenomena. The final word belongs to functional principles that govern human psychology and physiology: what people want and what means they have available to achieve it.

Below is the schematic summary of the explanatory argument for grammaticalization.

> **EXPLANANDUM** ((2) above)
> In the course of the history of Mandarin Chinese, a verb became a preposition and two conjoined clauses merged into a single clause.
>
> **EXPLANATORY PRINCIPLES**
> GOAL-RELATED:
> • The goals in linguistic communication are production and comprehension.
> • The speaker aspires to ease of production and the hearer aspires to ease of comprehension.
> MEANS-RELATED:
> • The production and comprehension skills of humans are limited.
> • If a word is frequently repeated in the same context, both form and meaning become predictable. Thus, the speaker can afford to produce only a reduced form and the meaning loses its original specificity.
>
> **BRIDGE STATEMENT**
> In Mandarin Chinese, the verb *bǎ* came to be used as a semantically light verb and since it occurred in front of the object, it came to be seen as an object-marking preposition.

This functional explanation is not nomological: the change might or might not have happened in Mandarin. Even in the light of the tendencies appealed to, Mandarin might have not undergone the changes that it has.

5 Conclusions

As Albert Einstein remarked in the quote that heads this chapter, the goal of science is to explain why things are the way they are and not otherwise. In linguistics, the primary explananda are facts about linguistic structure. There are four kinds of explanations that are available for such facts.

First, properties of individual sentences are explained by general grammatical rules. Why does the speaker of a language formulate a particular sentence the way he does? Because that structure is an instance of a general grammatical pattern of the language.

Second, why does the speaker follow the grammatical patterns of the language around him? Because he has acquired these patterns from the ambient language.

Third, why does his ambient language have exactly these patterns? Because these are the patterns that have evolved in the history of the language.

Finally, why have exactly these patterns evolved in the language rather than some others? Because of the functions of language, which dictate, or at least favour, or at the very least allow these patterns.

Thus, properties of structure may be explained by generalizations about structure; structure can be explained by its genesis: by the developmental and historical changes that have led to it; and changes ultimately derive from function. In short, history and development drive structure and function drives history and development.

But how can function itself be explained? Language function – the goals of language and the means available for people to achieve these goals – must be related to the overall goals and means of humans. The genetically given physical and psychological make-up of human beings must ultimately underlie all of language, just as it underlies everything that we do as we interpret and affect the world on our own specifically human terms.

Notes

Section 1   Preliminaries
On explanations in linguistics, see for example Cohen 1974; Hornstein and Lightfoot 1981; Butterworth *et al.* 1984; Hawkins 1988; Moore and Polinsky 2003.

Section 2.1   Wh-questions in English

- This discussion is based on Haegeman 1994: esp. 371–429. For an original source, see Chomsky 1986: esp. 28–42.
- For a demonstration of how simple learning procedures can account for child language acquisition and thus render the assumption of innate language universals unnecessary, see MacWhinney 2004.

Section 2.2   Relative clauses in Basque

- The examples in (2) are taken from Keenan and Comrie 1977: 72. For a more detailed account of Basque relative clauses, see de Rijk 1998a, 1998b.
- (3) is a somewhat simplified rendition of the constraint; for more detail, see Keenan and Comrie 1977. For a discussion of the constraint along with exceptions to it, see Newmeyer 1998: 316–20.

Section 3   Evolutionary explanations
For an interesting and highly influential account of explaining language change, see Keller 1994.

Section 3.2   Direct and indirect objects in English

- An alternative term for (2b) is 'dative-shift construction', originating from a version of transformational generative grammar where such sentences are derived by a movement rule relocating the Recipient from its underlying post-Theme position.
- Both conditions mentioned here regarding which verbs take double objects have exceptions. For example, *promise* and *offer* are Latinate verbs, yet they take double objects; and while one can *bake somebody a cake, cook somebody a dinner* is less grammatical in American English, even though in both cases the Recipient becomes the possessor of the food. For a detailed analysis of the problem, see Green 1974: esp. 70–154. For an analysis of the two constructions, see Dryer 1986.
- The developmental explanation of how double-object verbs are acquired by children follows mostly Pinker 1996, esp. 291–347, and Bowerman 1988.
- A well-known example to show that exposure to a language environment is vital for first language acquisition is the child known as Genie (Curtiss 1977).
- There is extensive literature on whether animals can or cannot be taught human-like languages. On relevant experiments involving chimpanzees, bonobos and dolphins, see for example Terrace 1979; Herman and Forestell 1985; Savage-Rumbaugh and Lewin 1994.
- On Noam Chomsky's ideas regarding innate linguistic knowledge, see for example Chomsky 2002.

Section 4   Functional explanations
On the difficulties of functional explanations, see Nettle 1998: 450–7.

Section 4.1   Co-ordinate ellipsis in English and Japanese

- 'Ellipsis' is a Greek word for 'omission'. The pattern is generally called co-ordination reduction in the literature.
- For evidence for the assumption that the listener's needs are favoured over the speaker's in language, see Gundel *et al.* 1988.
- The idea that simple structures are more frequent is independently documented in language as well; see the discussion about markedness in Chapter 4, Section 3.4.2.

Section 4.2   Constituent order in Mandarin Chinese

- In addition to works on grammaticalization mentioned in
  the course of the discussion, see also Harris & Campbell 1995:
  15–20, 92; Heine *et al.* 1991; Hopper and Traugott 1993;
  Lehmann 1995; Ramat and Hopper 1998; Newmeyer
  1998: 227–95.
- On the psychological roots of grammaticalization, see also
  Langacker 1977: esp. 98–116; Haiman 1994; Bybee 1988; Heine
  1997; Haspelmath 1998: esp. 318–22.

Exercises

1. In those English wh-questions where the question word is not the subject, the order of subject and auxiliary is inverted; for example, *Joe should wash the dishes* and *What should Joe wash?* However, if the wh-word is itself the subject, this does not happen; cf. *Who should wash the dishes? *Should who wash the dishes?* What might be the reason for the lack of inversion of subject wh-words?

2. In Chapter 6 (Section 4.2), we saw that children tend to acquire subject wh-questions before object wh-questions. The explanation proposed had to do with the actual position of the wh-word and its semantically expected position in the two kinds of questions. See if the same explanation might account for the ways in which the Accessibility Hierarchy proposed by Keenan and Comrie (discussed in Section 2.2) constrains the distribution of relative clauses across languages.

3. The data in Exercise 6 of Chapter 2 showed a similarity between the use of the English conjunction *that* and its Indonesian equivalent *bahwa*. How may the pattern be related to language function?

4. As seen in Section 4.1, the same constituent order rules for subject, verb and object hold in English for unreduced and reduced clauses. Consider the ordering of adjectives and nouns within noun phrases in examples such as the following. Do unreduced and reduced noun phrases show the same order pattern or do different order rules apply to them?

    (a) NO ELLIPSIS
            schema: ADJ   N   ADJ   N
            example: *yellow tulips and yellow roses*

(b) ADJECTIVE ELLIPSIS
　　schemata:　ADJ N __ N
　　　　　　　 *__ N ADJ N
　　examples:　*yellow tulips and* __ *roses*
　　　　　　　 __ tulips and yellow roses

(c) NOUN ELLIPSIS
　　schemata:　ADJ __ ADJ N
　　　　　　　 *ADJ N ADJ
　　examples:　*yellow* __ *and red tulips*
　　　　　　　 *yellow tulips and red __

5. As noted in Chapter 5 (Section 3.1.3.2), languages tend to place semantically related word next to each other. How can this observation be related to language function?

Glossary

ablative
see case

absolutive
see case

accusative
see case

adjacency
the 'next to' relation; for example, the garage is next to the house

adposition
a cover term for prepositions (e.g. English *about*) and postpositions (e.g. English *ago*)

agent
see semantic participant role

agreement
a pattern of word-form selection: one word (the 'target') has an affix or clitic whose feature value co-varies with that of another word in the sentence ('the controller'); for example, the English demonstrative agrees with the noun in number (*this boy, these boys*)

anaphoric pronoun
a pronoun that takes its referent from another noun phrase in the sentence or discourse, called the antecedent; for example, in *Jill said **she** was tired, she* is an anaphoric pronoun and *Jill* is its antecedent

antecedent
see anaphoric pronoun

argument
a noun phrase whose referent is semantically associated with a predicate; for example, *The bird* ate *the spider*

bimorphemic
consisting of two morphemes; for example, *happi-ly*

bridge statement
it establishes the link between an explanatory principle and a fact that the principle explains; for example, *The Earth is a planet* is a bridge statement between *All planets move* and *The Earth moves*

case
a marker (affix or adposition or a special form of the word stem) that indicates the role of a noun phrase in a sentence

- Nominative: the case of the subject (e.g. *He left.*)
- Accusative: the case of the direct object (e.g. *Jill left him.*)
- Genitive: the case of the possessor (e.g. *John's brother*)
- Dative: the case of the indirect object (e.g. *John gave a book to him.*)
- Ablative: the case indicating origin (e.g. *I took the book from him.*)
- Oblique: any case other than the nominative
- Ergative: the unique case of the active participant in two-argument clauses distinct from that of the subject of an intransitive sentence
- Absolutive: the shared case of the patient of two-argument clauses and of the intransitive subject
- Vocative: the case of the name of a person addressed

category (class, type)
a set of items grouped together because of some shared properties (e.g. birds)

clitic
a stressless word that forms a phonological unit with a stressed word: *He's tall*

compositional
a whole is compositional if its characteristics are the sum of the characteristics of its parts and their relations; for example, the number 15 is compositional relative to its parts 10 and 5 and the additive relation between them

conjuncts
terms of a co-ordinate structure; for example, the phrase *John and Jill* consists of two conjuncts

constituent
part of a whole; for example, constituents of *The sun rose* are the phrases *the sun* and *rose*

constituent structure
see partonomy

controller
see agreement

co-occur
occur together; for example, nouns and articles co-occur

demonstrative
see determiner

dependency
a syntagmatic relationship between two things where one (the 'Head') can stand without the other (the 'Dependent'); for example, the verb is a Head and its adverb is the Dependent

dependent
see dependency

determiner
cover term for article (*the*, *a(n)*) and demonstrative (*this*, *that*); *this* is a proximate demonstrative and *that* is a distal demonstrative

discontinuity
a linear pattern where two things that belong together are separated; for example, a cup on the table and its saucer left in the kitchen

discourse
a set of connected sentences, such as a lecture, a poem or a conversation

distal
see determiner

distribution
the description of the locations where members of a class of objects can be found; for example, the distribution of lions in Africa

ditransitive
a verb that takes two objects; for example, *give* in *I gave the puppy milk*

ergative
see case

explanandum
a fact to be explained; for example, that things fall

explanans
a principle that explains a fact; for example, gravity explains that things fall

evolutionary change
in this book, the term is used in reference to both historical and developmental change

finite verb
a verb that can be a predicate of a main clause; for example, *He is working*

gender
a grammatical characteristic of nominals – it may or may not be based on sexual gender; for example, Spanish *manzana* 'apple' is feminine gender

genitive
see case

governee
see government

government
a pattern of word-form selection: a word, such as a verb or an adjective (the 'governor'), calls for a particular case of a nominal (the 'governee') – for example, *love* requires the accusative: *love **her***

governor
see government

immediate precedence
the relationship of one event happening directly before another; for example, *the* immediately precedes *plum* in *the plum*

implicans
see implication

implication
one thing (the 'implicans') predicting the presence of another (the 'implicatum'); for example, rain implies wet ground

implicatum
see implication

interlocutor
participant of a conversation or of an exchange of letters

intransitive
a verb that takes no object; for example, *exist*

lexicon
dictionary

linearization
placing items in order in a one-dimensional arrangement; for example, arranging people in a single line

linear order
see linearization

main clause
a clause that can form a sentence by itself; for example, *Jill likes the house* that *I am going to buy.*

markedness
the asymmetric relationship between two items forming an opposition, where one member (the 'unmarked') is simpler and more frequent than the other (the 'marked'); for example, of active and passive sentences, the active is unmarked and the passive is marked

marker
an affix, clitic or word indicating a grammatical category such as tense or case; for example, *baked*

modality
cover term for 'must', 'may' or 'must/may not'

monomorphemic
consisting of one morpheme; for example, *book*

nominal
cover term for nouns and pronouns

nominative
see case

nomological explanation
an explanation that predicts something with absolute certainty; for example, gravity predicts the falling of objects

oblique case
see case

ontogenesis
changes within the life of an individual; for example, the development of a child

paradigmatic relation
the relationship among items in an inventory; for example, among the consonants of English

parameter
dimension, or scale of variation; for example, animals differ along the parameter of whether they eat plants or meat

partonomy (same as mereonomy, mereology, meronomy, constituent structure)
whole–part relations; for example, a corporation consists of departments and the departments consist of subsections

patient
see semantic participant role

permissive explanation
an explanation that says something is possible (but not necessary or even probable); for example, meteorological principles of temperate climates allow for rain in September

phylogenesis
historical change; for example, the evolution of apes

phrasal verb
a verb plus particle construction; for example, *call up*

phrase
a set of words that form a grammatical unit; for example, ***The blue bird*** *is nearby*

polymorphemic
consisting of more than one morpheme; for example, *un-pleasant-ness*

possessor
designates an entity that owns or is otherwise dominant over another; for example, ***the book's*** *cover*

possessum
designates an entity that is owned or is otherwise dominated by another; for example, *the book's **cover***

precedence
the relationship of one item coming before another, whether directly or indirectly; for example, *the* precedes both *blue* and *plum* in *the blue plum*

predicate
part of the sentence that describes the action, event or state that the sentence is about; for example, *The plane **arrived late***

probabilistic explanation
an explanation that says something is likely (but not necessary); for example, meteorological principles of temperate climates render snow likely in December

proper inclusion
a set is properly included in another set if the latter includes all the former plus some additional members; for example, the set of mixed-gender students properly includes the set of male students

referent
a person or thing that a word or phrase designates; for example, the referents of *Jill* and *herself* are the same in *Jill hurt herself*

schema
a statement or name formulated in terms of symbols representing the structure of an object; for example, H_2O for water

selection
a decision regarding what items should be part of a structure; for example, selecting tiles for covering the walls of a bathroom

semantic participant role (also called thematic role)
the role that noun phrase referents play in an action or happening; for example, *Jonas* is an agent and *the horse* is a patient in *Jonas hit the horse*

standard of comparison
the item that something is compared with; for example, *John is taller than **Bill***

subordinate
an item dominated by another, 'superordinate' item; for example, the boss is superordinate to employees, who are subordinates

superordinate
see subordinate

symbolic correspondence
the relationship between the form and meaning of a symbol, such as the relationship between the meaning and the form of a hand gesture

syntagmatic relation
the relationship among co-occurring items; for example, between *s* and *p* in *span*

target
see agreement

taxonomy (classification, categorization, typology)
the arrangement of items in groups based on some shared characteristics; for example, the taxonomy of schools includes primary, middle and high schools

temporal relation
the relation between items on the timescale; see precedence and immediate precedence

token
individual members of a class; for example, this computer is a token of the class of computers

topic
a known item of which something is said; for example, **My brother**, *he is in Chicago.*

transitive
a verb that takes an object; for example, *resemble*

type
see category

univerbation
two or more words merging into one in historical change; for example, *alright*

valence
the number of obligatory arguments a verb or other word takes; for example, *give* has three valences (*Jill gave the bone to her dog*)

well-formedness
the property of being constructed in compliance with a given set of rules; for example, *the world* is well-formed, **world the* is ill-formed

References

Aikhenvald, Alexandra Y., R.M.W. Dixon and Masayuki Onishi (eds). 2001. *Non-canonical Marking of Subjects and Objects.* Amsterdam and Philadelphia: John Benjamins.

Allan, Keith. 2001. *Natural Language Semantics.* Oxford and Malden, MA: Blackwell.

Anderson, Stephen R. 1993. 'Wackernagel's revenge: clitics, morphology, and the syntax of second position'. *Language* 69, 1: 68–98.

Ashton, E.O. 1944. *Swahili Grammar, Including Intonation.* London: Longman.

Baker, Mark C. 2003. *Lexical Categories: Verbs, Nouns, and Adjectives.* Cambridge and New York: Cambridge University Press.

Bakker, Dik. 1994. *Formal and Computational Aspects of Functional Grammar and Language Typology.* Amsterdam: Uitgave IFOTT Amsterdam.

Barlow, Michael and Charles A. Ferguson (eds). 1988. *Agreement in Natural Language. Approaches, Theories, Descriptions.* Stanford: Center for the Study of Language and Information.

Battistella, Edwin L. 1996. *The Logic of Markedness.* New York, Oxford: Oxford University Press.

Beaugrande, Robert-Alain de and Wolfgang Ulrich Dressler. 1981. *Introduction to Text Linguistics.* London: Longman.

Behaghel, Otto. 1928, 1932. *Deutsche Syntax. Eine geschichtliche Darstellung.* Volume 3 (1928), Volume 4 (1932). Heidelberg: Carl Winters.

Bhat, D.N.S. 1994. *The Adjectival Category. Criteria for Differentiation and Identification.* Amsterdam and Philadelphia: John Benjamins.

Bloomfield, Leonard. 1933. *Language.* New York: Holt, Rinehart and Winston.

Bowerman, Melissa. 1988. 'The "no negative evidence" problem: how do children avoid constructing an overly general grammar?'. In J.A. Hawkins (ed.), 73–101.

Brown, Cecil H. 1990. 'A survey of category types in natural language'. In S.L. Tsohatzidis (ed.), *Meanings and Prototypes. Studies in Linguistic Categorization.* London and New York: Routledge, 17–47.

Brown, Keith and Jim Miller (eds). 1996. *Concise Encyclopedia of Syntactic Theories.* Oxford and New York: Pergamon.

Bunt, Harry and Arthur van Horck (eds). 1996. *Discontinuous Constituency*. Berlin: Mouton de Gruyter.

Butterworth, Brian, Bernard Comrie and Östen Dahl (eds). 1984. *Explanations for Language Universals*. Berlin, New York: Mouton.

Bybee, Joan L. 1988. 'The diachronic dimension in explanation'. In J.A. Hawkins (ed.), 350–79.

Chomsky, Noam. 1984. *Lectures on Government and Binding*. Dordrecht: Foris.

Chomsky, Noam. 1986. *Barriers*. Cambridge, MA: The MIT Press.

Chomsky, Noam. 2002. *On Nature and Language*. Ed. by Adriana Belletti and Luigi Rizzi. Cambridge: Cambridge University Press.

Christie, Agatha. 1986. *The Clocks*. New York: Pocket Books.

Cisneros, Sandra. 1985. *The House on Mango Street*. New York: Vintage Books.

Cohen, David (ed.). 1974. *Explaining Linguistic Phenomena*. New York and London: Hemisphere.

Cole, Peter and Jerrold Sadock. 1977. *Grammatical Relations. Syntax and Semantics*. New York and San Francisco: Academic Press.

Comrie, Bernard. 1978. 'Ergativity'. In Winfred P. Lehmann (ed.), 329–94.

Comrie, Bernard. 1989. *Language Universals and Linguistic Typology*. 2nd edn. Chicago: The University of Chicago Press.

Comrie, Bernard, Stephen Matthews and Maria Polinsky (eds). 1996. *Atlas of Languages. The Origin and Development of Languages throughout the World*. New York: Facts on File, Inc.

Corbett, Greville G. 1983a. 'Resolution rules: agreement in person, number, and gender'. In Gerald Gazdar, Ewan Klein and Goffrey K. Pullum (eds), *Order, Concord, and Constituency*. Dordrecht: Foris, 175–206.

Corbett, Greville G. 1983b. *Hierarchies, Targets, and Controllers: Agreement Patterns in Slavic*. London: Croom Helm.

Corbett, Greville G. 1988. 'Agreement: a partial specification based on Slavonic data'. In M. Barlow and C.A. Ferguson (eds), 23–53.

Corbett, Greville G. Forthcoming. *Agreement*. Cambridge: Cambridge University Press.

Corrigan, Roberta. 1989. 'Linguistic and non-linguistic categorization: structure and process'. In R. Corrigan, F. Eckman and M. Noonan (eds). 1–28.

Corrigan, Roberta, Fred Eckman and Michael Noonan (eds). 1989. *Linguistic Categorization*. Amsterdam and Philadelphia: John Benjamins.

Croft, William. 1990. *Typology and Universals*. Cambridge: Cambridge University Press.

Croft, William. 2001. *Radical Construction Grammar. Syntactic Theory in Typological Perspective*. Oxford and New York: Oxford University Press.

Csikszentmihalyi, Mihaly. 1993. *The Evolving Self. A Psychology for the Third Millenium*. London: Harper Collins.

Curtiss, Susan. 1977. *Genie: A Psycholinguistic Study of a Modern-day 'Wild Child'*. New York: Academic Press.

Dainora, Andra, Rachel Hemphill, Barbara Luka, Barbara Need and Shevi Pragman (eds). 1995. *Papers from the 31st Regional Meeting of the Chicago*

Linguistic Society. Volume 2: The Parasession on Clitics. Chicago: Chicago Linguistic Society.

Darnell, Michael, Edith Moravcsik, Frederick Newmeyer, Michael Noonan and Kathleen Wheatley (eds). 1998. *Functionalism and Formalism in Linguistics. Volume I: General Papers, Volume II: Case Studies.* Amsterdam and Philadelphia: John Benjamins.

Dawkins, Richard. 1976. 'Hierarchical organization: a candidate principle for ethology'. In Patrick P.G. Bateson and Robert A. Hinde (eds), *Growing Points in Ethology.* Cambridge: Cambridge University Press, 7–54.

Day, Beryl. 1992. *Dependency: Personal and Social Relations.* Aldershot: Avebury.

Derbyshire, Desmond C. 1985. *Hixkaryana and Linguistic Typology.* Dallas, TX: Summer Institute of Linguistics.

Derbyshire, Desmond C. and Geoffrey K. Pullum. 1981. 'Object-initial languages'. *International Journal of American Linguistics* 47, 3: 192–214.

de Rijk, Rudolf P.G. 1998a. 'Relative clauses in Basque: a guided tour'. In de Rijk, Rudolf, 55–69.

de Rijk, Rudolf P.G. 1998b. 'Studies in Basque syntax: relative clauses'. In de Rijk, Rudolf, 71–149.

de Rijk, Rudolf P.G. 1998c. *De Lingua Vasconum: Selected Writings.* Bilbao: Universidad del País Vasco.

Diessel, Holger. 1999. *Demonstratives. Form, Function, and Grammaticalization.* Amsterdam and Philadelphia: John Benjamins.

Dik, Simon. 1978. *Functional Grammar.* Amsterdam: North Holland.

Dixon, R.M.W. (ed.). 1976. *Grammatical Categories in Australian Languages.* New Jersey: Humanities Press.

Dixon, R.M.W. 1980. *Languages of Australia.* Cambridge: Cambridge University Press.

Dixon, R.M.W. 1994. *Ergativity.* Cambridge: Cambridge University Press.

Dixon, R.M.W. and A.Y. Aikhenvald (eds). 2002. *Word: A Typological Framework.* Cambridge: Cambridge University Press.

Doi, Takeo, 1973. *The Anatomy of Dependence.* Tokyo and New York: Kodansha International Ltd.

Dryer, Matthew. 1986. 'Primary objects, secondary objects, and anti-dative'. *Language* 62, 4: 808–45.

Dryer, Matthew. 1989. 'Article-noun order'. *Chicago Linguistic Society* 25: 83–97.

Dryer, Matthew. 1992. 'The Greenbergian word order correlations'. *Language* 68: 81–138.

Farb, Peter. 1984. *Insects.* (Illustrated Library of Nature, Volume 3) Westport, CT: Stuttman.

Gil, David. 1994. 'The structure of Riau Indonesian'. *Nordic Journal of Linguistics* 17: 179–200.

Gil, David. 2000. 'Syntactic categories, cross-linguistic variation and universal grammar'. In P.M. Vogel and B. Comrie (eds), 173–216.

Givón, Talmy. 1976. 'Topic, pronoun, and grammatical agreement'. In C.N. Li (ed.), 149–188.

Givón, Talmy. 1981. 'On the development of the numeral "one" as an indefinite marker'. *Folia Linguistica Historica* II, 1, 35–53.

Givón, Talmy. 1984. *Syntax. A Functional-Typological Introduction, Volume I.* Amsterdam and Philadelphia: John Benjamins.

Givón, Talmy. 1990. *Syntax. A Functional-Typological Introduction, Volume II.* Amsterdam and Philadelphia: John Benjamins.

Givón, Talmy. 1995. *Functionalism and Grammar.* Amsterdam and Philadelphia: John Benjamins.

Givón, Talmy (ed.). 1997. *Conversation. Cognitive, Communicative, and Social Perspectives.* Amsterdam and Philadelphia: John Benjamins.

Givón, T. 2002. *Bio-linguistics. The Santa Barbara Lectures.* Amsterdam and Philadelphia: John Benjamins.

Green, Georgia M. 1974. *Semantic and Syntactic Regularity.* Bloomington, IN: Indiana University Press.

Greenberg, Joseph H. 1963. 'Some universals of grammar with particular reference to the order of meaningful elements'. In Joseph H. Greenberg (ed.). *Universals of Language.* Cambridge, MA: MIT Press, 73–113.

Greenberg, Joseph. 1966. *Language Universals.* The Hague: Mouton.

Greenberg, Joseph H. *et al.* (eds). 1978. *Universals of Human Language. Volume III: Word Structure; Volume IV: Syntax.* Standford, CA: Stanford University Press, 249–95.

Greenberg, Joseph H. 1978. 'Generalizations about numeral systems'. In Joseph H. Greenberg *et al.* (eds), 249–95.

Gregory, Bruce. 1988. *Inventing Reality. Physics as Language.* New York: John Wiley.

Gundel, Jeanette K., Kathleen Houlihan and Gerald Sanders. 1988. 'On the function of marked and unmarked terms'. In M. Hammond, E.A. Moravcsik and J.R. Wirth (eds), 285–301.

Haddon, Mark. 2003. *The Curious Incident of the Dog in the Night-time.* New York: Doubleday.

Haegeman, Liliane. 1994. *Introduction to Government and Binding Theory.* 2nd edn. Oxford and Cambridge: Blackwell.

Haider, Hubert and Martin Prinzhorn (eds). 1986. *Verb-second Phenomena in Germanic Languages.* Dordrecht: Foris.

Hailman, Jack P., Millicent S. Ficken and Robert W. Ficken. 1985. 'The 'chick-a'dee: calls of *Parus atracapillus*: a recombinant system of animal communication compared with written English'. *Semiotica*, 56, 3/4: 191–224.

Haiman, John. 1985a. *Natural Syntax. Iconicity and Erosion.* Cambridge: Cambridge University Press.

Haiman, John (ed.). 1985b. *Iconicity in Syntax. Proceedings of a Symposium on Iconicity of Syntax.* Stanford, 24–26 June 1983. Amsterdam and Philadelphia: John Benjamins.

Haiman, John. 1994. 'Ritualization and the development of language'. In W. Pagliuca (ed.), 3–28.

Hale, Kenneth. 1973. 'Person marking in Warlbiri'. In Stephen R. Anderson and Paul Kiparsky (eds), *A Festschrift for Morris Halle*. New York: Holt, Rinehart and Winston, 308–44.

Hammond, Michael, Edith Moravcsik and Jessica R. Wirth (eds), 1988. *Studies in Syntactic Typology*. Amsterdam and Philadelphia: John Benjamins.

Hammond, Michael, Edith Moravcsik and Jessica Wirth. 1988. 'Language typology and linguistic explanation'. In Michael Hammond, Edith A. Moravcsik and Jessica R. Wirth (eds), 1–22.

Harris, Alice C. and Lyle Campbell. 1995. *Historical Syntax in Cross-linguistic Perspective*. Cambridge: Cambridge University Press.

Haspelmath, Martin. 1998. 'Does grammaticalization need reanalysis?' *Studies in Language* 22, 2: 315–51.

Hawkins, John A. 1983. *Word Order Universals*. New York: Academic Press.

Hawkins, John A. (ed.). 1988. *Explaining Language Universals*. Oxford: Blackwell.

Hawkins, John A. 1994. *A Performance Theory of Order and Constituency*. Cambridge: Cambridge University Press.

Hawkins, John A. 1999. 'Processing complexity and filler-gap dependencies across grammars'. *Language* 75, 2: 244–85.

Heine, Bernd. 1994. 'Grammaticalization as an explanatory parameter'. In W. Pagliuca (ed.), 255–87.

Heine, Bernd, Ulrike Claudi and Friederike Hünnemeyer. 1991. *Grammaticalization: A Conceptual Framework*. Chicago: The University of Chicago Press.

Heine, Bernd and Tania Kuteva. 2002. *World Lexicon of Grammaticalization*. Cambridge: Cambridge University Press.

Hempel, C.G. and P. Oppenheim. 1948. 'Studies in the logic of explanation'. *Philosophy of Science* 15: 135–78.

Herman, Louis M. and Paul H. Forestell. 1985. 'Reporting presence or absence of named objects by a language-trained dolphin'. *Neuroscience and Biobehavioral Reviews* 9: 667–81.

Hopper, Paul and Elisabeth C. Traugott. 1993. *Grammaticalization*. Cambridge: Cambridge University Press.

Hornstein, Norbert and David Lightfoot (eds). 1981. *Explanation in Linguistics. The Logical Problem of Language Acquisition*. London: Longman.

Huck, Geoffrey J. and Almerindo E. Ojeda. 1987. *Discontinuous Constituency. Syntax and Semantics*. Orlando, FL: Academic Press.

Jacobs, Joachim, Arnim von Stechow, Wolfgang Sternefeld and Theo Vennemann (eds), 1995. *Syntax. An International Handbook of Contemporary Research*. Berlin: Walter de Gruyter.

Jacobson, P. 1996. 'Constituent structure'. In K. Brown and J. Miller (eds), 54–67.

Jackendoff, Ray. 1997. *The Architecture of the Language Faculty*. Linguistic Inquiry Monographs 28. Cambridge, MA: The MIT Press.

Javarek, Vera and Miroslav Sudjic. 1963. *Teach Yourself Serbo-Croat.* London: The English Universities Press.

Keenan, Edward. 1974. 'The functional principle: generalizing the notion of "subject of"'. *Papers from the Tenth Regional Meeting of the Chicago Linguistic Society.* Chicago: Chicago Linguistic Society, 298–309.

Keenan, Edward L. 1978. 'The syntax of subject-final languages'. In P. Lehmann (ed.), 267–327.

Keenan, Edward and Bernard Comrie. 1977. 'Noun phrase accessibility and universal grammar'. *Linguistic Inquiry* 8, 1: 63–99.

Keller, Rudi. 1994. *On Language Change: The Invisible Hand in Language.* London: Routledge.

Kiparsky, Paul. 1973. 'The role of linguistics in a theory of poetry'. In Morton Bloomfield and Einar Haugen (eds), *Language as a Human Problem.* New York: W.W. Norton, 234–46.

Kirby, Simon. 1998. 'Constraints on constraints, or the limits of functional adaptation'. In Darnell *et al.* (eds), Volume II, 151–74.

Koutsoudas, Andreas. 1966. *Writing Transformational Grammars: An Introduction.* New York: McGraw-Hill.

Koutsoudas, Andreas. 1969. *Workbook in Syntax.* New York: McGraw Hill.

Krámský, Jiří. 1972. *The Article and the Concept of Definiteness in Language.* The Hague: Mouton.

Lakoff, George. 1987. *Women, Fire, and Dangerous Things: What Categories Reveal about the Mind.* Chicago: University of Chicago Press.

Langacker, Ronald W. 1972. *Fundamentals of Linguistic Analysis.* New York: Harcourt Brace Jovanovich.

Langacker, Ronald W. 1977. 'Syntactic reanalysis'. In Charles N. Li (ed.), *Mechanisms of Linguistic Change.* Austin, TX: University of Texas Press, 59–139.

Langacker, Ronald W. 1999. *Grammar and Conceptualization.* Berlin and New York: Mouton de Gruyter.

Langton, Christopher G. 1995. *Artificial Life: an Overview.* Cambridge, MA: The MIT Press.

Lederer, Richard. 1993. *More Anguished English.* New York: Dell.

Lehmann, Christian. 1982. 'Universal and typological aspects of agreement'. In H. Seiler and F.J. Stachowiak (eds), *Apprehension: das sprachliche Erfassen von Gegenständen. Teil II: Die Techniken und ihr Zusammenhang in Einzelsprachen.* Tübingen: Gunter Narr, 201–67.

Lehmann, Christian. 1995. *Thoughts on Grammaticalization.* München and Newcastle: LINCOM EUROPA.

Lehmann, Winfred P. (ed.). 1978. *Syntactic Typology. Studies in the Phenomenology of Language.* Austin, TX: University of Texas Press.

Lehtinen, M. 1963. *Basic Course in Finnish.* Bloomington, IN and The Hague: Indiana University.

Lewis, M.B. 1956. *Teach Yourself Malay.* London: The English Universities Press.

Li, Charles N. (ed.). 1976. *Subject and Topic.* New York: Academic Press.

Li, Charles N. and Sandra A. Thompson. 1974. 'An explanation of word order change SVO → SOV'. *Foundations of Language* 12, 2: 201–14.

Li, Charles and Sandra A. Thompson. 1976. 'Subject and topic: a new typology of language'. In C.N. Li (ed.), 491–518.

Li, Charles N. and Sandra A. Thompson. 1981. *Mandarin Chinese. A Functional Reference Grammar.* Berkeley and Los Angeles: University of California Press.

Lyovin, Anatole. 1997. *An Introduction to the Languages of the World.* New York: Oxford University Press.

MacWhinney, Brian (ed.). 1999. *The Emergence of Language.* Mahwah, NJ: Erlbaum.

MacWhinney, Brian. 2004. 'A Multiple Process Solution to the logical problem of language acquisition'. *Journal of Child Language* 31, 4: 883–914.

Matteson, Esther. 1965. *The Piro (Arawakan) Language.* Berkeley, CA: The University of California Press.

McLendon, Sally. 1978. 'Ergativity, case, and transitivity in Eastern Pomo'. *International Journal of American Linguistics* 44, 1: 1–9.

Merian, Maria Sybilla. 1994 (reprint). *Das Insektenbuch. Metamorphosis insectorum Surinamensium.* Frankfurt am Main: Insel.

Merrifield, William R. *et al.* 1987. *Laboratory Manual for Morphology and Syntax.* Dallas, TX: Summer Institute of Linguistics.

Mervis, Carolyn B. and Eleanor Rosch. 1981. 'Categorization of natural objects'. *Annual Review of Psychology* 32: 89–115.

Moore, John and Maria Polinsky (eds). 2003. *The Nature of Explanation in Linguistic Theory.* Stanford, CA: Center for the Study of Language and Information.

Moravcsik, Edith. 1978a. 'Agreement'. In Joseph H. Greenberg (ed.), Volume IV: *Syntax,* 331–74.

Moravcsik, Edith. 1978b. 'On the distribution of ergative and accusative patterns'. *Lingua* 45: 233–79.

Moravcsik, Edith A. 2000. 'Infixation'. In Geert Booij *et al.* (eds), *Morphology. An International Handbook on Inflection and Word-formation,* Volume I. Berlin: Walter de Gruyter, 545–52.

Moravcsik, Michael J. 1981. 'Dependence'. *Human Systems Management* 2: 268–74.

Nettle, Daniel. 1998. 'Functionalism and its difficulties in biology and linguistics'. In M. Darnell *et al.* (eds), Volume I, 445–67.

Nettle, Daniel. 1999. *Linguistic Diversity.* Oxford: Oxford University Press.

Newmeyer, Frederick J. 1998. *Language Form and Language Function.* Cambridge, MA: The MIT Press.

Newton-Smith, W.H. 2000. 'Explanation'. In W.H. Newton-Smith (ed.), *A Companion to the Philosophy of Science.* Malden, MA: Blackwell, 127–33.

Nichols, Johanna. 1992. *Language Diversity in Time and Space.* Chicago: Chicago University Press.

Noonan, Michael. 1992. *A Grammar of Lango.* Berlin and New York: Mouton de Gruyter.

O'Grady, William. 1997. *Syntactic Development.* Chicago: The University of Chicago Press.

Pagliuca, William (ed.). 1994. *Perspectives on Grammaticalization.* Amsterdam and Philadelphia: John Benjamins.

Pais, Abraham. 1994. *Einstein Lived Here.* Oxford: The Clarendon Press.

Peirce, Charles. 1932. *Philosophical Writings. Volume II.* Cambridge: Harvard University Press.

Pinker, Steven. 1996. *Language Learnability and Language Development.* Cambridge, MA: Harvard University Press.

Plank, Frans (ed.). 1979. *Ergativity. Towards a Theory of Grammatical Relations.* London: Academic Press.

Plank, Frans (ed.). 1986. *Folia Linguistica* (special issue on typology) 20: 1–2.

Plank, Frans. 1995. 'Ergativity'. In J. Jacobs, A. von Stechow, W. Sternefeld and T. Vennemann (eds), Volume 2, 1184–99.

Pullum, Geoffrey K. 1977. 'Word order universals and grammatical relations'. In P. Cole and J. Sadock (eds), 252–77.

Pullum, Geoffrey K. and Arnold M. Zwicky. 1986. 'Phonological resolution of syntactic feature conflict'. *Language* 62, 4: 751–73.

Pullum, Geoffrey K. 1991. *The great Eskimo vocabulary hoax and other irreverent essays on the study of language.* Chicago: The University of Chicago Press.

Radford, Andrew. 1988. *Transformational Grammar. A First Course.* Cambridge: Cambridge University Press.

Ramat, Paolo. 1987. *Language Typology.* Berlin: Mouton de Gruyter.

Ramat, Anna Giacalone and Paul J. Hopper (eds). 1998. *The Limits of Grammaticalization.* Amsterdam and Philadelphia: John Benjamins.

Riemsdijk, Henk van. 1981. 'Adjacency in phonology and syntax'. *Proceedings of the Eleventh Meeting of the North Eastern Linguistic Society.* Amherst, MA: Graduate Linguistics Student Association, 399–413.

Rijkhoff, Jan. 2002. *The Noun Phrase.* Oxford: Oxford University Press.

Rosch, Eleanor. 1973. 'Natural categories'. *Cognitive Psychology* 7: 532–47.

Rosch, Eleanor. 1984. 'Prototype classification and logical classification: the two systems'. In Ellin Kofsky Scholnick (ed.), *New Trends in Conceptual Representation: Challenges to Piaget's Model?* Hillsdale, NJ: Erlbaum, 73–86.

Rosch, Eleanor and Carolyn B. Mervis. 1975. 'Family resemblances: studies in the internal structure of categories'. *Cognitive Psychology* 7: 573–605.

Samarin, William J. 1972. *Tongues of Men and Angels. The Religious Language of Pentecostalism.* New York: Macmillan.

Sanders, Gerald A. 1970a. 'On the natural domain of grammar'. *Linguistics* 63: 51–123.

Sanders, Gerald A. 1970b. 'Constraints on constituent order'. *Papers in Linguistics* 2, 3: 460–502.

Sanders, Gerald A. 1972. *Equational Grammar.* The Hague: Mouton.

Sanders, Gerald A. 1977a. 'Functional constraints on grammar'. In Alphonse Juilland (ed.), *Linguistic Studies Offered to Joseph Greenberg on the Occasion of His Sixtieth Birthday.* Saratoga: ANMA LIBRI and Co, 161–78.

Sanders, Gerald A. 1977b. 'A functional typology of elliptical coordinations'. In Fred R. Eckman (ed.), *Themes in Linguistics*. Washington: Hemisphere, 241–70.

Sanders, Gerald A. 1982. 'An intermediate syntax problem from Indonesian'. *Innovations in Linguistics Education* 2, 2: 99–105.

Savage-Rumbaugh Sue and Roger Lewin. 1994. *Kanzi. The Ape at the Brink of a Human Mind*. New York: John Wiley.

Schachter, Paul. 1976. 'The subject in Philippine languages: topic, actor, actor-topic, or none of the above?' In C.N. Li (ed.), 491–518.

Schachter, Paul. 1977. 'Constraints on coordination'. *Language* 53, 1: 86–103.

Schachter, Paul and Fe T. Otanes. 1972. *Tagalog Reference Grammar*. Berkeley: University of California Press.

Senn, Alfred. 1966. *Handbuch der litauischen Sprache. Band I: Grammatik*. Heidelberg: C. Winter.

Siewierska, Anna. 1988. *Word Order Rules*. London and New York: Croom Helm.

Song, Jae Jung. 2001. *Linguistic Typology: Morphology and Syntax*. Harlow: Longman.

Stassen, Leon. 1997. *Intransitive Predication*. Oxford: Clarendon Press.

Taylor, John R. 1995. *Linguistic Categorization. Prototypes in Linguistic Theory*. Oxford: Clarendon Press.

Terrace, Herbert. 1979. *Nim: A Chimpanzee Who Learned Sign Language*. New York: Knopf.

Thompson, Sandra A. 1989. 'A discourse approach to the cross-linguistic category "Adjective"'. In R. Corrigan, F. Eckman and M. Noonan (eds), 245–65.

Tinbergen, Niko. 1963. 'On aims and methods of ethology'. *Zeitschrift für Tiergeschichte* 20: 410–33.

Tomlin, Russell S. 1986. *Basic Word Order. Functional principles*. London and Sidney: Croom Helm.

Traugott, Elizabeth Closs. 1972. *A History of English Syntax*. New York and Chicago: Holt, Rinehart and Winston.

Traugott, Elizabeth Closs and Mary Louise Pratt. 1980. *Linguistics for Students of Literature*. New York: Harcourt Brace Jovanovich.

Tversky, Barbara. 1990. 'Where partonomies and taxonomies meet'. In S.L. Tsohatzidis (ed.), *Meanings and Prototypes. Studies in Linguistic Categorization*. London and New York: Routledge, 334–44.

Vogel, Petra M. and Bernard Comrie (eds). 2000. *Approaches to the Typology of Word Classes*. Berlin: Mouton de Gruyter.

Waugh, Linda R. 1977. *A Semantic Analysis of Word Order. Position of the Adjective in French*. Leiden: Brill.

Whaley, Lindsay. J. 1997. *Introduction to Typology: The Unity and Diversity of Language*. Thousand Oaks: Sage.

Wierzbicka, Anna. 1988. *The Semantics of Grammar*. Amsterdam and Philadelphia: John Benjamins, 463–97.

Winters, Margaret E. 1987. 'Innovations in French negation. A cognitive grammar account'. *Diachronica* 4, 102: 27–52.

Wirth, Jessica R. 1983. 'Toward universal principles of word formation: a look at antonyms'. *Proceedings of the XIIIth International Congress of Linguists,* 967–71.

Wittgenstein, Ludwig. 1963. *Philosophical Investigations.* Oxford: Blackwell.

Wurm, Stephen A. 1976. 'Accusative marking in Duungidjawu (Waga-Waga)'. In R.M.W. Dixon (ed.), 106–11.

Zwicky, Arnold M. 1996. 'Syntax and phonology'. In K. Brown and J. Miller (eds), 300–5.

Index